TENS AND NERVOUS

Derby C(

2(

Volume One: 2010–2015

By Ollie Wright

To Gene,
With apologies

Preface

This was the period in which Nigel Clough patiently built a team that Steve McClaren took to new heights, only for crushing disappointment to follow as the Rams twice fell short of promotion in dramatic style.

But alongside the desperate lowlights were fine performances to savour – not least the unforgettable 5-0 – as the likes of Craig Bryson, Will Hughes and Chris Martin rose to become Derby County heroes.

Ollie Wright's Derby County Blog turned ten years old in 2020. This book compiles the highlights from his first five years of Rams coverage.

Foreword

Through the ups and downs, the wins and the defeats, the joy and despair, there is one constant truth of following Derby County Football Club; it is never boring.

This is by no means a recent phenomenon. Perhaps it goes all the way back to the gypsy curse that was supposedly put on the Baseball Ground when the Rams moved in. Derby did eventually win their FA Cup, though they needed the drama of extra-time to do it.

Then there was the rollercoaster that was Brian Clough & Peter Taylor's reign. From the titles and the glory to the protests and player strikes, it was never dull.

I am never sure where to start with the Robert Maxwell era. Then there's the ascent under Jim Smith, the struggles since, the Three Amigos, Billy Davies's paranoid delusions, that awful record-breaking Premier League campaign, the numerous play-off heart-breaks, plus everything else.

Like I say, it is never boring.

Long before I ever had the honour of covering Derby County in any official capacity, I was a supporter. In many ways I miss the simplicity of that relationship, and having – at least in theory – the opportunity to occasionally step away. Covering this club is all-consuming, exhausting. It is partly the reason I have such huge admiration for the work Ollie has done over the last decade or so.

You don't need me to tell you that the sports media landscape has transformed over the last 20 years. I remember when BBC Radio Derby, the Derby Telegraph and Ceefax were the only ways to stay up to date with club news and comment.

Things have changed. Supporter-led journalism has become more important than ever, and the Derby County Blog has been at the forefront from a Rams perspective. I have been an avid reader pretty much since the beginning, and remain so to this day.

I didn't always agree with Ollie's conclusions, and still don't, but I can invariably see the merit in his arguments and always trust the genuine intent of his efforts. That said, it is remarkable reading back through these first five years of his work to see just how often he was right!

Owen Bradley
June 2021

Introduction

2010 was not so long ago, but nevertheless it feels like a different world entirely. Sir Alex Ferguson was still the manager of Manchester United. DVDs and CDs still roamed the land. Twitter was still a relatively new innovation. Even when I joined a press office as a junior staff member, in late 2011, one of my earliest tasks was to file huge stacks of dusty, print newspapers. Most of those titles would be extinct within a few years as the concept of paying for a daily paper was made largely redundant by technology.

Back then, if you wanted to express your opinions about Derby County, or find out what other people thought, you went on to a fan forum. I tried this for a while and soon realised that it wasn't for me. Threads spiralling away from the original topic, constant in-jokes and disagreements, and people wanting the last word meant it felt to me like chaos and not a space where I could usefully contribute.

But I still wanted to write about the Rams and that's where the idea of setting up my own blog came from. It was initially dubbed "The Power of Clough" but that name was swiftly and rightly junked when a much more tech-savvy friend, Joe Burns, pointed out that if I went for a "Ronseal" approach and simply called the website "Derby County Blog", it would be a lot easier and more natural for people to find online. This also meant that the site was no longer tied in name to the Rams' manager of the time.

In the first five years, which are covered in this book, I was writing an awful lot, trying to find my feet and my voice. I went down many cul-de-sacs and rabbit holes. As a trainee journalist, I was providing regular Fanzone blogs for Sky Sports and countless Q&As for blogs from other Championship clubs. I became fixated on statistics and how they could be applied to football, after reading Moneyball by Michael Lewis. I posted sometimes overly lengthy articles using whatever new metric was currently floating my boat.

Putting together this edited version of my work from 2010 – 2015 involved cutting out a lot of that stuff as, frankly, it didn't stand the test of time. This volume seeks to distil my story of what it was like to be a Derby County supporter through a short, at times relatively uneventful, but crucial period that saw the Rams wading through treacle for several mediocre seasons, before exploding into life in 2013.

This book is not an exhaustive history of the era and should not be read as such. You may want or need to consult the records at times to remind yourself of particular games. If so, I would recommend using www.soccerbase.com or www.whoscored.com. However, additional context and footnotes around selected posts will help you fill in the gaps.

Ollie Wright
June 2021

The Seasons

2010/11 – 19th
W13 D10 L23 F58 A71 (-13) **Pts 49**

2011/12 – 12th
W18 D10 L18 F50 A58 (-8) **Pts 64**

2012/13 – 10th
W16 D13 L17 F65 A62 (-3) **Pts 61**

2013/14 – 3rd
W25 D10 L11 F84 A52 (+32) **Pts 85**

2014/15 – 8th
W21 D14 L11 F85 A56 (+29) **Pts 77**

2010/11

Season Preview 2010/11 for Sky Sports[1]
August 6, 2010

It's not been the most memorable of off-seasons for Derby County.

Our transfer business was conducted in a low-key, unfussy fashion before everybody got all worked up about the World Cup. In fact, one contributor to a fans' forum described it as the most boring pre-season for the Rams he could remember. I say that's a good thing.

Derby's tumultuous recent past has provided more managerial changes, squad overhauls and boardroom shenanigans than anybody with the club at heart would care to remember. So it's refreshing to go into a new season with a feeling that what is required is not revolution, but simply a continuation of the evolutionary process Nigel Clough is attempting to foster.

That said, our squad is still light on numbers, especially given the poor fitness record of many of our first-teamers, so it seems inevitable that Clough will be obliged to dip into the loan market again.

He actually used it well last season, with the likes of Freddie Stoor, Lee Johnson, Paul Dickov and DJ Campbell all making useful contributions. However, it would be much better if our own players were able to fill the first-team positions regularly, with our youngsters used as back-up.

Clough has already outlined that he wants to bridge the existing gap between the youth team and the first team. To this end, young players such as Ben Pringle are being nurtured in the reserves, but it will take time to develop the kids and in the meantime, the first XI must not struggle in the way they did last term.

---

[1] Around this time, I was invited to write a column for the 'Fanzone' section of the Sky Sports website. Fanzone, now long-deceased, was fan-created content, giving the opportunity for Sky to get lots of free articles from starry-eyed aspiring football journalists such as myself.

The signs in that regard are no better than OK, if, as is inevitable over the course of a gruelling Championship campaign, we lose a couple of players to injury.

The main change for the new season is set to be the formation, rather than the personnel. At the suggestion of coach Johnny Metgod, who spent the World Cup scouting for the Netherlands, Clough has decided to adopt a 4-2-3-1 system, as notably deployed by the Dutch, Germans and Spaniards in South Africa.

Of course, Derby's players are nowhere near as technically adept as the likes of Andres Iniesta and Xavi but we do have a squad of players who like to pass the ball, and in Kris Commons, we have an individual talent tailor-made for the modern set-up.

Playing with two holding midfielders – on Saturday at Leeds the positions will be filled by 35 year-old Robbie Savage and his 21 year-old protege James Bailey – theoretically allows the forward-thinking midfielders to concentrate on attacking.

Hence the likes of Paul Green, Commons and the young Pole, Tomasz Cywka, who has joined from Wigan Athletic after a successful loan spell last season, will be allowed to roam and search for space in between the lines, as Derby look to build from the back.

The full-backs have an important role in the 4-2-3-1, as in addition to their defensive work, they need to get forward to support the attack. New players have been brought in this summer to fill these roles. John Brayford, an adventurous young right-back Clough developed at Burton Albion, was signed from Crewe Alexandra at the same time as Bailey.

Veteran left-back Gareth Roberts has joined from Doncaster Rovers and has already treated Pride Park to a thumping goal, smashing in from range during the friendly against Birmingham City.

All has been calm at Derby since the end of last season, with only the irritation of the continuing speculation about Rob Hulse's future causing a ripple on the otherwise placid surface.

Clough would have liked to have signed Gary Hooper from Scunthorpe but was unable to match the financial muscle of Celtic, so we go into the season with what we've got and the possibility of a long-term loan to replace the luckless Steve Davies, who is sidelined yet again with knee ligament damage.

A young, talented, albeit slightly lightweight squad will go into this season unfancied and that could help them. I believe that the Championship is wide open this season and while I think the play-offs are beyond us, my expectation is a top-half finish with some attractive football along the way. Hopefully good results against the likes of Leicester, Leeds and most importantly Nottingham Forest will also be achieved.

I would also like to see Commons' contract extended – it runs out at the end of the season – on the proviso that he can keep himself fit, as he has been far too susceptible to injury over the last couple of seasons.

As for Saturday's clash with Leeds, I'm looking forward to stepping into Elland Road for the first time as our old muckers make their comeback to the second tier. I expect a real bear-pit atmosphere, which will provide a tough test for our new system – and for the youthful trio of Brayford, Bailey and Cywka.

The more experienced players, like Savage and the centre-backs, Russell Anderson and Dean Leacock, will need to stand up to the 'Dirties' and help the younger lads through the game. It's a great chance to put down a marker and three points would be a magnificent way to start the new season.

Bring it on.

***

'You were brilliant, every one of you'
August 10, 2010

In the novel *The Damned United*, David Peace puts those words into Brian Clough's mouth after another Derby County victory. And it would be no surprise if Nigel Clough said something similar in the dressing room at Elland Road on Saturday evening,

I'd been warned by Tommo to expect an intimidating atmosphere at Leeds – he'd been there in the late nineties, when a capacity Yorkshire crowd helped the Whites to blow Derby away. It seemed, back then, to be their natural right to beat Derby at home. When the Billy Davies team finally got a typical 1-0 out of them, as Leeds sank towards League One in 2006/07, it was the first time we had won there since 1857[2].

So the first thing that surprised me when we walked into Elland Road was just how many empty seats there were. This was the opening day of the season, their return to the Championship after three seasons languishing in League One, against a club with whom their most successful team jousted so memorably in the seventies.

Yet the attendance of less than 27,000 – while not much less than Derby can expect against Cardiff City next Saturday – made Elland Road look much too big for the current Leeds United era. The top tier of the hulking, cavernous main stand was entirely empty.

Derby's magnificent support, of course, was in fine fettle and never really got dominated by the home fans.

Watching the game back on the BBC iPlayer, the first thing I noticed was how much louder the home crowd seemed on the telly than they did in the stadium – because I was buffered from the volume by the constant noise that our lot generated. Going to away games is often so much more fun, because it's truly a privilege to be a part of the band of

---

[2] Actually, it was 2 November 1974.

lunatics that so loyally follow the Rams o'er land and sea.

The match in summary – Leeds huffed, puffed and hoofed with little reward. Their front three of Becchio, Watt and Sam were not terribly threatening and when we took the lead, it felt like we deserved it. Kris Commons had already slalomed through the defence and shot just over in the first minute, before ten minutes of inconclusive Leeds pressure were followed by a classic breakaway goal. Paul Green nicked the ball in midfield and simply set off, with Commons and Rob Hulse in hot pursuit. As Leeds panicked, Green found Hulse with a simple pass behind the defence and the big man obliged with a deeply satisfying finish.

Much as Nigel Clough has talked about how hard it is to choose between Hulse and Chris Porter to lead the line, in my opinion, so long as Hulse is with the club, he has to be first choice. He is strong, holds the ball up well whether received on the ground or aerially – and certainly leaves centre-backs well aware that they've been in a contest. Plus his finishing is excellent.

By this time, the pattern of the match had emerged. Leeds were going to rush us and battle for everything, while Derby were going to attempt to play out from the back. Leeds very rapidly realised that if they put our centre-backs, especially Russell Anderson, under pressure, they would not enjoy having the ball, but the Rams stuck to the plan – even after disaster struck in the 16th minute.

Dean Leacock's lateral pass to Robbie Savage was miscontrolled and led to total confusion between Savage and Anderson. Jonny Howson (a local hero, if the T-shirts bearing his name are anything to go by) nipped in and pulled the ball across to a blissfully unmarked Becchio, who couldn't miss with an open net at his mercy. All the good work was undone.

Fortunately, Derby's commitment to passing football continued — and paid off. In the aftermath of the goal, it was nice to see Hulse walk over and signal the defenders to stay calm and keep playing. That's exactly what they did and very soon, we'd pinged the ball through the Leeds lines for Commons, who fed Tomasz Cywka in the box. From our angle (bottom tier behind the opposite goal), it seemed that the lunging Sam had managed to nick the ball and I was surprised when the ref pointed to the spot. My mate Morgan received texts from Leeds fans and neutrals in short order, informing him that 'it was never a pen'. However, TV replays were inconclusive, so you have to go with the ref's call.

Commons coolly sent Kasper Schmeichel the wrong way and the Rams now had a moral responsibility not to cock it up again.

At half-time, as we sat in the Bowels of – if not the Beast (we weren't at the City Ground), at least one of Satan's more annoying helpers, we felt quite exhilarated. Derby had passed it well and strung together some really progressive moves. OK, there had been a couple of howlers, but we had also created two goals, without recourse to a single long ball. John Brayford, from right-back, provided some of the most probing runs forward, but in the final analysis it was Commons and Green, in their attacking midfield roles, who had caused Leeds all manner of trouble.

It hadn't been all our way – both Leeds centre-backs managed to hit the bar from set-pieces and the second opportunity was actually a free header from close range, which was planted straight into the turf rather than the gaping net. But the man of the match for Leeds was most assuredly Schmeichel.

A shock of white hair, a hyperactive ability to command his box, a booming kick, swift distribution and an apparent impenetrability in one-on-one situations. Who does young Kasper remind you of? In form like that, Sir Alex Ferguson wants to think very seriously about bringing him to Old Trafford. He was magnificent throughout.

When he somehow pulled off a double save of Schmeichel Snr proportions in the second half, I was on to my Manchester United supporting mates in a flash – he's just like his f**kin dad.

The second half was more of a battle for Derby. I think Simon Grayson must have given his lads a rocket at half-time, because Leeds came out scrapping. Stephen Bywater was forced to launch a few more pragmatic long clearances, but Derby did continue to attempt to pass it. Leeds were swarming around us like angry, albino Yorkshire wasps, but when they did hustle us off the ball, they simply weren't composed enough to create meaningful chances. The nearest they got to a clear sight of goal was when Bywater's lax pass out towards Brayford was intercepted – but fortunately, Derby had the answer to that.

Shaun Barker, who missed out on pre-season as he recuperated from his knee operation, wasn't even meant to be on the bench. And then, suddenly, there he was. As we finished our half-time pints, we saw, on the concourse monitors, the number five going up on the substitution board. There was our finest defender, with his black hair longer and more slicked back than before, but still attached to a head which acts as a magnet when the ball enters the Derby County penalty area.

Barker it was who blocked the shot after Bywater's horrific rick. Barker it was who took a venomous free kick square in the face, for the team. Barker it was who repeatedly rose like a salmon to clear the danger as Leeds turned our final third into the Alamo by hurling the ball into the box at every opportunity.

In the final analysis, we struggled to come up with a man of the match; we were so thrilled with the team performance. Brayford and Cywka will do nicely, thank you very much. Brayford is quick (Sam was in his pocket the whole game), intelligent and brave. Cywka is quick and extremely skilful. On watching the game back, it became clear that the chief thorn in Leeds' side been Commons, but Commons is a player who needs his team to support him. Without the ball at his feet he can do nothing. Every one of them played their part.

As we strode away from the ground, Tommo Jr got a worried call from Tommo Sr, who was watching a ruck transpire in the Elland Road car park. We were well away from the danger zone by then. Soon we were ensconced in The Angel, eating nuts, drinking pints and feeling – at least I was feeling – drained from the tension of holding a 2-1 lead for an hour.

It really shouldn't have been that taxing. We should have been out of sight. And but for an exceptional young goalkeeper, we would have been.

Sky blog – post-Rob Hulse sale
September 3, 2010

Finally, the moment many Derby fans were dreading has come and Rob Hulse has left the club. The big number nine has been the subject of endless transfer speculation for the past year and in some ways, it's a relief that it's finally over.

We knew that Hulse wouldn't be staying past the end of the season anyway, as Nigel Clough had already stated that the club were not prepared to offer him an extension of his reportedly lucrative contract. As Hulse is nearly 31, I can see the logic in moving him on and investing in a younger replacement.

Our American owners continue to do their best to reassure the fans of their honesty and in fairness, we have known for some time of the intention to move Hulse on, as part of a drive to reduce the wage bill to a realistic Championship level. Derby have finally got rid of those who weren't required and have recruited eight new players this summer – all of whom look really useful.

The newest signing is the Spanish forward Alberto Bueno. From the limited amount we know about Bueno, he is not a direct replacement for Hulse, as he prefers to play in the gaps between the frontman and the midfield. This leaves us with only one target man in the squad – the seemingly perma-crocked Chris Porter. But within the tidy new 4-2-3-1 system we're using, what if we don't even need an orthodox English centre-forward to lead the line? I can hear the gasps from the gallery and the whispers of 'burn the heretic!' But hear me out.

If you study our six league goals this season, you'll notice that the ball barely leaves the ground as we pick our way through opposition defences with precise passing. Spain's World Cup winners, using the 4-2-3-1, deployed the diminutive David Villa as the out-and-out forward, but he spent as much time in wide areas and joining up play as he did in the box waiting for the ball to be delivered. Football has evolved beyond the old certainties of 4-4-2 and England, both internationally and domestically, would do well to start catching up.

And who better than a Spaniard to play in this formation? After all, Bueno played in all of Spain's age group sides – and they are set up to mimic the senior team's formation, thus preparing young talents for the step-up when it comes.

Championship centre-backs are used to heading the ball a long way and the physical test of repelling a strong number nine, like Hulse. But it seems likely that we will play at least some games this season without any such player, instead looking to pull defences out of position with our passing and movement.

I think the new system looks really promising. We score terrific goals these days – I was delighted with both strikes against QPR, especially the second from James Bailey[3] – and it suits the personnel really well.

Tomasz Cywka has pace and trickery, Kris Commons has trickery and Paul Green has a happy facility for nicking the ball from opponents and initiating counter-attacks. Robbie Savage and Bailey sit deeper in midfield, while full-backs Gareth Roberts and John Brayford scamper forward whenever they can. Even centre-backs Shaun Barker and Dean Leacock are given license to carry the ball over half-way.

It's really refreshing to watch players creating space and time – and goals – through judicious use of the ball. Of course it doesn't always come off and they have made their fair share of mistakes, but when it does work, it's a lot more satisfying than watching grim long-ball 'percentage' football.

When I saw the reports confirming Hulse's departure, panic set in and my itchy Twitter finger started moving. But when I think about it, I'm not so sure it isn't a good move for the club. A front four of Bueno (if he

---

[3] 28 August 2010, Derby 2 QPR 2. The Rams had led 2-0 going Into injury time, before collapsing. The draw left the Rams with four points from their opening four games, after the opening day Leeds win was followed by 2-1 defeats to Cardiff City and Coventry City.

lives up to his name), Commons (if he can stay fit), Cywka and the ever-willing Green could give any defence at Championship level real problems. Then there are Porter and Stephen Pearson to return from injury and further additions to come once the loan window opens next week.

As much as I would like to see Derby in a position to splash transfer fees around, the bottom line is, at the moment, I like the team and I haven't been able to really say that for a long time. Our brand of football would make Nigel's dad proud and I firmly believe that somebody will be on the end of a stylish thrashing before too long.

So far, we have played two of the strongest teams in the division at home – Cardiff and QPR – and two traditionally tough opponents away, in Leeds and Coventry. Four points is not a disaster from those games and in truth, we've deserved far more.

Once the players pick themselves up from the devastating late collapse against QPR, they will realise that they should be proud of the way they are playing in the league and are set for a really good season ahead – unless there's another injury crisis, of course.

Let's hope that Bueno fits in to the Clough *tiki-taka*, because if he does, we could be a force to be reckoned with. If he doesn't, the goals of Hulse, which have kept us in the second division for the past two seasons, will have to be replaced somehow. I, for one, remain confident.

***

Sky blog (post Hull City defeat, 14/9/10) September 16, 2010

It's hard to know where to begin.

If you'd told me as I walked through the grim, damp streets of Leeds, trying to hide my delight at Derby's opening-day win at Elland Road, that five games later we'd only have got one more point, I'd have laughed at you.

True, it was a fiendishly tricky run of fixtures. QPR and Cardiff are now the top two, newly relegated Hull still have some quality players (not least Jimmy Bullard), Sheffield United are never a pushover – but we were so impressive against Leeds. Whereas the Whites resorted to aerial bombardment, we cut them open by keeping it on the deck. It was refreshing, it was easy on the eye, it was good.

I was cross when we lost at Crewe in the League Cup, but I still wasn't really worried when I saw us lose narrowly, undeservedly, to Cardiff. I was upset when we lost at Coventry, but more because it was such an injustice.

Even though we threw away two points against QPR, I felt OK – we'd scored two lovely goals – but I grimaced when Rob Hulse was sold, gnashed my teeth awaiting a replacement, then listened on Rams Player as Matt McCann, the club's press officer, attempted to paint a picture of the awful home defeat against Sheffield United that was so palpably false, it threatened to make the club a laughing stock. Then the loss at Hull had the numbing feel of a 'routine away defeat', already, so early in the season – and it set the alarm bells clanging.

And I won't deny that I was underwhelmed by last week's loan signing of Shefki Kuqi as a target man, even though we are told he won't be the only signing. Apparently, New Zealand striker Chris Wood of West Brom is still a loan target – but then again, we've been told things before.

In a pre-match interview with BBC Radio Derby, Adam Pearson, now working for Hull after selling Derby to the American GSE group, stated that the new owners have invested £30m cash into the Rams. He also said that the club's debt had been cut to 'single figure' millions and it was now 'all about making money for Derby'. Yet there is still huge mistrust and massive paranoia amongst the supporters, as Hulse's sale on transfer deadline day brought back so many bad memories.

To me, it makes no sense to put £30m into a club, cut its debts right down, but then allow the team to suffer by not loosening the purse strings just a little bit to bring in two or three more players, which would make a massive difference.

*

Derby have been so bad for so long that it simply can't be sorted out overnight – and by overnight, I mean a couple of seasons.

Consider the fact that Robbie Savage is reportedly still taking £15,000 per week out of the club – once he goes, Clough can bring in one, two or even three younger, better players. I'm not blaming Sav, who took a wage cut in return for a one-year extension to his contract, but frankly, he is clogging up the wage bill and is the one high earner we can't shift. Young Conor Doyle, the Texan forward recruited from an American university, disclosed last week that he earns about £34,000 per year – one Savage (at £780,000 per year) would fund around 23 Doyles.

But a lot of Derby fans see things very much in black and white, in more than one sense of the words – and all they see is Hulse gone, replaced by an even older player who couldn't get a game at Swansea. And this makes them angry. All it would take is for James Vaughan – who Clough wanted to sign, but who has gone to Palace instead – to score the first goal when the Eagles come to town and the howls of rage could start in earnest.

I think the board are sailing quite close to the wind at the moment and a recent tweet from one of our reported investors, the Canadian gazillionaire W. Brett Wilson, was quite galling, for its timing.

Whilst Derby were losing at Hull, Wilson tweeted that he was in London, having a wonderful meal with Michael Palin and 'Freud's grandson'. I can only assume that as he took time out from enjoying the fruits of his success to update the Twitterverse about his huge happiness, he wasn't casting an eye on the scores in the English second division, where one of his lesser playthings, a regional football team named Derby County, are struggling and in need of some help. The squad – threadbare. The fans – restless. The manager – under pressure. The chief executive – constantly promising things he seems unable to deliver.

There was a day, recently, when all my optimism about how the team were doing simply vanished and it will take more than a couple of positive results to change my mood. And worst of all, I know that there's nothing I can do, except for go to the games and cheer, rather than boo. The cost of my match ticket makes no difference at all – only the whim of multi-millionaire investors can genuinely make a difference.

The gulf between the Premier League and everybody else is now so monstrous that even a £30m cash investment is a drop in the ocean. Think of how Lionel Pickering sent Derby roaring into the top tier with an eye-watering £15m splurge on players. £15m! Derby spent that on players last time they got promoted and came back down humiliated – the 'worst team in history'. Yes, Billy Davies had wasted it all on disasters like Claude Davis and Benny Feilhaber, but that's not the point. The point is that it takes huge, sustained investment to get anywhere close to stability in the Premier League.

Johnny Metgod, massively off-message, said after the Hull defeat, 'This squad isn't good enough for the top half, let alone promotion, so what do you expect?' This stark analysis of our current situation – 'we've got to be realistic' – is something fans won't accept for long without demanding change. Because everyone is, at root, concerned that the club, by not moving forward with an increasingly competitive Championship, might slide inexorably towards the wasteland of League One. Just like Forest, just like Leeds, just like Sheffield Wednesday, or Southampton, or any of the other faded has-beens of the English game.

For me, it still isn't Clough's fault. He's brought in the best players he could on the budget he's been given. He's done what he was told to do, which was to cut the wage bill. He's tried to get his young lads playing good football. He's been forced to deal with a load of permanently injured players his predecessors signed. But none of this registers with the blowhards who want his blood.

I think these people need to think very seriously about who they would have to replace Clough. Do they expect Alan Curbishley? Because they won't get him. The only managers who would be interested would be the 'young and hungry' – think Phil Brown, when he took the reins from George Burley under the 'Three Amigos' – or the old and jaded. Paul Hart was on Sky Sports News the other day, touting himself for work. Any takers?

Last season, Clough was on a knife-edge after we got thrashed by Scunthorpe and I'm not sure he could get away with another such disaster. He kept the wolves at bay by pulling off a few big results when he needed them – the defeat of Forest, especially, was absolutely vital[4]. With the current squad, can he do it again this season?

The bottom line is, we need new players. And we need to not be depressed by constant home defeats. Or a lot of people will simply stop going – and the ones who would never, ever stop going, will start protesting. Peter Gadsby, who wants the land around Pride Park, is watching and waiting. Rightly or wrongly, I don't think it will take many more defeats before the calls for both manager and board to go start in earnest.

Except that suddenly and unexpectedly, things turned on their heads in the weeks that followed.   Having failed to win in six league games, Derby suddenly burst into life, winning four of their next five in some style. My next blog came just after a 3-2 win at Doncaster Rovers – remarkably, Derby had scored 14 goals in their last five games…

***

---

[4] Derby finished the 2009/10 season 15th, with 56 points. On the way, they suffered a harrowing 4-1 loss to Scunthorpe at Pride Park, but did beat Forest 1-0 at home, thanks to a late goal from Rob Hulse.

Not much to say this week, really, apart from 'jolly good, chaps, carry on'.

I was intending to go to Doncaster, but couldn't go because getting back to Manchester on the train would have necessitated leaving before the end, something I don't do (apart from once when we lost 3-0 to Millwall, when Dennis Wise was playing for them).

Anyway, before the Donny game, I was having a chat with my good mate Morgan on Facebook about the possibility of going together. This conversation was rudely interrupted by one of Morgan's mates, who is, unfortunately, a Nottingham Forest supporter. The Forest berk's jibe was something along the lines of 'Derby fans going to away games? Makes a change', before he started bragging about Forest's 'magnificent away support', which he claims is much larger than Derby's. He was unable to provide statistical proof for this, instead assuring us that we could take his word for it.

I hope that Forest's magnificent away support enjoyed their most recent jaunt, a 3-1 defeat at Barnsley. It's not going particularly well for their much-loved manager, Billy Davies – the Red Dogs have managed just three wins and 13 goals in 12 games and that pesky transfer acquisition panel still won't let him bid on Zlatan Ibrahimović. Derby have scored more goals in their last five games than Forest have managed all season.

The East Midlands derbies this season should be really spicy. I'm also looking forward to us whupping Swingin' Sven in his leopard-print crisp bowl. Bring them on!

*

Suddenly, it's clicked. The early-season promise, which was temporarily derailed by the sale of Rob Hulse and the scramble to recruit replacements, has finally flowered, with Derby embarking upon an excellent six-game unbeaten run. Since losing to Hull City, it's 15 goals scored, only four conceded, a settled system, players knowing their jobs and proving more than capable of beating any team at this level.

Crystal Palace (5-0), Middlesbrough (3-1) and Preston North End (3-0) have not been able to live with us at Pride Park. That's understandable, given that all three are in the bottom four of the Championship, but more settled teams like Doncaster Rovers (3-2), Barnsley (1-1) and Swansea City (0-0) have been unable to beat us in their own back yards.

Last season, we were dreadful on our travels – notably so at Doncaster and Swansea – so to have gained five points from those three difficult away games shows a very clear improvement in team shape, personnel and attitude. As Tommo pointed out before Donny, every outfield player who started against Preston North End has scored this season, except for John Brayford, the right-back – and he's made three assists. New loanee Luke Moore started against Doncaster and joined the fun by bagging the first goal of the night.

It is easy to become overly excited in the face of a run of victories, just as it is easy to start contemplating your navel after a couple of consecutive defeats. But essentially, Nigel Clough and his backroom team have assembled a talented squad, without being able to spend like QPR or Cardiff City. A big part of Clough's job was clearing out the players he didn't fancy and, Luke Varney's brief flash of form in the Premier League aside[5], he has not been proved wrong by anybody who has left yet.

And the signings he's made are proving to be great acquisitions. Brayford and James Bailey, whom we thought had been signed to learn and develop, are our only two Championship ever-presents this season and have improved the team massively. I believe that Brayford has the ability to be a Premier League right-back, while Bailey's astute passing game has seen him fit in to the team beautifully. Both players have

---

[5] Varney signed for Ian Holloway's Blackpool on loan in August 2010, scoring five goals in 30 appearances for the Seasiders that season.

made a mockery of the 'step up' to Championship level and whatever we paid to Crewe Alexandra, it was worth it.

Meanwhile, Alberto Bueno, the little Spaniard from Real Madrid via Real Valladolid, is brilliant. There is always a danger that a young man coming to a new country might not settle, but Bueno has been magnificent almost from game one. He is a natural for the position in the hole behind the mainline striker and is thriving by popping up between the lines in pockets of space and receiving the ball to feet. He's ably aided and abetted by the energy of Paul Green and the tenacious little technician Tomasz Cywka, players with determination and drive going forward.

All of this has helped to finally unlock the potential of Kris Commons. He seems to be missing a sitter a game at the moment, but as long as he's also scoring at a rate of better than one in two, he can be forgiven. In the past, the pressure has been on Commons to be the creative spark, but in the new system, the attacking threat comes from many different sources. If the opposition focus their energies on nullifying Commons, then Bueno, Cywka, Green or even Brayford have the ability to pop up and hurt them instead.

The only slight cloud on the horizon is the ongoing uncertainty over Commons' long-term future. Kris has stated repeatedly that he wants to stay and genuinely seems to be busting a gut at present – although the old issues of his fitness came up when he was forced off late on against Donny with cramp. That said, Robbie Savage recently commented that 'the penny seems to have dropped' with Commons and hopefully, we will have a real player on our hands for the rest of the season and beyond.

Since briefly dipping into the bottom three by losing at Hull, the Rams have surged up the table to seventh. I'm trying not to get carried away, but as I've said before, I really like the team at present and there have been many times in recent years when I couldn't really say that. The performances I've seen so far this season tell me that the current run of form is not a flash in the pan. So long as injuries don't bite as hard as they did last season, so long as Commons stays fit and motivated and so long as we are able to adequately replace Hulse on a longer-term basis, Derby can continue to improve at a rate of knots – and the DVD of goals this season will be well worth the money.

On another note, can I offer my sympathies to supporters of Portsmouth, who at the time of writing, may be on the verge of liquidation. It's a 'there but for the grace of God go I' situation, as any club could be put into such a predicament by cowboy owners.

English football has a duty to ensure that those who seek to become custodians of institutions such as Portsmouth, Derby County, or Manchester United for that matter, are not just self-interested parasites, or irresponsible, amoral fools prepared to spend unrealistic sums and then simply walk away when they lose interest.

***

Post-Watford[6]
November 3, 2010

I was just emailing a friend who supports Stoke City and explaining that it's apparently harder to blog when you're winning by three, four and five every week than it is to churn out reams of doom when you're lurking around the relegation line. Derby fans are loving it at the moment – but what do you write?

I'm not sure I'm psychologically geared for success. All these brilliant, brilliant goals, the style of play, the superiority, the talent. It may well not last through the whole season – our luck might turn, the young players might need a bit more help than is currently available, Robbie Savage might start to struggle to play as much as he did last season and there is still no long-term replacement for Rob Hulse – but the important thing is that the curve is upwards and the pattern is improvement. This run of form is the first flowering of Nigel Clough's Derby. Who knows where it will end?

---

[6] Derby had just walloped Watford 4-1 at Pride Park, with goals from Brayford, Cywka (2) and Kuqi

When Clough was appointed, there were plenty of people who were concerned by his lack of league management experience. The 'non-league Nigel' jibes of Forest fans were shamefully taken up by some of his nay-sayers as Derby struggled to cope with an epic injury crisis last season. Three consecutive home defeats in the bleakest of midwinters, the last by Scunthorpe, 4-1, could have triggered the board to panic and sack him. It's possible that their lack of experience of English football – who the hell would they appoint? – saved Nigel then, but an upturn in performances saw us safe in the end.

Nobody could have predicted that the coaching staff would get together over the summer, overhaul the tactical system and bring in two absolutely cracking young English players – James Bailey and John Brayford – plus two gifted foreign technicians – Tomasz Cywka and Alberto Bueno – thus radically reinventing a Derby County side which had lacked on-field cohesion or purpose since the promotion season of 2006/07. And crucially, although the Billy Davies way produced winning football, the Clough way is infinitely more entertaining. The players are young and have ability, the fans love them and the team has not been assembled by overspending in a way that would threaten the mid-to-long-term future of the club.

When Clough was touted as a possible replacement for Paul Jewell, I posted on a forum (I know, I know – I don't do it any more) that I thought he would be a great appointment. I immediately found myself in a minority of one. In rubbishing the suggestion, one usually sensible commentator cited Clough's lack of top-level experience and then astounded me by saying 'I want Paul Ince' – Ince was, at the time, manager of MK Dons, with only a prior short spell at Macclesfield Town behind him. Clough, I pointed out, was actually far more experienced than Ince, who went on to a disastrous spell at Blackburn Rovers and ended up back with the Dons.

What attracted me to Clough as a candidate was the work he had done at Burton Albion. OK and the name a bit, too. But think about it – Clough had played for England and at the top level for most of his career. His knowledge, experience and contacts put him in a position to apply for jobs at a higher level, but he'd never done it. He and his family lived in this area and I would suggest that here is a man who put his family first and didn't want to uproot them for the sake of his work.

Even after he managed Burton to a draw with Manchester United in the FA Cup, after helping the Brewers to move to their new stadium, he was not tempted away until finally, after he had taken the club to the brink of promotion to the Football League, the opportunity to move up to Derby came.

The impact of his long tenure at Burton is something that I sincerely hope he can duplicate at Derby, because if he can, the club will without a doubt end up as an established force in the Premier League. This will take seasons, but Clough has certainly bought himself plenty more time with the current, scintillating run of form.

And the scintillating form continued for a couple more weeks. Derby won three of their next four games to sit fourth in the league table by 20 November 2010.

However, it didn't last. A month later, Derby had lost four straight games to drop to ninth at Christmas. After their Boxing Day clash with Doncaster Rovers was postponed, they faced a trip to the City Ground…

***

Afterthoughts on a disaster
December 30, 2010

For f**k's sake.

Firstly, Forest are not that good and they certainly didn't thrash us. We thrashed ourselves[7].

Cloughie needs to explain the decision to start with Leacock as right-back and Brayford at centre-back in words of one syllable, because it

---

[7] Oh, Ollie….. For the record, this article refers to Nottingham Forest 5 Derby County 2

was wrong-headed and in fact just wrong. Not only did we lose the aerial power of a tall centre-back, we also lost Brayford's rampaging raids down the flank. By the time they switched back over, Leacock had been rinsed down the flank for a goal, Marcus Tudgay had won two headers for goals and the horse had not so much bolted as run two laps and hit the paddock for a nice hose-down.

Without Savage, we lacked leadership and organisation. We were loose, open and I said to Gav at half-time that it didn't matter if we scored two or three, because we would probably concede five or six. In fact, my half-time prediction was 3-6, which wasn't far off, in the end.

Essentially, we play with four forwards, none of whom are particularly powerful. Forest did what teams need to do to us, which is pressurise us hard and high up the pitch, ensuring we can't play out from the back. When we did manage to string a few passes together, or when a defender was invited to run into Forest territory, the final ball was invariably dreadful. Paul Green was one of the worst offenders – he is in an utter slump at the moment – but the whole lot of them are playing like they need someone to pick them up and drag them to a result.

We're short of something. I can't put my finger on it. A lot of fans think we miss Kuqi, or Hulse, really – that big man up front who can chest the ball down and hold it up. I think Moore does his best in that role, but he wants the ball in to his feet more. Give him the ball to feet and he will score goals. Toss it down the channel and he will chase after it. He also gets his fair share of flick-ons. I don't think it was Luke Moore's fault that we lost today. But the majority of fans seem to think that we need a big strongman up front. I actually like Moore and think we should sign him long-term, but most supporters seem to need a centre-forward in the old-fashioned Stevie Howard mould to roar on.

Personally, I think that what we need more than a big number nine is a new central midfielder to do the Savage role and I don't think that January is too early to make the move. If we had a proper, combative ball-winner to go in, break up play and launch our creative players, we might not look so maddeningly weak and easy to score past. Clough had said he expects new signings early in the window and it will be very interesting to see who they are.

We must take a minimum of four points from the next two games, put this slump firmly behind us and move forward into the new year with positivity. We should be cheerful about the future, because the club is moving in the right direction, but it doesn't feel that way right now. Tonight, it's just anger and fear and more anger.

Derby did as I asked and stopped the rot. They picked up four points from the next two games by winning 2-1 at Preston North End through a Chris Porter brace on New Year's Day 2011, then drawing 0-0 at home against Millwall on 3 January.

Next came a week-long break, before an FA Cup trip to non-league Crawley.

What could possibly go wrong…?

***

Sky blog (pre-Crawley Town[8]) January 7, 2011

The January transfer window is a time of uncertainty for fans of most clubs and it remains to be seen how it will pan out for Derby. The main talking point is still the future of our best player, Kris Commons. As second-top scorer in the Championship, on a contract that expires in summer, it seems inevitable that somebody will nip in and make him an offer and the club can't even expect much in the way of the transfer fee if he is sold this month. This seems like a no-win situation for Derby.

Such is the general air of austerity around the club that nobody seriously expect Commons to stay, or even anybody to be signed to replace him, with the possible exception of a promising kid from somewhere. After all, Rob Hulse was sold in August and still hasn't been

---

[8] Derby had been drawn to face non-league Crawley in the third round of the FA Cup.

replaced. The major problem for the club is that replacing players of the calibre of Commons, Hulse and Robbie Savage is impossible without serious investment, something the current board are clearly not prepared to countenance.

Nobody objects to Derby bringing through young starlets and the emergence of John Brayford, James Bailey and Tomasz Cywka under Clough is heartening, but the younger lads do need a guiding hand on the pitch, sometimes. Savage is currently filling that role and doing it well, but once he leaves – presumably at the end of the season – there will be a void to fill and none of our other experienced players have quite the same sort of character. But then, does anyone have the same character as Sav?

Results in January, especially the FA Cup tie at Crawley Town and the home leg of the East Midlands derby, will probably influence whether reinforcements are sought; however, I doubt we'll see more than a couple of loans coming in. Other than Commons, who may go to Celtic this month, I don't foresee much in the way of outward transfer activity, either – although some clubs might fancy Paul Green, who is currently doing penance for missing a load of chances by filling in at right-back, while Brayford covers at centre-back.

That Brayford is currently playing in central defence is a shame, as the team misses his pace, skill and driving runs from his natural position. We could seriously do with having him at full-back for the Forest match, because he adds so much to our attack, as well as being able to cope with a pacy wideman running at him. Forwards such as Commons and Alberto Bueno can sometimes be marked out of games, but it is difficult to shut down Brayford, whose marauding raids cause panic in opposing defences.

We need the boost of wins at Crawley and against Forest, because the season seems to have gone flat. The play-off positions seem light years away, even if we're only a few points off them and while I backed us for a cup run earlier in the season, right now, I'm just hoping that we don't become the victims of a major giantkilling. To have to go to Crawley in front of the TV cameras on a Monday night is a major test of character for our players, who badly flunked their last such examination at the City Ground.

Ah yes, about that. In the most part, I had a fine time on 29th December. We wandered around the quieter, non-footballing Nottingham hostelries for the majority of the day, sporting no colours and sampling some good local ales. The journey to Forest's lair is never pleasant for a Derby fan, but walking across the River Trent for a night match, with the mist illuminated by the floodlights, is a truly evocative footballing experience. Then you get to laugh at Forest's naff anthems ('Mull of Kintyre' and 'You've Lost That Lovin' Feelin') and settle in for what is usually a strongly contested affair. Only this time, we kept simply giving goals away.

Fortunately, I was numbed from the worst excesses of the pain by the liberal quantities of ale I'd quaffed in the build-up. I vented my 'enthusiasm' by yawping unkind words in the direction of Billy Davies and the Derby-born Forest goalie Lee Camp and by giving the Rams the benefit of my years of coaching experience, screaming 'MOVEMENT!' and 'WANT IT MORE!' at regular intervals.

Our defending was staggeringly poor on the night and Dean Leacock may well have paid for it with his future at the club. One particularly perceptive Derby blogger – Chris from Ramspace – noted that Nigel Clough's post-match laceration of Leacock's performance was reminiscent of the gaffer's singling-out of Martin Albrechtsen, who was drummed out of the club in the aftermath of some unacceptably milky defensive displays. Albrechtsen is now back in his native Denmark and one wonders if Leacock will be gone by the end of the season too.

Memories of the scintillating win against Crystal Palace, amongst others, remind us of what the current squad is capable of, but when they drop below their best level, we end up with experiences like the defeat at the City Ground. We have the opportunity to put it right by taking revenge at Pride Park in a couple of weeks – but another defeat, either in the FA Cup or in the East Midlands derby, will ramp up the pressure on the board to come up with a major new signing.

***

Post-Crawley Town debacle
January 11, 2011

Lingy[9] and I recorded a podcast last night and I think in some ways, attempting a live commentary of the game allows you be to be slightly more dispassionate than you would be in the stands. I've avoided message boards and Twitter as much as possible since the result and will limit myself to a couple of observations before I get down to editing the podcast files.

My theory is that Brayford was deployed at centre-back because Clough was worried that a lack of pace in that position would leave us vulnerable to balls tossed over the top for the nippy striker, Tubbs, to chase. It worked, to an extent, but of course, we lost the ability of Brayford to make game-changing bursts from right-back. Clough no longer trusts Leacock and so there was nobody else to play centre-back alongside Barker.

Clough obviously wants his defenders to show spirit and tenacity; hence he loves Barker and Brayford and has apparently given up on Leacock. Unfortunately, the team is suffering, as we lose the best qualities of Green and Brayford while they cover positions they aren't particularly suited to.

It would seem that Clough is desperate to change personnel, but it would also seem that there is no money to do it, so players will have to leave first. I would imagine that Clough will accept the departure of Leacock, Green and Commons in order to recruit new blood.

Back to the team selection – no Bueno. Lingy theorised that Clough felt it might be best to hold him back until Crawley had tired a little (Tubbs' despicable tackle on Savage showed he might have had a point), but in fact, Bueno wasn't risked at all. I just don't get why Cywka was intro-

---

[9] Lingy = my friend Matt Ling, a brilliant guy who I met while working at Reveal Records, in Derby city centre. For the Crawley game, he came up to visit me at my flat in Chorlton, Manchester. We recorded a pre-game conversation and then I attempted a live commentary of the whole match, with Matt on 'co-comms' (which partially involved rolling and passing me joints).

duced for Pringle, rather than Bueno – and Clough wasn't available to take questions after the match.

On the plus side, Miles Addison made it through 90 minutes and showed his strength by scoring (and celebrated like it meant something). His strength and character might well be exactly what we need. I thought Bailey played quite well too – although his panic after we conceded was betrayed, when he was booked for a rash tackle after missing his kick to give away possession. It was a rush of blood caused by embarrassment. Unfortunately, he was also the defender on the edge of the box when the low, skidding 90th-minute corner fizzed straight across the box and allowed Sergio Torres to become a Crawley Town legend.

The media blackout led to speculation that Clough might be sacked and nobody was more relieved than me to read his statement of apology, which turned up on the club's website this afternoon.

BBC Radio Derby were extremely cross that he refused to speak to them after the game, which won't have helped his cause any – especially when there are no end of people of limited intelligence who've been desperate for him to be sacked since the day before he was appointed and like to ring the Colins[10] up every week.

It's a mess. The season has threatened to drop into freefall and the last thing we need is the visit of a well-drilled Forest prepped for the Billy Davies promotion push, after a trip to Watford. What we do need is a couple of new players, to freshen things up. The squad is palpably too thin and has been since the start of the season. We're now reaping the 'rewards' of that.

I've always defended Clough from his most egregious critics, because in the past two years, he's done a lot of good things. He's also made

---

[10] Colins = Colin Bloomfield, who was working as Radio Derby's commentator, and Colin Gibson, the veteran journalist who went on to 'cross the aisle' by accepting a job at Derby County. Bloomfield, who was a real gentleman, was the first person to give me an opportunity to appear on BBC Radio Derby's Monday night *Sportscene Talk-in*. Very sadly, he passed away in 2015, having been diagnosed with stage 4 melanoma in 2013 (https://www.skcin.org/ourWork/colinBloomfieldMelanomaAppeal.htm).

plenty of mistakes and his team selections for the Forest and Crawley games must have lost him support. He knows himself it's a results business and the fans will desert him if we stop winning.

Attendances are already in decline (around 24,500 at the moment). That said, the board know damned well that they owe Clough for implementing their cost-cutting measures while managing to retain some vestiges of class – not that this will save him if the bottom drops out of the team's form.

For Christ's sake, Tom Glick, back your manager in this transfer window. It won't take multi-millions to get this squad to top-eight level.

In the next fortnight, things just got worse. First Derby lost 3-0 to Watford and then they were beaten 1-0 by Forest at Pride Park…

***

Rip It Up and Start Again
January 29, 2011

OK, so Kris Commons is history, blah blah blah. For all that he's done exceptionally well this season, I am genuinely not arsed. In the modern era, it's dangerous to get overly attached to players, when they aren't tied to clubs in the same way that the fans are. Even the sainted Miles Addison might be tempted away one day. I could conceivably weep on that day, but that's a different case entirely.

Anyway, I think it's more important to focus on the players we have got, either for now, or for the long term. Everybody's view seems to be clouded by the temporary bleakness of the picture – and of course I can see why, of course I don't particularly enjoy watching us get hacked and bullied off the park by a bunch of cloggers from Sussex, or capitulating like muppets at the City Ground, or huffing and puffing our way towards an inevitable Billy Davies away-day classic result. I do not like any of these things. But I refuse to indulge in 'board out' tantrums, I refuse to believe that the current squad are going to get us relegated and am not going to start ranting because an instant, gift-wrapped Commons replacement isn't going to be announced before the end of the window.

The way I see things, the summer is absolutely pivotal and the recruitment has to be spot on. Clough has a major opportunity to reshape the squad in his image, with the albatross Robbie Savage (God bless him) finally due to be off the bill, Commo gone and very possibly a couple of others in line to be released.

With this in mind, I thought I'd look at the first team players' contract expiry dates and see if that helped me to feel more positive about the future of the club. The answer is – yes it does, actually, assuming that GSE don't cut Clough's wage bill any more than they already have done and the signings we make in the summer work out.

CONTRACT TO EXPIRE END OF 2010/11 – Saul Deeney, Jake Buxton, Robbie Savage, Ben Pringle, Steven Davies, Alberto Bueno, Chris Porter

Deeney will probably be retained for another year, to sit on the bench. As outlined in *Why England Lose* by Simon Kuper (and noted by Ramspace previously), it makes absolutely no sense to have two highly paid goalkeepers at the club, unless you're Man City. At one stage, we had Stephen Bywater and Roy Carroll on the bill (thanks, Paul Jewell), which was just nuts. You have your number one, then ideally a talented young number two. If your number one gets a bad injury, you can go out and loan in a competent keeper to man the fort.

Bucko hasn't played all season and could well be on his way in May. Savage has already been told it's time for him to bow out and anybody who saw the home defeat to Forest will agree with that decision. The Vancouver Whitecaps thing would have been the perfect resolution as far as Derby were concerned. Pringle will probably be renewed for another year and let's hope he kicks on. Which leaves us with the strikers.

Davies is the one I lament the most – clearly a talent, the poor lad simply can't get himself fit. His cameo at the City Ground recently was the saddest thing, at least until he came on for the return leg at Pride Park for five minutes and did nowt except for jump for the same ball as Chris Porter – a moment which rightly sparked a mass exodus from the stadium (no, of course I didn't leave). Unless Davies plays regularly for the rest of the season and delivers on his promise, it could well be time to wave him goodbye. That would be really sad, but unfortunately, his record of ten starts in 2008/09, eight in 2009/10 and none yet this season outweighs his talent in my reckoning at this time.

Porter is an odd one and his much-vaunted 'goals to games' ratio could do with being tested by a prolonged run in the team. His nine goals have come from three starts in 2008/09, 13 in 2009/10 and six so far this time around. The fans got extremely cross with him against Forest, because he had a bit of a "Rick Witter" – and also managed to miss a sitter[11].

Bueno, we know, will be offski.

CONTRACT EXPIRES END OF 2011/12 – Stephen Bywater, Dean Leacock, Miles Addison, Russell Anderson, Gareth Roberts, Dean Moxey, Paul Green, Jeff Hendrick, Stephen Pearson, Conor Doyle, Lee Croft, Dave Martin, Tomasz Cywka, Luke Varney

The one that leaps out of me, from this list, is Addison – I want that extension dusted, pronto. The second one is Green. I've been a bit worried for Green of late; the poor lad has missed a bunch of chances, but his energy and drive are serious attributes. I hope Derby see the best of him again soon; it might just be that he can't quite fit into the current system properly – but then, I almost got the impression that the current system had been introduced for Commons' benefit and he's gone now. If we don't agree an extension with Green, other clubs will bid for him in summer, without a doubt.

Leacock, Bywater and Pearson are all on good money and will be under pressure to earn it from now on. You can't help but wonder if Clough regrets extending the injury-prone Pearson's deal. Bywater is an interesting one. The manager used to praise his goalkeeper quite

---

[11] For the uninitiated, Rick Witter was the frontman of nineties indie band Shed Seven

regularly, even talking him up for the World Cup squad before summer, but that's all gone quiet and even though he's a good age for a goal-keeper (29), his contract has been allowed to reach the dreaded 18-month mark. Maybe Frank Fielding's performances turned Cloughie's head.

What about Deano? He has fallen out of favour and the stubbornness Clough exhibited by refusing to play Leacock at centre-back despite having no viable alternatives was the key factor to the 5-2 at Forest – putting Leacock at right-back, up against Tyson, was a dreadful de-cision and he was only restored to his natural position once the game at Watford was lost and it was threatening to get embarrassing. He put in a better performance in the Forest home game, but is now suspen-ded for two matches and has forced Clough to try to replace him with Liverpool youngster Daniel Ayala. If Ayala gets in and stays in, who knows what the future holds for Deano.

Cywka has ability and seems to have a good attitude too. I hope he comes off. The left-backs can both sod off tomorrow, for all I care (I used to think Moxey was really promising, but he seems to lack brains and I've lost faith in him. Roberts – bleh). The wingers Croft and Martin have been rendered redundant by the new system and anyway, Croft failed on loan at Huddersfield recently. We'll not see much more of An-derson due to his injuries, unfortunately – if he can't get right, we might even see a mutual termination in the summer. Varney will stay at Blackpool and fingers crossed, he won't come back and haunt us, like all of other our former strikers do.

2012/13 – Mark O'Brien, John Brayford, James Bailey, Ben Davies
2013/14 – Shaun Barker

These are the players who Clough sees as the long-term nucleus of the squad. I enjoyed Barker's rant on Rams Player when he signed his extension, which very much seemed to me like one long dig at Com-mons. His commitment in the home game against Forest was truly in-spirational and my heart went out to him as he stood alone applauding the fans, after the final whistle, with everyone else having made their way back to the safety of the dressing room. It seemed that he simply couldn't bear to leave the field. His headers, blocks, tackles and covering that day were all superb and it's little wonder that he has been rewarded with such a long extension and the captaincy.

I think the key point is that there aren't many on long contracts anymore and I think all those that are, the fans would agree should be. The club tried to keep Commons, but he stayed true to the pattern of his career and ran down his contract before moving on. Good luck to him.

Now I'm off to start my 'Extend Addison's Contract' campaign. Who's with me?

After a 1-1 draw with Portsmouth on 5 February 2011, Derby had won only one of their previous 12 games in all competitions and were sliding rapidly down the table, sitting 17th.

***

Fear and Loathing in DE24
February 8, 2011

In 1971, Brian Clough signed Colin Todd for Derby County from Sunderland for a fee of £175,000, while the club's chairman Sam Longson was on holiday, blissfully unaware of what was going on. Just prior to this deal being concluded, Rolls-Royce had announced lay-offs in Derby and the mood around the place was not good. Clough's rationale for spending big, in the wake of so many job losses? It's said that he declared, 'I thought the town needed cheering up.' Longson was alerted to the transfer by telegram.

Cheering up, of course, is something that Derby could sorely do with right now, but Brian's son Nigel won't be going to another club with a chequebook and returning with their star player any time soon – and certainly not Saturday's opponents Leicester City, where money is now seemingly no object. And so as another season ebbs rapidly into nothing, Derby people, down-trodden by the government's agenda of cuts, tax increases and more cuts, are receiving no cheer from the one institution in the city with the power to bring them unconditional joy – the football club.

These days, Derby County is being dispassionately run as a business. The wage bill has been capped at what is in effect a middling Championship level and the chief executive, Tom Glick, seeks to increase revenues by negotiating all sorts of sponsorship deals and offering 'football fans, specifically Derby County fans', as he recently put it, great deals on anything he can stick a club badge on. The £175,000 that Clough Snr paid for Todd is peanuts in today's football, but Clough Jnr couldn't spend even that without Glick's approval.

That's not necessarily a bad thing in itself, but the problem is that somewhere in the midsts of all this book-balancing, the squad got lost. There was little wrong with selling the contract-hopping mercenary Kris Commons and even less wrong with offloading the full-back Dean Moxey – who is not very good and at 25, can't really be regarded as one for the future – but the lack of new signings in January, when we were told the cavalry was coming, was intensely frustrating. And not just for the fans.

After the Portsmouth draw, complete with soul-destroying last-minute equaliser, Nigel's frustration spilled over into his most personal and questionable beasting of a player yet, with poor Tomasz Cywka the recipient. Fans were shocked – nobody expected a young tryer to get a roasting like that – but it had in fact been brewing for a while. After the City Ground debacle, Clough gave Cywka a dishonourable mention, before expressing his disappointment with the Pole after an unfruitful sub appearance in the defeat to Ipswich Town.

I can think of reasons to defend Clough for his actions. I have no problem with his policy of criticising players when they err – it's a man's game, the players are extremely well paid by anybody but bankers' standards and the pressure they pile on the manager with their mistakes could cost him his job – but in my heart of hearts, I didn't like it. Colin Bloomfield, the BBC Radio Derby journalist, broke with his usual equanimity to publicly criticise Clough and a disgruntled little band of Rams fans are on Twitter, sticking the boot in as we speak.

I stopped using message boards long ago because I got sick to death of all the moaning. Twitter has started to feel the same. Mostly now, all I read when I search for Rams news on the site is people saying they've heard we're about to sign Nathan Tyson, slating Gareth Roberts, or Clough, or GSE, or a mixture of the above. It's depressing, but you have to say that the board have brought it upon themselves.

If there are, as is rumoured, to be protests during the televised game against Leicester, Glick has only himself to blame. He had January to bring in players and with the exception of Ben Davies – who might be a good player, but has the misfortune to be stepping into Commons' shoes – he failed to do so. A couple of unfortunate defeats have been compounded by a slew of colossally demoralising losses and even the point at crisis-ridden Portsmouth was turned into a negative by Clough's verbal laceration of Cywka.

To the current board, Derby is just another franchise, to be run as a tight ship and sold on if they get a good offer. And it is right not to run at a dangerous loss, it is right to be financially sensible – nobody wants to see a Portsmouth scenario at Pride Park. However, to many people in Derby, the Rams are a personal obsession, a much-cherished, lifelong love, with the potential to be a light in the darkness, to raise spirits when times are hard. These passionate, ardent fans are a powerful force when riled, as the criminal Three Amigos found, in days we choose not to think about, but will never forget.

The board would be well-advised to give Clough the two strikers he has asked for before Saturday's game against Leicester, to give us a chance of arresting a ruinous run of five home games without a win and offer some indication to the people whose money they take that they might actually be worthy custodians of it – because plenty of supporters have run out of patience already.

***

Derby County sign Jamie Ward on season loan
February 16, 2011

Derby County completed a deal today to sign the Sheffield United striker Jamie Ward on loan until the end of the season. Ward, 24, has been allowed to leave Bramall Lane after falling out of favour with the Blades' new manager, Micky Adams. Ward takes over the number ten shirt recently vacated by Kris Commons.

Nigel Clough told Rams Player that he would have liked to have signed Ward from Chesterfield at the time he moved to Sheffield and is pleased to have brought in a player with 'a bit of pace' and 'a bit of an edge to him'. He also revealed that there is a possibility for Ward to sign at Derby permanently this summer, if the initial loan move is a success.

Ward, an Aston Villa youth product, was a big hit at Chesterfield, scoring 31 goals in 62 starts and nine substitute appearances, but had a mixed spell at United after signing from the Spireites for a reported £333,000 in January 2009. He has scored only once this season, in a 3-1 home defeat to Aston Villa in the FA Cup, and was sent off after coming on as a sub in the loss to Leeds United at Elland Road last September.

Ward was candid enough to admit to Rams Player that moving to Derby was his 'only option' at this point in his career and it's fair to say that he was not Clough's first choice, given that moves for Martyn Waghorn and Conor Sammon failed in recent weeks. That said, there is an opportunity for a young striker to make himself a hero at Derby County, especially the way things are going at present. Let's hope that Ward takes that chance.

***

Sky Blog, post Doncaster Rovers March 3, 2011

I haven't written for a while, principally because I've been experiencing feelings of shock, denial, anger and depression, which have engulfed all fans of this benighted club for the past three months.

During that time, we have won twice, drawn three times and lost 11 games, most notably 5-2 at Forest, 2-0 in a one-sided joke match against Leicester, 3-1 at home to Doncaster, who had 12 players out injured and were in the bottom six at the time (now replaced there by us) and, of course, 2-1 at Crawley in the FA Cup. Only one of the pathetic total of nine points we've 'amassed' since 27th November 2010 has been earned at home. The teams who still have to play us will be licking their lips.

The really distressing thing about Nigel Clough's current team is their total lack of character. This season, we have come from behind to get a win or a draw a grand total of once – and that was because of the brilliance of the now-departed Kris Commons, upon whom, it turns out, we were almost totally reliant for goals and inspiration. If we ship the first goal, we lose. Clough's Derby of 2010/11 know exactly when they're beaten and that's the first time their defences are pierced. This is unacceptable.

The numbing home defeat to Doncaster was as good an example as any – for 40 minutes, Derby had a go and pegged very beatable opposition back. Until, with pretty much their first opening, the visitors managed to get Billy Sharp away. Sharp did what million-pound strikers do. Derby then conceded another crass goal straight after half-time and with fans booing, scuffling among themselves and screaming at Clough for subbing Theo Robinson, the team had no chance of mounting a comeback.

Probably, most of the players don't like playing at Pride Park, with good reason. The fans are unhappy and certain players have become easy targets. Porter and Pearson have plenty of detractors and Ben Davies' substitution against Doncaster was met with cheers – sadly, he is going the same way. The alleged dead-ball specialist has shown little of that expertise at Derby and is doubtless feeling the pressure of the tag.

But even if he does manage to ping in a few good set-pieces, I would question the recruitment of this 29 year-old, who has never played above League One level, simply on physical grounds. He is possibly the slowest player I've ever seen and when Clough has been so busy complaining about a lack of pace in his team, adding someone even more pedestrian than the rest of them made no sense whatsoever.

The 4-2-3-1 system used earlier in the season stopped working as soon as teams caught up to the tactical innovation. The consequent switch to 4-4-2, which was necessary, has stuttered because we don't actually have any wingers. That Dave Martin, the only genuine left-winger in the squad, has been loaned to Notts County, reveals that something has gone badly wrong for him during his first full season at the club. The only right-winger, Lee Croft, has also been excommunicated to the point that he was sent to the club's official pub, the fantastic Woodlark, to meet and greet fans before the Doncaster disaster. The last manager, Paul Jewell, was guilty of freezing players out – most notably Robbie Savage – and it breeds disharmony and discontent within the squad, to the point that his ultimate resignation was a relief to everyone.

There's not much sympathy left in the stands for anybody now – players, management, certainly not the board – and revolution is in the air. Attendances are dropping, but those who are too hard-bitten to stay away are becoming more and more vocal in their discontent.

Mistakes have been made at all levels – not least the witless failure to recruit sufficiently during January – and the cumulative weight of cock-ups could very conceivably see the club relegated to the third tier for the first time since 1983/84. I have never seen the team I love sink so low and I suppose I always thought we had a divine right not to be relegated out of the Championship, but that's not so. You just wonder if a combination of a lack of investment, underachieving senior players, managerial mistakes (both in the transfer market and tactically), an inexperienced, arguably incompetent chief executive and disinterested, bean-counting board across the Atlantic have finally caught up with us.

Certainly, relegation starts to seem inevitable when both your goal-keepers get injured within a day, leaving the youth team goalie to miss a corner so you lose a game you shouldn't have lost (Hull, at home). But the odd thing like that will go against you in a season and it was only one goal that the kid conceded. It's how you bounce back from setbacks like that. And at the moment, Derby's players are not showing the type of resolve that's needed to get out of a crisis.

If we do stay up, it will only be because three teams are in an even worse mess than we are. I can think of only three candidates – Scun-thorpe, Sheffield United (who just lost to us at home, which shows how poor they are[12]) and Preston. If we can make it through to summer – and it's a big if – we might be able to build a new squad on the nucleus of good young players, such as Addison, Bailey, Brayford, Steve Davies and hopefully Frank Fielding in goal, along with the captain, Shaun Barker. But fans are sick of the promise of 'jam tomorrow'. A good friend of mine isn't sure whether to renew his season ticket and when I thought about it, I couldn't think of a single reason why he should. It's a question only Tom Glick can answer.

A radical change in fortunes is required and that may only be possible under new ownership, or new management, or maybe both. One thing's for certain – something has got to change and fast.

***

---

[12] Derby beat Sheffield United 1-0 at Bramall Lane on 26 February 2011. It was their first win since New Year's Day and only their second in 16 games.

'Rat' Jumps Sinking Ship – Bywater departs Derby County for Cardiff
March 4, 2011

Stephen Bywater may well have got his rat ahhhtt[13] for the last time as a Derby County custodian.

'The Nutter' departs on loan to Cardiff City for the rest of the season, after the England under-21 goalkeeper Frank Fielding returned to Derby for a second loan spell from Blackburn Rovers. Fielding was originally ostensibly signed as cover for the injured Rams number one, but his popularity with the fans paves the way for the departure of the more experienced, presumably better-paid Bywater, whose contract expires at the end of the 2011/12 season. Derby have inserted a 24-hour recall clause into the loan agreement, in case of any emergencies.

Bywater recently caused controversy by issuing a series of cryptic tweets, which were interpreted by some followers as containing thinly veiled criticism of the club's management. He also made national newspapers in September last year when neighbours complained about a bizarre 'art installation' he kept in his back garden. The installation involved a graffiti-daubed portaloo and prominently featured two blow-up sex dolls[14].

The *Derby Telegraph* reported today that 'Bywater is close to fitness and the Rams are keen for him to get some games'. This pronouncement from the club seems somewhat disingenuous; Bywater has only been missing for a couple of matches, so can hardly be described as a player in need of regaining match practise, having played for the majority of the season. The loan deal is more likely to be part of a longer-term strategy of moving Bywater on.

---

[13] A reference to Bywater's bawdy interruption of Giles Barnes' interview immediately after Derby's 2007 play-off final victory over West Bromwich Albion.

[14] https://www.bbc.co.uk/news/uk-england-derbyshire-11393407

A problem with this move is that it could necessitate the use of another loan to provide goalkeeping cover. Matt Duke of Hull City is reportedly the most likely candidate, having previously played for Nigel Clough at Burton Albion. The problem with this would be that with Duke on board, the Rams would be up to five domestic loanees, the maximum number that can be named in a matchday 18.

Derby are already extremely short of defensive cover, with Paul Green filling in at right-back and John Brayford shifted to left-back in the absence of Gareth Roberts and, erm, anybody else, so it's not ideal to have to fill up the fifth loan slot with a reserve goalkeeper, who is unlikely even to be called upon.

One would hope that Cardiff are at least paying a reasonable loan fee for Bywater. Looking further down the line, it's possible to see a scenario in which Duke is viewed as a potential number one goalkeeper for next season, if the worst happens and Derby are relegated to League One.

***

Stephen Bywater Timeline – Those Tweets in Full
March 9, 2011

22nd January – Derby County 0 Nottingham Forest 1, Derby's seventh defeat in nine games

25th January @sbywater1 – Titanic!!!!

26th January @sbywater1 – In baseball, do they say??… He's outta here!

28th January – Kris Commons signs for Glasgow Celtic for a fee of around £300,000, on wages of about £1m per year

30th January – @sbywater1 You pay peanuts.... You get monkeys. You pay coconuts.... You get gorillas. FACT!

30th January – @sbywater1 Stayed in big hotel this weekend. The people running it know what there doing. That's what made the difference!

31st January – @sbywater I'm off.........

31st January – @sbywater .... to the shop!

1st February – Derby County 1 Ipswich Town 2 – first Ipswich goal by Jimmy Bullard, a long-range shot which should have been comfortably saved.

5th February – Portsmouth 1 Derby County 1 – Clough in now-notorious 'Cywkagate' incident, wherein the young Pole is extremely harshly pilloried for losing the ball in the build-up to Nugent's 89th-minute equaliser

6th February – @sbywater1 Commons...
GooooooaaaaaallIIIIIIIIIIIIIIIIIIIIIIIIIIIIIIIIIIIIIIIIIIIIIIIIIIIIIIIIIIIIIIIIIIIIIIII

7th February @sbywater1 How can you lose a dressing gown? Seems quite an achievement to me. Yep, mine is gone...I'll blame someone else.

7th February @sbywater1 Nope. Looked around and the dressing gown is definatly gone. Gutted.

9th February @sbywater1 Coffee... Did you say coffee. No I'm not keen on coffee. Tee 1 sugar plz.

22nd February – Derby County 0 Hull City 1 – Bywater substituted with a muscle injury, leaving youth team goalkeeper James Severn to miss a corner and condemn Derby to another damaging defeat

25th February – Frank Fielding signs as cover for the injured Bywater. Clough – 'The deal lasts until the end of the season, so when Stephen is back fit it gives us some really strong competition for the number one jersey, which will be good for both of them and ultimately the team.' Derby Telegraph – *'Regular number one Stephen Bywater is expected to be out for a few weeks with a strained muscle in his side'*

4th March – Bywater loaned to Cardiff until end of season. Clough – 'Stephen has recovered from his injury and Cardiff made an inquiry about taking him on loan until the end of the season and he seemed keen to go. Frank Fielding has got the shirt and we are happy for Frank to be in goal.'

5th March – Cardiff City 0 Ipswich Town 2, with Bywater starting.

7th March @colinbloomfield Frank Fielding can only play the next 3 games for Derby before his emergency loan comes to an end – full details at 1635.

8th March (RT by @sbywater1) @stokesy69 give us a retweet if you think the bluebirds are going 2 get back on track with a win tonight !

***

Porter and Ben Davies dropped as Derby County take a step towards redemption March 14, 2011

To my confusion and delight, Derby County made a mockery of my doom-laden prediction[15] and toughed their way to a massively important 2-1 victory over Swansea City on Saturday.

At a point when any realistic hopes of a recovery had gone and relegation was starting to look like a very serious threat, Ashley Williams and Dorus de Vries lost the plot under pressure and scored the best own

---

[15] I'd predicted a 3-0 thrashing for the Rams

goal at Pride Park since Andy King's last season[16].

Derby don't do things the easy way and although Steve Davies doubled the advantage with a deflected header from Conor Doyle's corner, there were serious fears that the Rams might buckle once Darren Pratley made it 2-1. However, although Williams and Stephen Dobbie both hit the bar and Scott Sinclair somehow failed to slide in Dobbie's centre, ultimately Derby did what they have failed to do on too many occasions this season and held out for the points.

I was delighted by Nigel Clough's decision to recall Alberto Bueno. I feared that there would be no meaningful changes made to the side that lost at Middlesbrough, other than the recall of Robbie Savage, but the fulcrum Bueno was restored, playing behind the promising Steve Davies.

However, a glance at the subs' bench brought a major surprise – the omission of Ben Davies and Chris Porter from the matchday 18, at the expense of the academy duo Callum Ball and Jeff Hendrick, both of whom have reportedly impressed Clough in training.

Porter has been in and out of the team throughout another injury-ravaged season and with his contract due to expire in summer, this latest development is not a good sign for the striker. It's starting to look increasingly likely that he will be playing his football elsewhere next season.

Porter made an extremely promising start to his Derby County career, scoring three goals in his first three starts. Sadly, injuries intervened and he has made a total of just 19 starts in the past two-and-a-half seasons. At 26 years old, he can't be regarded as a prospect in the same way that the 23-year old Steve Davies can and, barring an incredible last-ditch flurry of goals before the end of the season, has to be chalked into Nigel's 'Flop' column, along with excommunicated Huddersfield reject Lee Croft.

---

[16] King's backpass rolled straight over the foot of Foxes' goalkeeper Chris Weale, giving Derby a 1-0 win in March 2010.

Signed by Clough in January, Ben Davies has failed to make any impression on the Derby fans, or the team's fortunes, so far. Even allowing for the fact that it's difficult to look good in a struggling team, Davies does not seem to be the sort of player who can make a difference at Championship level. He is ponderously slow and seems to have no obvious natural position. Much therefore depends on his set pieces, but seemingly weighed down by the pressure of his 'dead-ball specialist' tag, he has struggled to get any consistency on his corners or free kicks for Derby to date.

Even worse, it was his 89th-minute mistake which cost the Rams a share of the points at Middlesbrough on Tuesday and while Clough refrained from giving him a public tongue-lashing, the action of omitting him from the matchday squad for Swansea is a more extreme, albeit less visceral, decision. Cutting Ben Davies and Porter from the squad surely refutes the accusations of anti-Clough commentators who accuse the manager of favouring 'special' players.

Perhaps leaving Ben Davies out was meant to be a kick up the backside for a player who might well be wondering why the hell he went through the hassle of leaving Paul Ince's Notts County. Incidentally, a world where a footballer receives death threats for joining a second division club from a third division club, as Ben Davies claims to have done, is a world gone mad.

***

Bizarre transfer rumour links Nathan Tyson with Derby County
March 16, 2011

I've heard some nonsense in my time, but surely this takes the cake.

The *Mirror* yesterday reported that Nathan Tyson is in line to join Derby County on a free transfer in summer, as his unsuccessful spell at Notts Forest winds down. The story quotes Nigel Clough's recent line – that he will be looking to add experienced players to the squad in summer –

adds the striker-cum-wide man Tyson's availability and calls that a transfer rumour.

The *Mirror* seem blissfully unaware of Tyson's 'previous' with the Rams. On that fateful day last season when Derby lost 3-2 at the City Ground, the Derby supporters stood to applaud their players' efforts, only to be confronted with a red-shirted buffoon trailing a corner flag, replete with Forest logo.

This action certainly incited the fans, caused Derby players to remonstrate with him, before the entire Forest squad descended *en masse* and an embarrassing brawl ensued. The imbecilic Tyson's smirk was captured on camera and the image has been a favourite of Forest fans ever since – notwithstanding the fact that the incident cost his club an initial £15,000 in FA fines.

To think that this pillock would be offered a contract at Pride Park is frankly bizarre. And it's also worth considering whether he's actually any good.

Tyson started his career with Reading, but didn't make the grade there and scored only one goal for the club, against (guess who?) Derby County. After a series of loans to lower-league and non-league clubs, he moved to Wycombe Wanderers in 2004, who were a League Two outfit at the time.

At Wycombe, he did well, scoring 39 goals in 68 appearances. He then joined Forest in 2006, but has never been a roaring success for the Red Dogs. He managed 12 goals in League One in 2007/08, seven the next season after Forest's promotion and just two in 2009/10 – one of which came on the day when this Reading-born lad showed his fealty to Forest by parading around with a flag. The fact that he has scored just once this season has presumably prompted Billy Davies to allow his contract to elapse.

I'm going to file this one under 'bulls**t'.

***

Derby County – International Break Review
March 28, 2011

On 24th February, things looked pretty terminal. Derby County had just suffered a depressing 1-0 defeat at home to Hull City, the Rams' sixth defeat in a winless streak of nine games, including the sickening cup exit at Crawley. Before that disgraceful streak, we had beaten crisis club Preston North End – how bad were they at the time? – but before that, we'd lost another five consecutive league games.

As nosedives go, it was pretty much vertical. The goals had completely dried up, Kris Commons had, probably reasonably, decided to sod off, Alberto Bueno couldn't get a game and creativity had deserted us to the extent that we had scored just three goals in our previous 810 minutes of football.

By 24th March, things looked slightly better. Eight points had been added to the tally, with a slightly less embarrassing seven goals scored in the last six games. The horrific run of nine home games without a win had finally ended and with sides below us still stuttering, survival looked far more likely than it had done in the dark days of February.

We may well be due a couple of fearful drubbings in the next eight games – Cardiff and QPR away, anyone? – but overall, fingers crossed, it looks like we'll just about be OK and can start to plan for another Championship campaign in 2011/12.

That said, I've been unimpressed with the PR slant emitting from the official Rams Player of late. In interviews, Matt McCann and his staff keep telling players and staff that our current points tally (44) is probably enough to keep us up, which is, in my opinion, demented. Forty-four points would not have kept us up in any season since 2006/07 and until this club is mathematically safe from relegation to the third tier, I want those players out there fighting tooth and nail to prevent any such disaster. Sheffield United, Crystal Palace *et al* are all capable of winning games, as they have proved in recent weeks. Preston North

End are the only club who look doomed and nobody will go down without a fight.

With all this in mind, I thought I'd review the (unanswered) questions I sent to Derby County's press office on 24th February, as the club readies itself for the last eight games of the season and prepares its transfer moves for the summer.

What is the club's response to the recent lifetime ban imposed on the former investment manager Jeffrey Martinovich, given that the ban is related to malpractice involving investment made into our club?

This story was finally addressed by Ed Hill in the *Derby Telegraph* one month after Derby County Blog posted an article about Martinovich's financial meltdown. The *Telegraph* article also revealed confusion over the future of the ten per cent of Derby County shares purchased by Martinovich. Where those shares end up is, at present, anybody's guess. Wouldn't it be wonderful if the fans could purchase them?

The club's public response to this issue has been consistent. 'Martinovich has never been a director, he was not a major investor, look at the reputation of our main players.' However, in an email to Derby County Blog techie Joe Burns, Andy Appleby revealed his exasperation with the situation saying, 'The news keeps resurfacing. We've had to explain it three or four times.'

Martinovich has gone under, but for the foreseeable future, General Sports Derby Partners LLC is going nowhere.

Do you accept that the debt-reduction plan the ownership embarked upon was 'too deep, too soon', to the point where our Championship status has now been needlessly jeopardised?

I think the board understand now that whatever the amount of money they've invested (Glick claims a total figure of £24m since the takeover), the squad for this season was well short of what was required, even before it was weakened by the departures of Rob Hulse and Kris Commons.

Hopefully, the experiences of the past couple of seasons have shown GSE that a) the fans' bare minimum expectation is a winning team in home games at Championship level and b) you're very lucky if you get away with a season of cost-cutting as radical as the one the Rams have just undergone. If you don't go forwards in this division, you go backwards.

Glick referenced these concerns in a recent interview with Rams Player, in which PR guru McCann played the role of Jeremy Paxman. Much better was a BBC Radio Derby interview with Phil Trow, in which Glick explained that the club's income has not been enough to cover costs, hence we are making a loss despite additional investment from the owners and the massive wagebill cut.

Competing at the top end of the division becomes even more difficult given the bumper payments due to the three relegated teams who'll be joining us next season. Despite this, Glick claims that the board have committed to financing a promotion push for 2011/12.

Would you agree that the failure to make more signings in January was a huge mistake, especially considering the departure of Kris Commons?

Glick did take responsibility on Radio Derby for Derby's failure to sign their January targets, Martyn Waghorn (loan) and Connor Sammon (permanent). The Sammon move could have been tied up if the club had been prepared to pay a little more. Regarding Waghorn, Leicester clearly messed Derby around, but looking in from the outside, it seemed that Clough and Glick stuck with it for far longer than they should have done.

Given the calibre of the recent signings, it is clear that there has been no decision to invest in the sort of proven player who would be likely to make a big impact and keep us out of the bottom three. Was there no temptation to spend money on at least one more established player, or even a gifted youngster from the Premier League, especially considering the savings that have been made by releasing Commons and Rob Hulse (plus the transfer fees)?

Calibre of signings remains an issue and one which Glick has attempted to address with his recent public pronouncements. Ben Davies has thus far bombed horribly. Theo Robinson has missed a series of sitters, but appears to have done enough to convince Clough that he's worth keeping. On the other hand, Jamie Ward clearly has some ability and Frankie Fielding, while still a little raw, has the potential to be a top goalkeeper. Glick and Clough are both on record recently stating that they hope to sign the player permanently in the summer.

There's no doubt that next season is a massive season for Nigel Clough. Clough has implemented the board's cost-cutting measures, while just about keeping us afloat and rummaging in the transfer bargain bins. Now Glick says that the ownership group are prepared to stump up more money to propel us up the league. We'll have to wait and see, but Glick's 'money back guarantee' on season tickets is certainly a very bold move. That said, Early Season Optimism is a legendary phenomenon amongst football supporters and one which Glick is surely banking on.

In the event that relegation is avoided, can we expect to see serious investment in the playing squad in summer, especially considering that Robbie Savage will no longer be on the wage bill?

What Glick doesn't say, of course, is that the incoming transfers will, at least to some extent, be funded by fees and wage savings on outgoing players. Already, we've seen the back of Hulse and Commons and with Savage set to retire, a huge chunk of wages has been saved already. Surely joining them on the way out this summer will be Stephen Bywater, Dean Leacock, Alberto Bueno and maybe even Paul Green, who is approaching the last summer of his Rams contract.

Do GSE have contingency plans if the worst happens are Derby County are indeed relegated?

Of course, Glick has never publicly countenanced the possibility of relegation, but for a while there, he must have been s**tting himself.

I know I was.

If we are relegated, will the manager's position be reviewed?

There are plenty of Derby fans who believe that the manager's position should be reviewed in any case. I'm not among them, but of course, when you go through a run of results as punishingly bad as we did earlier this year, people have every right to criticise. For me, Clough deserves at least one more season to prove the doubters wrong, especially if money is going to be made available for new players.

Even the anti-Clough brigade cannot deny that signings such as James Bailey, John Brayford and Shaun Barker were inspired. Clough also identified other good players, such as Gary Hooper and Jamie Mackie, who would have made a hell of a difference if he'd been backed sufficiently to buy them.

***

Derby County release accounts for year to June 2010
March 28, 2011

Derby County's accounts for the year up to 30th June 2010 clarify the current financial health of the club and contain some data regarding its future direction.

In their annual report, the directors write that the financial position of the club has improved 'in comparison to its recent past'. The report states that the ownership group, General Sports Derby, injected £8.3m in share capital and loans during the financial year 2009/10, with a further £5.6m having been invested since that date. Despite this investment, Derby County made a loss of £2.2m in 2009/10.

The wage bill for all 201 club employees was £16.1m at the end of June 2010, which equalled around 55 per cent of the club's turnover of £29.754m. Given the high-profile departures of Rob Hulse and Kris Commons during the current season, along with the pending departure of Robbie Savage, there is clearly room to add quality to the current squad in the summer.

The directors' 'emoluments' (pay) for the year totalled £424,000, with £326,444 paid out to the 'highest paid director'. Directors' pay decreased by £323,000 from 2008/09.

The net debt of the club was reduced by £3.2m, from £22.3m at the end of June 2009 to £19,1m by the end of June 2010. Glick told Radio Derby that the main debt, £15m, is a 'mortgage' secured against Pride Park (which is valued at £55m). He describes the extra £4.1m debt as a 'revolving facility on a portion of season ticket income, which shows on the accounts as an additional debt, but actually comes in and out every year'.

The accounts state that 'additional working capital financing is required to enable the company to fund its business plan' and that this money will be provided by General Sports Derby Partners LLC. Derby County is funded by 'a mixture of parent company capital injections and the revenue that is raised through its business activities'.

The directors' report also states that 'in order to compete in the world's most competitive league, significant investment is required on an ongoing basis'. It also states that they have increased investment in the club academy year on year for the past three seasons and that no dividends have been paid out for 2009/10.

When the dust settles, the recalcitrant finally renew their season tickets and the overpaid, underachieving players of the past are offloaded, it may well turn out that this season, as generally unpleasant as it has been, paves the way for a better future. Numbers on a balance sheet don't really mean much to supporters – we just want to see a winning club – but the figures do at least show that the club is not in the hands of asset strippers, but of an investment group who are sticking to a plan designed to keep the club going in a sustainable way, without splurging dramatically on big-name players. The proof of that will have to come in the summer, when the promised new signings are actually unveiled.

***

Post-Leeds happiness
April 13, 2011

What a difference a win makes, especially one against Leeds[17]. I am tired, emotional and frankly hungover. Even the famously reserved Nigel Clough admits that beating Leeds is special, in perhaps the only concession he does make to his family history as the Derby County manager.

With the gap to 22nd position now 11 points – essentially 12, given that our goal difference is -7 to Scunthorpe's -40 – safety has been all but assured, with five matches to go. While this season seemed to have the makings of a relegation disaster a couple of months ago, our slump in form, as prolonged and as worrying as it was, was arrested in the nick of time.

So far in his time at Derby, Nigel Clough has always managed to find a big result when the pressure threatened to become too much. So, an embarrassing defeat against Scunthorpe was followed by a win over Forest last season. A poor start to this season was put to bed with a delirious thumping of Crystal Palace, which prompted a wonderful, if ephemeral, Rams resurgence. A dreadful run of home form was broken by a mixture of good fortune and hard work against a good Swansea City outfit. It seems that when the chips are down and Clough needs the players to turn up for him, they manage to pull a result out of the bag.

The 11 who went out against Leeds all worked themselves into the ground for the cause. Perhaps certain players have not taken to Clough's methods, but it looks increasingly likely now that the manager will outlast them, replace them and move on.

I'm sure that Derby's owners would have liked to have extended Nigel's contract, which expires at the end of next season, before now,

---

[17] 12 April 2011 – Derby County 2 Leeds United 1. The Rams recovered from a goal down to win, courtesy of a memorable, thumping volley from Ben Davies

but our nosedive in form made that impossible. Many supporters lost patience with Clough this season, but the board still have faith and I would be very surprised if the manager's contract is not extended this summer.

Critics will point to Clough's failure to improve the team's league position this season. However, this should be weighed against the very challenging cost-cutting exercise he has been asked to carry out on behalf of the club, which lost about £15m in 2008/09. Losses of that sort are simply unsustainable. Look at Sheffield United, whose financial instability has dumped the club into what now looks like a relegation fight they cannot win. The Blades' loss of £19m, announced in November 2010, shows what can happen to Championship clubs who flirt with the Premier League but can't stay in the top flight.

Coventry City are another problem club, recently described by their own chief executive as a 'basket case' and kept afloat only by a begrudging, last-minute injection of cash from their shadowy owners SISU – a hedge fund which Jeremy Keith tried to sell our beloved club to, in the days when darkness reigned.

So, in my opinion, the plan of action at Pride Park should run something like this: –

Get Shaun Barker booked in for his operation now. He's been truly incredible this season, especially given that he's never been fully fit. He deserves to be named in the PFA Championship Team of the Year, although I doubt that he will be, given our lowly league position.

Get Clough's contract extended. This brings stability and allows him to focus on the job in hand, which is remodelling the squad, bringing in more players like Brayford, Bailey and Barker to develop a winning team.

Transfers. There are set to be quite a few ins and outs this summer and the sooner we can get cracking, the better. I would imagine that at the very least, Porter and Leacock will leave, making space for more players to join the likes of Fielding, Ward and possibly Robinson in signing up. Inevitably, rumours are flying around – Lee Bowyer, Billy

Jones, Darren Pratley, even Danny Graham – and while I'd be surprised to see more than one or two of those come in, certainly, the Rams can offer players good wages, great facilities and the chance to play for one of the best-supported clubs in the country.

***

Derby County's Player of the Year vote is on
April 24, 2011

My vote has gone to Shaun Barker.

A recent poll I ran on Facebook suggested that fans are split between Barker and John Brayford. Brayford is a worthy contender, having played every match, looked assured at right-back and slotted in at centre or even left-back when necessary.

But Barker has played every game but one this season in spite of a knee injury which has prevented him from training. Despite being unfit, he has shown inspirational leadership and valiant defensive qualities. There would also be a nice symmetry to the fact that the last Rams player to win the Jack Stamps Trophy for two consecutive seasons was Mark Wright.

Brayford was a fine signing by Clough, as was Barker. Brayford will go on to be a big player for the Rams and surely a contender for Player of the Year trophies in future seasons. The goal he scored in the 4-1 home win against Watford typified his tenacity, spirit, desire and ability. For now, in my opinion, he rates as a very good runner-up to his skipper.

Some votes will doubtless go to the blond bombshell himself, Robbie Savage. Sav has his ardent fans (judging from Twitter, many of them are female) and some supporters may plump for him out of sentimentality. Certainly, his effort and determination have impressed and while his passes are variable, it's clear that he understands the game and his experience will be missed. Realistically, he is no longer athletic enough to chase the best Championship players – his stiff-legged shuttles around the park are almost reminiscent of Paul McGrath's cameo at the Baseball Ground – and he's bowing out at the right time.

The only other realistic contender is Kris Commons, whose goals have still not been replaced. We had a tantalising glimpse of the player at his best this season, but it was all too brief. One would like to think that Rams fans would cast their vote in a different direction, simply because a Player of the Year *in absentia* would be a somewhat embarrassing first for the club.

2011/12

Derby County splash the cash as Tom Glick pre-empts a run on the bank
June 23, 2011

Tom Glick must feel confident that his 'money back guarantee' offer on Derby County season tickets won't be attracting too many takers, after signing six new players within six weeks of the end of the 2010/11 season. There is also the promise of up to five more arrivals to follow.

The six new players signed so far are Frank Fielding, Jamie Ward, Theo Robinson, Craig Bryson, Jason Shackell and – controversially – the Forest 'legend' and flag-waver extraordinare, Nathan Tyson.

I have said my piece about Tyson. When I wrote that blog, I didn't believe for a second that Derby would sign him, but you have to learn to expect the unexpected when a Clough is in charge. Now it's time to prepare for the somewhat surreal prospect of watching Tyson play for my team, having previously considered him the ultimate embodiment of all things Anti-Ram.

When asked by PR assistant Tom Loakes what his biggest concern was about coming to Derby, Tyson responded, only half in jest, 'They hate me.' He also knows, as Clough must, that if he doesn't get off to a flying start in Rams colours, there's a danger that he could find himself on the end of some unpleasant fan 'intolerance', as has previously occurred at Pride Park with ex-Forest striker Stern John.

Tyson has said he's sorry. He accepted the FA fine he deserved without appealing and claims to have been embarrassed by the Forest fans who approached him to congratulate him on the incident in the aftermath. He might also have been embarrassed by the T-shirts printed in his honour by Nottingham punk band Red Dogs.

He has also said that if he scores against Forest, he won't celebrate, dashing any childish hopes of a tit-for-tat flag/scarf incident … that I might have harboured.

One does wonder, however, if the doubtless heinous abuse set to rain down him from all corners of the City Ground might change that stance. Kris Commons and Lee Camp, to give an example from either side of the fence, certainly celebrated with gusto when their time came.

It could well be the case that the fans who are most viscerally opposed to Tyson's signing are amongst those who were actually at the match when the flag-waving incident happened. As this is of course a minority of Rams fans – we took 4,376 to the City Ground that day – perhaps the club have surmised that most supporters, who only saw what happened on TV, heard about it on Radio Derby or read of it in the papers later, won't be nearly as fussed as some of the Rams fans who were at the game.

It's also perfectly possible, even probable, that the incident never entered into Clough's thinking at all. And as long as Tyson does OK, the more intransigent minority will not grumble too loudly – so goes the theory, at least. It will be fascinating to see what happens when Birmingham City's visit opens the new season.

Whatever your opinion on Tyson, it should be remembered that he attracted a lot of interest from Championship clubs this summer and it was Derby who were able to secure his signature. Ditto Shackell – and even more so.

Shackell was Barnsley's captain and reigning Player of the Year. At 27, he is approaching his peak and has committed to a three-year contract with the Rams, who were able to outbid Burnley and see off reported interest from Portsmouth in concluding the deal.

In his first interview with Rams Player, Shackell said, 'You hear rumours that people are starting to get excited about the faces that are getting brought in and it's nice to be part of that... They had a great start to last season... adding six or seven players to that can only be good for Derby.'

Adding Tyson and Shackell to the current England under-21 goalkeeper, plus Ward, who is a goalscorer and Bryson, who captained Kilmarnock, and you're looking at a significant investment in the squad from

GSE (and the season ticket holders).

I don't believe that the new signings will be sufficient to build a promotion-ready side, although if the loan market is mined effectively in addition to the new signings, we could well have sufficient squad depth to challenge in and around the top half of the table. That in itself would be a major development given the club's generally wretched state in recent and not-so recent years. Simply to be in a position to add good loans to an already decent squad, rather than desperately patching up gaping holes with any player we can get, represents real progress and is a great start.

None of the new signings are monumental bank-breakers and it was obvious to any sensible observer that a Sky Sports article linking Derby with Venezuelan midfielder Ronald Vargas, at €3m, was nonsense. Further, it should be remembered that the new signings have been in part made possible by the release of at least six players, Robbie Savage, Stephen Bywater and Dean Leacock chief amongst them.

Glick and GSE are attempting to show what a club of Derby's size can do without overspending and they are doing this ahead of pending regulations which will force all Championship clubs to follow suit. This being the case, it becomes important for the academy to constantly feed players into the squad and a few youngsters are already starting to emerge, such as Jeff Hendrick, Mark O'Brien and Callum Ball.

One cloud does remain in the shape of Clough's contract situation. Despite allowing the manager to bring in new signings, Glick told the *Derby Telegraph*, 'We [Glick and Clough] both know that we need to have a good season and that is what we are preparing for. There will be plenty of time for us to talk about his contract situation but at the moment, we are focused on putting a squad together, having a great pre-season and getting a good start to next season.'

A poor start to the season could see Clough come under serious pressure and, while I think we will be OK, signs of underperformance will presumably not be tolerated.

Certainly if a new manager did come in at some point during 2011/12, he would inherit a reasonably strong squad and a solvent, well-supported club capable of pulling in 30,000-plus crowds. If Clough is the man to bring success to the football club, then the time to start proving it is nigh. The potential at Derby County is tremendous, especially now that the Championship is to be protected from the sort of wild, unsustainable spending that has driven clubs from Portsmouth to Cardiff to Preston into troubled waters in recent years.

All in all, the six new signings have been just the tonic for jaded Rams fans and should be enough to keep the vast majority of current season ticket holders coming back for more in August. Glick will also know that the old rogue, Early Season Optimism, will be on his side and the policy of making the signings early, before worrying about shifting unwanted players out, has alleviated a lot of the pressure on both him, as a representative of the owners, and the manager.

In the aftermath of the unforgivable FA Cup defeat at Crawley Town, I tweeted Derby investor W. Brett Wilson to ask his opinions on the dark clouds that were gathering over Pride Park. His reply seemed a little cryptic at the time, but with hindsight, makes far more sense. 'All is not as it seems,' he said. 'Patience is a virtue.'

Much remains to be proved and there is still business to attend to. And plenty of people – Glick, Clough and Tyson included – will go into this season feeling like they have a point to prove. I wish them all the best and hope this turns out to be a cracking season for the Rams. It's about time we had a good one!

***

Do Derby County Really Need a Director of Football?
July 3, 2011

In the wake of Derby County's dismal 2010/11 season, it was clear that far-reaching changes were needed if the club was to enjoy an upturn in fortunes. Some Rams fans pointed the finger of blame squarely at manager Nigel Clough. Others were more inclined to criticise the board of directors, personified by chief executive officer Tom Glick, for under-investing in the squad; and as the season progressed, it became clear that Clough himself had lost patience with certain senior players, including Lee Croft, Dean Leacock and Stephen Bywater.

Whatever your opinion on who was at fault, it was clear that something had to give before the start of the new season. Glick therefore came out as early as April to declare that further investment in the squad was coming and told the BBC on 19th May that the management team would be strengthened by the recruitment of a director of football.

The English game has traditionally invested all responsibility for the playing side of the club in the manager, while the purse strings are held by the board of directors. It is for the manager and the board to come to an agreement on transfer and wage budgets and reach decisions about the acquisition or otherwise of players. As an example of where this relationship can founder, Mark Robins recently resigned as manager at Barnsley over the budget his board were prepared to sanction for the coming season. In other situations, managers have been able to manipulate directors into overspending on new players, or directors themselves have been keen to splash non-existent cash, putting clubs in long-term jeopardy by their selfish pursuit of short-term success. A director of football (DoF) can be defined as a board member who acts as a bridge between the businessmen and the football men at the club. Sometimes he will have managerial experience himself, therefore being able to 'interpret' between the two sides of the operation and help them to work together more smoothly, but DoFs can come in different forms and at some clubs, the position is merely symbolic. Sir Bobby Charlton fills a comparable role at Manchester United, as an emblem of the Red Devils' past; however, it is clear that the Rams' DoF will be actively involved in the day-to-day running of the club.

Damien Comolli is a famous current example of a DoF who is heavily involved in the recruitment of new players, formerly at Tottenham Hotspur, but now with Liverpool. Interestingly, Comolli himself has no track record in playing professional football, having started coaching at the age of 19 before spending seven years working as a European scout for Arsène Wenger's Arsenal. He is a friend of the celebrated baseball coach Billy Beane, with whom he shares a commitment to using statistical analysis to establish the value of players. Given our American ownership and Clough's frequent references to Prozone in his interviews, it's not beyond possibility that the new Derby DoF may be something of a number cruncher, or at least further the Rams' use of data when looking at potential acquisitions.

As some DoFs are more hands-on in terms of recruitment than others, this does raise the possibility of disagreements between the post-holder and the manager. After leaving Spurs, Martin Jol complained that certain players had been recruited by Comolli without his approval, highlighting the importance of manager and DoF being on the same page when it comes to transfers. In 2008, Kevin Keegan resigned as Newcastle manager over the 'imposition' of players such as Xisco and Ignacio Gonzalez upon him by DoF Dennis Wise, after James Milner was sold to Aston Villa without Keegan's knowledge.

Jim Smith was offered a DoF role at Derby in October 2001, with the Rams struggling to stay afloat in the Premier League under his management, but rejected the offer and walked away, leaving Colin Todd and John Gregory to oversee the club's subsequent relegation (incidentally, applicants for the Rams job in the wake of Todd's sacking included a globetrotting manager named Roy Hodgson, who had recently been fired by Serie A outfit Udinese). In even less glorious times, 'Mystic' Murdo Mackay acted as Derby's DoF during the post-Lionel Pickering reign of the Three Amigos – but the less said about that odious bunch of crooks, the better.

Glick recently told the BBC, 'We're looking for someone who will add talent and depth to our football operation, working with myself and the manager... It's a behind-the-scenes position, helping make sure the first team, scouting, recruitment, academy, youth development and medical team are all working well together... It's another brain, another set of hands, another pair of eyes and ears that will help us.'

Asked whether this brought Clough's position under question, Glick responded that it didn't, while admitting that the new season, the final year of Clough's contract, was an important one, in which there was an expectation for Derby to do well.

According to former Leicester director of football Dave Bassett, it's a good idea for the DoF to be in place before the manager is appointed. He told the BBC in 2004, 'The director of football has to be involved in the selection of the manager, so that when the manager gets the job, he knows the director of football is fully supportive because he selected him.'

In Derby's case, this could be inverted. Will Clough be involved in the selection of a board member who will presumably be his superior? Will the appointment of the new man depend upon whether he accepts that Clough should continue as the Derby County manager?

According to Bassett, the DoF can sometimes be responsible for ensuring that the club doesn't run over its player wage and transfer budgets. This doesn't seem to be an issue at Pride Park, where Clough has stuck rigidly to the board's financial plans for the last two seasons, donning his tin helmet as the team's form suffered the effects of the 'financial adjustment' necessary after the 2007/08 Premier League fiasco.

But Bassett adds that the DoF typically 'knows how to operate the market in terms of transfer fees and whether a club is paying the right money for a player', while Martin Samuel of the *Daily Mail* describes Liverpool DoF Comolli as 'a man who knows the market and can advise [Liverpool's owners] on value'.

This could be the key to the Derby DoF appointment. In the wake of his unsuccessful pursuit of Conor Sammon in the 2011 winter transfer window, Glick openly confessed that he was at fault after the Rams were outbid by Wigan Athletic. As Derby's initial rejected offer was reportedly in the region of £425,000, with Wigan's successful bid estimated at an initial £600,000, the comparatively piddling difference was a major embarrassment for the Rams and must have been a source of serious frustration for Clough. Many supporters, at that time, were seething with rage, with accusations of 'asset-stripping' becoming more and more prevalent and protests outside Pride Park following repeated home defeats.

Glick does seem to have learned the lessons of that situation, quickly concluding eight signings in the current window, but it should be said that not many other Championship teams currently appear to be ready to splash out very far on acquisitions – especially given the forthcoming self-imposed 'Financial Fair Play' regulations that will limit the amount clubs can spend on wages to a safe level (probably between 60-70 per cent percentage of their total revenue). It should be noted that based on 2009/10 figures, Derby are one of only six clubs in the top two tiers compliant with the 60 per cent ratio, according to the *Independent on Sunday*. The other five clubs named in Glenn Moore's report are Manchester United, Spurs, Arsenal, Wolves and Burnley.

In May 2011, Glick told the BBC that the proposed appointment of a DoF would 'sharpen' Derby's operations in the transfer market, so expect someone who will be heavily involved in the deal-making process, as well as presumably in the scouting of new players. At present, the Rams are picking up players solely from the domestic market – the recruitment of Alberto Bueno via Johnny Metgod's contacts being the only exception during the Clough era – so perhaps the new man will be possessed of sufficient foreign contacts to widen our net. Given that Glick's stated long-term aim for the club is promotion to the Premier League, the ability to uncover players from further afield than Aberdeen – and beat the competition to sign them – is ultimately going to be a necessity.

***

Reasons to be Cheerful ... Grounds for Optimism ahead of Derby County's 2011/12 season
July 31, 2011

On the back of another pre-season defeat to lower-league opposition (Exeter City, 1-0), it's fair to say that a cloud of gloom has fallen upon many Derby fans. Judging the mood from Twitter, at least, there is a general grumpiness about the losses at Crewe and Exeter, the failure to add to the glut of early pre-season signings – not helped by a lack of any meaningful titbits of speculation to get into – as well as the seemingly endless series of injuries which have disrupted Nigel Clough's preparations for what is a vitally important Championship season[18].

But hey – it's not all bad! Things might not have gone 100 per cent to plan this summer, but there are still some genuine grounds for optimism and better times could be ahead.

1. Frank Fielding – Brilliant signing. If the undisclosed fee is indeed, as reported, in the region of £400,000, then how the hell did we pull that one off? We all thought he was marvellous last season and it's great that he didn't turn out to be one of those rare loan successes you get, who promptly bogs off to his parent club to become a hit. In Tommo's words, 'It's a good job Blackburn is currently run by idiots.'

2. A new formation – Never mind the 4-2-3-1. The basic set-up will be 4-1-3-2. Clough and the gang have decided that playing with two holders in midfield and one out-and-out striker isn't sufficiently aggressive – perhaps Robbie Savage's lack of mobility enforced it as a policy last season.

Whatever the reasons, from watching the pre-season games, you can see that we will not suffer from a lack of men in and around the box this term. Two strikers up top, three midfielders given license to push

---

[18] Before losing at Exeter that pre-season, Derby beat Burton 3-1, drew 2-2 at Macclesfield, 1-1 at Morecambe and lost 2-1 at Crewe.

on and the buccaneering John Brayford storming forward from right-back. If we can get the right sitting midfielder to shield the defence, it has the potential to be an exciting system.

3. The injuries aren't that serious – OK, a fair few players have picked up knocks and strains during pre-season, leaving some to suspect that the training regime is too hard on the squad. However, the likes of Jason Shackell and Craig Bryson have already returned to the team and with Nathan Tyson among those who have been gradually building their match fitness ahead of the big kick-off, there aren't too many long-term absentees. Granted, it's not ideal to have Barker missing for the start of the season, but between Shackell, Russell Anderson and Chris Riggott, we should be covered there.

4. Lots of forwards – One of the major bugbears of the fans during the Clough Jr era has been a lack of striking options. Rob Hulse was never replaced, Shefki Kuqi didn't stay for long, Dean Moxey pressed into service as a number nine, etc. Not the case now. Suddenly we have a range of forwards and will be able to shuffle the pack during a game if things are going against us.

Tyson is one of the quickest strikers in the division. Jamie Ward is no slouch either and has a hammer of a long-range shot. Steve Davies has presence and a footballing brain. Chris Maguire looks to be a clever player, at his happiest dropping into space and linking up play with cute passes. Theo Robinson is a whippet and looks like a useful option to set on tiring defenders late in the game. Then there's the industrious Tomasz Cywka and even the raw potential of Callum Ball, who seems to be developing nicely.

5. Don't rule out the possibility of more signings – We have bid for Martyn Waghorn and John Eustace, which means that there must be more money available to Clough, if the right players can be identified. Permanent signings can be made until the end of August and removing the likes of Stephen Bywater and Dean Leacock from the wage bill will create more room to manoeuvre.

Then there's the loan market to consider. Rams fans have become jaundiced about loans, because they have been used excessively over the past couple of seasons. However, consider the possibility of adding a couple of talented youngsters from the Premier League to the current group. If we can get in some loans who are there to genuinely add to the squad, rather than just to paper over the cracks, then it could help us to have a good season.

6. James Bailey – Unfortunately, he's been out for a while through injury, but J-Bails will be back in full effect eventually. He might even have a scrap on his hands to get into the team, if an experienced holding midfielder is brought in – but competition for places can only be a good thing for a young player with bags of potential.

The 2011/12 season kicked off on 6 August 2011 and Derby hared out of the traps. Granted, they suffered the embarrassment of being knocked out of the league cup by Shrewsbury Town, but they won their first four Championship matches, beating Birmingham City 2-1, Watford 1-0, Blackpool 1-0 and Doncaster Rovers 3-0.

Their first defeat came against Burnley in the last game before the summer transfer window 'slammed shut'.

***

Transfer Deadline Special
August 31, 2011

Transfer deadline day was blissfully quiet at Pride Park. The first team got on with their training camp in Spain and Tom Glick issued a statement to say that we'd be looking at more loan signings when the window reopens on September 8th.

The club made it clear that they were looking to move out some 'dead wood' before making any further permanent signings, with Dean Leacock, Stephen Bywater and Stephen Pearson the obvious candidates. The trio, all Billy Davies signings, are out of contract at the end of the season and out of favour with the current management. I also have a feeling that Paul Green will depart as a free agent when his contract expires in 2012.

Martyn Waghorn, who has been a target for Clough all year, was finally told by Sven-Göran Eriksson that he could leave Leicester, having agitated for a move for some time. Disappointingly, he was not placed into a taxi and driven straight to Pride Park to ink a three-year contract. Instead, Southampton, cash-rich from the proceeds of Alex Oxlade-Chamberlain's move to Arsenal, were linked with a £1.5m bid, before more substantial reports linked the player with a loan move to Hull City, which was confirmed tonight.

Fans are always disappointed when transfer deadline day passes and no new players are presented to them in a last-gasp coup worthy of thoroughly aerating the worthies at Sky Sports News. However, as is usually the case, one has to remember boring old yesterday's news – the ten new signings since May. A reputable source has suggested that the Rams' spending on new players during this window has been in the vicinity of £5m.

That said, the club haven't been able to balance their spending by off-loading many players as yet, so it's clear that at least a modicum of investment has come from the owners. Pennies when compared to the money that has been lavished on Leicester City by Vichai Raksriaksorn, but investment nevertheless.

One or two keyboard warriors have taken to the internet to lambast Derby for their 'failure' to bring anybody else in today, but the reality is, the transfer window system is a weird, artificial construct that helps nobody except for Rupert Murdoch. Fans panic, thinking that because 'the window' is 'closing', something has to happen NOW, or we'll be up the proverbial creek without a paddle. Whereas in fact, the loan market opens next week and we could quite easily get somebody in then, on top of the ten blokes we've signed since May. All in all, the Rams have signed 11 players during the previous two transfer windows, while selling only three.

Furthermore, if it's right for all parties, a loan can become a permanent (as happened with Ward, Fielding and Robinson of late) and if the player turns out to be rubbish, you can send them back – as happened with Nathan Ellington, for example. Ellington was a waste of an initial loan fee, but at least we weren't lumbered with the Duke for a further two seasons after we'd worked that much out.

I would much rather be in Derby's position than Forest's or Coventry's or Birmingham's, to take three examples. Coventry, languishing under the corrosive ownership of SISU, have lost most of their best players this summer, with another, Ben Turner, leaving today. At Forest, meanwhile, a manager saddled with unrealistic expectations of promotion publicly criticised the board for a lack of signings just before the deadline, much as the last one did. And they have signed no players today, putting Steve McClaren in a very difficult position.

And how about Birmingham City, where the exodus continues and an owner facing criminal charges has just borrowed $10m at 12 per cent interest, to keep the club afloat?

These things are not happening at Pride Park.

It should also be remembered that one very important signing was made in the build-up to the Burnley game. Future captain John Brayford inked a new contract, extending his stay at Pride Park until summer 2014. One assumes this new contract is on improved terms – in any case, it prevents any speculation about the future of arguably our best player.

If there is criticism to level at Tom Glick, it is that his lack of experience of the English game has been exposed over the past few months. The Conor Sammon fiasco from January has gone down in legend and is doubtless used in manuals of How Not To Play the Transfer Window. The club went on to do the right thing by bringing in many of their summer targets as early as possible, but then raised expectations of more signings – only to find that the factor these extra moves were predicated on (offloading the unwanted players) would not be as simple as they expected. As a result, some fans consider Glick to be a 'liar' and resent what they describe as his 'broken promises'.

Wheeling and dealing gets tricky when all you have to offer other clubs are players with extremely patchy records, who are sitting on nice contracts. It was therefore unrealistic to expect Leacock, Bywater and Pearson be snapped up, although we did at least get a good deal for Luke Varney[19]. The reality is, we have to pay these players until such a time as they become free agents or somebody else takes them.

If the transfer window didn't exist, maybe fans' attention would rest more on the fact that Derby have signed a lot of players of late, not on the fact that we haven't signed anybody in the last few weeks. It really frustrates me when anti-board cynics use the window system as yet another stick to beat the club with – especially when we've just got off to our best start to a league season in over 60 years.

No, we're not promotion-ready and no, there have been no massive, 'raise the roof' deals, but the players who have come in (or been developed internally) are doing a good job and the club is on an even keel for the first time in too long.

Now that we have a genuine platform to build on, let's see how far we can go over the next couple of seasons.

***

East Midlands Derby Special
September 20, 2011

'You've got some problems here, haven't you?' – Johnny Rep to Kevin Keegan, during England 0 Holland 2, Wembley, 1977

After subsiding to defeat at Coventry's Theatre of Mediocrity, Derby County faced an early-season trip to the City Ground, Nottingham, where the ever-baleful Red Dogs awaited them.

Under the stewardship of Steve McClaren, Forest made an unpromising start to the season, losing to Millwall, West Ham and Southampton and beating only rock-bottom Doncaster. In the run-up to transfer

---

[19] Varney was sold to Portsmouth, for a reported fee of £750,000.

deadline day, McClaren followed in the footsteps of Billy Davies by openly criticising Forest's failure to back him in the transfer market. So the Reds were in dire need of a morale-boosting home win, which would be the first of the McClaren era. Defeat to 'Direby' was unthinkable.

Nigel Clough abandoned the 4-4-2 formation he tried at Coventry, reverting to his now-standard 4-2-3-1. Steve Davies was dropped for the first time this season, giving Theo Robinson his first start. Lee Croft also missed out, allowing Tomasz Cywka to return from the wilderness, his first inclusion in a league matchday squad all season. In defence, Kevin Kilbane[20] was replaced by Gareth Roberts, also for his first start of the campaign.

As has been the case in our previous two visits to the City Ground, disaster struck within seconds, only this time even more spectacularly than usual.

McClaren's new striker Matt – ahem – Derbyshire flicked the ball into the path of the equally new Ishmael Miller, about eight yards from goal. Miller knocked the ball past the onrushing Frank Fielding and bulldozed straight into him as the covering Gareth Roberts cleared off the line. Referee Scott Mathieson had no choice but to give the penalty, but did he really need to send Fielding off?

Firstly, it could hardly be described as a professional foul. Fielding had rushed out to block Miller's shot and at such close range, there was no way he couldn't make contact with the striker once the ball went past him. Especially as Miller locked on to him like an Exocet missile.

Secondly, Roberts was back in position to clear the ball away, meaning that Fielding was not the last defender in this situation and there was no way that Miller could have scored – even if he hadn't been intent on impersonating a Chicago Bears offensive lineman.

Forest's players surrounded Mathieson instantly. The ever-annoying Chris Cohen popped up in front of him, like a playground toadie, ac-

---

[20] Left-back Kilbane signed from Hull City on a six-month loan deal in August 2011.

cusing Fielding of stealing his Penguin and calling teacher a bad word. Meanwhile, Jonathan Greening and Andy Lard delivered pious sermons on the laws of the game to the man paid to administer them. Mathieson duly made the wrong call.

With seconds gone, the Rams were down to ten men, a goal down once Lard had waddled up to fire home the penalty and a substitution down, sacrificing Cywka for Adam Legzdins. Due to one questionable decision – and an equally questionable rule – Derby had been triply punished.

As Tommo pointed out, a Billy Davies team would surely have gone on to win the game from such an insanely favourable position. Fortunately, Davies has long-since saddled his Labrador and quit the East Midlands. McClaren teams are clearly less skilled in the art of shutting down games 'professionally'. But we'll get to that.

Forest controlled possession for the next half-hour, pushing the ball around their midfield diamond while Miller and Derbyshire took turns to drop into space between the lines. It was pleasing enough on the eye, in the bland manner of a traditional landscape painting – and about as threatening.

Derby were unable to mount much of an offensive response, but hung in there, repelling the occasional Forest cross and defending a few unthreatening corners without much difficulty. If there were moments of alarm, it was only when Rams defenders committed to tackles in the box.

Then Cohen pulled up *en route* to a challenge on Hendrick, with what later proved to be a bad leg injury. However, there was no foul and it wasn't a head injury, so Mathieson was not obliged to stop play. A couple of Forest players pointed out Cohen's plight, but Derby kept the ball and as the boos of the home fans mounted, worked it from right to left, to Jamie Ward.

At this point, a goal was not on the cards. On the contrary, there were plenty of defenders between the wide man and the goal.

Radoslaw Majewski essayed a wild lunge masquerading as a tackle, which Ward shrugged off easily. That put him through to the byline. He might have been expected to send in a cross at this point – presumably that's what Chris Gunter expected, because Ward was able to nutmeg him and continue serenely towards goal. And presumably Lee Camp also expected a cross, because when Ward slipped a shot in at the near post, he could offer only a confused, wrong-footed attempt at a save.

Goalkeepers are taught to protect their near post as kids. A 'keeper playing international football will be extremely disappointed to be beaten in such a fashion.

Players are taught to play to the whistle as kids, as Clough pointed out in his post-match interviews. McClaren agreed.

So in summary, Forest were the architects of their own downfall. Firstly, for trying to referee the game and expecting their arch-rivals, a man and a goal down in the East Midlands derby, to meekly submit to their demands and put the ball out of play. How many times, in such situations, has the 'injured' player proved not to be hurt at all?

Secondly, all they had to do to stop the incident from escalating was make one tackle.

Thirdly, the goalkeeper should have covered his near post. If the ball flashes across him, he has to trust his defenders to deal with it. He should never commit the cardinal sin of being beaten at the near stick.

And so the Forest supporters howled with rage at Derby's perceived lack of sportsmanship – and the cocky Ward didn't hold back in his celebrations, which hardly appeased them – but their anger should have been directed at their own players, for failing to manage a passage of play that was in no way likely to end in a goal.

This said, Ward deserves huge credit for jinking his way through the defence so adeptly and slotting home such a cheeky finish. He made right mugs of Forest, not least Lee Camp – and for that, we thank him.

Forest continued to dominate possession for the rest of the half, without being able to pierce the Rams' defence. Moved into the wide midfield roles of a 4-4-1, Ben Davies and Ward tracked back indefatigably, essentially playing as extra full-backs while Robinson ploughed a lone furrow and even dropped back into midfield himself to help out quite regularly. Consequently, Derby's attacking threat was zero, but quite rightly, their only thought was to get through to half-time on level terms.

The second half continued in much the same vein. Derby saw little of the ball and when they did get it, they simply pumped it in the general direction of Robinson, whether he was there or not. It was unreconstituted, old-fashioned, negative long-ball football and it was absolutely necessary in such extenuating circumstances. Forest huffed and Forest puffed, but their lack of guile was palpable. They seemed happy to keep the ball and Derby were happy to let them have it.

And Forest's inability to grasp the nettle should have been punished when, out of nothing, an utterly unmarked Jeff Hendrick was granted a free header within no more than two yards of the back post. Somehow, he planted it wide.

It could have been a moment of torment, but Ward and Robinson raced in to drag him back to his feet. And you just wonder, given their generally stressed and fractious air, whether Forest's men would have been as quick to reassure one of their own number had the situation been reversed.

Throughout, the body language of the Forest players was not great, with much sulking, gesticulating, pointing and complaining. They seem an unhappy camp at the moment, without much togetherness. The pressure of a run of negative results can do this but there doesn't seem to be much leadership in the Red Dogs current team.

Public complaints from the manager about the lack of new signings cannot have helped, but neither has the pedestrian nature of the ageing players McClaren has recruited. A pacy, sparky team could have worn The Ten Men down, but veteran midfielders Lard and Greening, along with the defensively-minded Moussi, provided little offensive gusto. The wispy Majewski was presumably supposed to provide the trickery, but didn't turn up on the day.

Too many red shirts were missing in action. And you couldn't say that about a single Ram.

And soon enough, Hendrick's moment came.

The emotion released by Hendrick's winner – to beat the auld enemy in their own yard, to do it with ten men, to have played with ten men for essentially the whole game and yet still tough them out, to do it through determination, to do it through hard work, that it fell to a youth product, who had already missed a gaping sitter, who had been pulled back to his feet by his team-mates, who had played only six games before, who still had the confidence to make the right decision and run on to the ball at the right angle, to take responsibility when a more senior pro was on hand, just a brilliant finish, an unforgettable moment of triumph – will rarely be topped in all our days as Derby supporters.

Derby are unlikely to pass anyone to death at present, depending on work-rate, discipline and organisation to stop their opponents before looking to play on the counter attack. And so we were better equipped than most to cope with the disaster of Fielding's dismissal. There is definitely something in Clough's habit of collecting other clubs' captains, as the loss through injury of our own – Shaun someone-or-other? – has simply not been a problem, with Shackell unfussily assuming the role. His assured defending and vocal leadership have been key to our successes this season – and hugely important to his protege, O'Brien.

Moments of individual brilliance from Steve Davies and Ward have spurred us on to excellent results this season and we do rely upon those two players, plus the dead-ball accuracy of Ben Davies, to create goals. Those three won't come up with the goods every time and so we will inevitably suffer our share of disappointing results this season.

This, however, was one of the best days in Derby County's recent history, certainly at least since the time of Clough senior. It was a monumental display of graft, resilience, bravery and steely will to prevail. To achieve victory in any game with ten men for over 90 minutes is surely with few precedents. To do it in one of England's major derby fixtures is unbelievable.

***

Leicester City (A) + International Break
October 9, 2011

Derby headed into the October international break on the back of a 4-0 drubbing at Leicester City. The defeat, which was arguably as comprehensive as anything we've seen since the 2007/08 season, acted as a thorough reality check for a Rams side who, nevertheless, remain within touching distance of top spot after ten games. Southampton, the league leaders, visit Pride Park next.

Derby's fine start to the season has been made possible by the players' laudable work ethic and desire, as well as the odd illuminating moment of star quality from the likes of Steve Davies, Ben Davies and Jamie Ward. However, in Leicester, they faced an expensively assembled promotion favourite, who were simply too strong. The Foxes' Thai-funded team is stuffed with experienced internationals, while the Rams rely mostly upon unproven players without the same level of reputation, or price tag.

The two teenagers who have done so well for Derby this season, Mark O'Brien and Jeff Hendrick, both endured moments that they need to learn from rather than forget. As Leicester built a counter attack, O'Brien was left flatfooted by Switzerland midfielder Gelson Fernandes's deft lob, which set David Nugent free to run beyond the young Irishman and slot home.

Hendrick, meanwhile, was lucky that the referee was Howard Webb, who famously forgave Nigel De Jong's kung fu kick in the 2010 World Cup Final. Most refs would have instantly sent Jeff off after he jumped, two-footed, into a tackle on Darius Vassell, in a panicky attempt to win back a ball he had just lost. Webb probably took Hendrick's inexperience into account because regardless of the obvious lack of intent to hurt Vassell, it was a dangerous challenge and there could have been no argument if he had gone.

Derby were unable to cope with Leicester, who were full of running. Their crisp passing and attacking movement proved too good for a jaded-looking Rams side.

In the aftermath of the defeat, Nigel Clough revealed that Hendrick had been playing with a hamstring strain, which then kept him away from Ireland duty this international break. Relying upon a teenage midfielder is one thing – relying upon a slightly injured teenage midfielder is another. In fact, all four of Derby's Irish internationals – Kevin Kilbane (Republic of Ireland), Jamie Ward (Northern Ireland), Hendrick and O'Brien (Rep. of Ireland U21) were forced to pull out of their respective squads last week.

Tom Glick has stated that Derby will act in the loan market if they consider the squad to be 'light' in any particular area. Presumably then, having only two players available to play central midfield doesn't qualify as 'light' in that area. What this seems to tell us is a loan signing will only be brought in when there isn't anybody else fit to play in the particular position.

When Mansfield Town defender Tom Naylor impressed Clough during his recent trial period at Derby, it seemed reasonable to assume that the player would sign, given that the Stags were reportedly asking for a fee of £50,000. However, when an offer was submitted, Mansfield were cross enough to declare on their official website that they did not want to be 'messed around' and that talks between the two clubs were dead. A later report stated that while the fee offered was about right, the terms of payment were unacceptable.

If the club is so skint that we can't afford to pay such a relatively piffling amount for a prospect the manager fancies, it follows that there isn't any room for a loan signing unless it's absolutely essential, or the parent club are desperate enough to let the player out while still paying some or all of his wages. So we'd better hope that nothing happens to the likes of Jason Shackell, John Brayford or Craig Bryson, until one or more of the unwanted players in the squad are moved on.

Meanwhile, the uncertainty over Clough's future continues, with the *Mirror* reporting 'exclusively' (and probably erroneously) that Forest are preparing a bid to take the Derby manager back to the City Ground, where he served with distinction as a player. This report caused BBCs Derby and Nottingham to put their heads together and sound out their respective clubs. The Beeb's inquiries from both ends of Brian Clough Way led them to conclude that the rumour is false.

BBC Nottingham has already reported that Forest are not in a position to pay a considerable sum of compensation for a manager, so the new man would have to be somebody out of work, or possibly a lower-league manager who would be relatively inexpensive to take from their current club. Yet the speculation about an approach for Clough continues.

Forest have, it seems, lost faith in the idea of trying to spend their way to promotion and now look set to copy Derby's tighter financial policy – spending within their means and resisting pressure to splash out on the kind of marquee, 'stellar' signings constantly demanded by the likes of Steve McClaren and Billy Davies. Forest have repeatedly cited the impending Financial Fair Play regulations for their 'failure' to back McClaren in the transfer market, above and beyond the costly Premier League signings he had already been allowed to make.

Sadly for Forest, they have allowed McClaren to pay out good money for a bunch of overrated journeymen, who look set to hold back the club's progress for seasons to come. And it would beggar belief if Clough disappeared to the wrong end of the A52 only to be faced with the same kind of onerous spadework and burdensome, 'big club' expectations he was forced to deal with for the first two-and-a-half seasons of his Derby career. Yes, his Rams experience would equip him well for the massive task of stabilising a club which has spent beyond its means for some time, but why would he want to go through all that again?

However, the questions remain. Why has Clough's contract been allowed to run to within less than a year of its expiry date? Is Glick hedging his bets and waiting for the next couple of months' results to come in? Is Clough so loyal that finding himself within a few months of potential redundancy genuinely won't affect his thinking? Will Clough's players ultimately be affected by all the uncertainty? And who the hell else would Tom Glick appoint in Clough's place?

Until Glick's 'Nigel's our guy' platitudes are backed up with a formal contract offer, these distracting, irritating tabloid reports about Clough's future will inevitably continue. We can only continue to ask the questions, until the truth about the board's intentions are revealed.

At the end of September, Derby were second in the table. However, by the time of the next international break in November, they had endured a run of just one win in eight games and dropped to seventh.

***

Peterborough United (A) + International Break
November 17, 2011

I had a bad feeling about the Peterborough United game and unfortunately my gut instinct – that trouble was brewing, that the injury problems were finally starting to really bite (again) – proved to be accurate. In the most depressing way possible.

It started well enough. The Rams buzzed around with plenty of confidence, bossing proceedings early doors, before Peterborough started to force their way back into the game. They got most of their joy on the left, where the callow Conor Doyle and the out-of-position Jake Buxton were repeatedly exposed. The moment after about 20 minutes, when Doyle received a routine pass from Buxton only to stumble over his own feet and concede possession in a very dangerous area, was quite extraordinary.

Overall, the American's performance showed why he has failed to force his way into the first-team reckoning with any regularity during his time at the club and he was subbed early in the second half. The gritty Ben Davies might have been better-equipped to help Buxton on the right-hand side, but with so few strikers available, Nigel Clough felt he needed to deploy Ward at centre-forward, forcing Davies to move over to the left and leaving a gap in right midfield.

I have to confess that despite his appearances for Republic of Ireland U21 and USA U23, Doyle is a player I simply don't get. I have no idea what his best position is, or exactly what it is that makes him a promising player. Here's hoping that he proves me wrong before the season is out.

Anyhow, Theo Robinson exploited Posh's naive defending to bag a quickfire brace and become Derby's top scorer for the season. And that should have been that. New season, new squad, new start. The frailties of previous campaigns, when Derby would contrive to throw points away from winning positions like confetti, were behind us... weren't they?

Not so. The experienced likes of Shackell, Roberts, Bryson and Ben Davies are good pros, but they need a bit more help than they're getting. And after Robinson missed a glorious chance to complete the first league hat-trick by a Derby player since 1847, the team capitulated.

Passive defending allowed the first Peterborough goal, then Shackell, of all people, made an incomprehensible error to give away the equaliser just after the break. And with that, any semblance of control Derby had was swept away. Posh, desperate for the three points, played at a breathless tempo and attacked their patently rattled visitors in remorseless waves. But still, Derby were able to withstand the pressure until deep into injury time.

Then, with the job seemingly done, a free kick (awarded apparently for nothing) on halfway was dumped into the box, cleared to the edge and screamed into the back of the net from 25 yards by an unmarked Grant McCann. By that point, two schoolboy substitutes had increased the number of teenagers on the pitch for Derby to five[21].

I have no wish to criticise the youth products, but when you end the game with that many kids in the team, it's obvious that the balance has shifted too much. Youth requires the guidance of experience and experience benefits from the energy of youth. And the aggravating fact is, even something approximating the Rams' first choice XI would have easily beaten a Peterborough side whose defensive fallibility is palpable.

In the aftermath of the Posh collapse, reports surfaced that Derby had finally agreed a fee with Mansfield Town for the defender Tom Naylor, who duly signed on an initial loan ahead of the Hull game. Naylor can reportedly play right-back or centre-back and reports from those who've seen him play locally – whether for Mansfield or Belper Town, where he spent a long loan spell – are good.

On the plus side, Paul Green, Shaun Barker and Chris Riggott all played a part against Sheffield United reserves – and those three players returning will make a massive difference to our chances this season.

Those who chunter about the lack of cover at full-back will probably be cross to note that Clough again mentioned Green as a potential fill-in right-back in his pre-Hull interview with Rams Player. Clough and the PR man, Matt McCann, were ambivalent about Green's longer-term future, only insisting that his expiring contract would not be a distraction to the player as he seeks to force his way back into the Republic of Ireland reckoning ahead of Euro 2012.

For what it's worth, I doubt that Green will sign an extension, simply because the cost-cutting measures that have been forced upon the club since the Paul Jewell-era mean that wages are not as generous. A good player like Green might well be able to find a club able to match or better his current terms, which Derby might struggle to do at present. A sale for a modest fee in January is probably the most likely

---

[21] The five were Mark O'Brien and Jeff Hendrick, who started the game, plus substitutes Callum Ball, Mason Bennett and Will Hughes.

90

outcome.

Sadly, things continued to deteriorate for Nigel Clough's men as winter drew in. After the Posh collapse, three more straight losses followed, to Hull (2-0), West Ham (3-1) and Brighton (1-0), dropping Derby into the bottom half of the table for the first time in the season.

***

You Can't Always Get What You Want: Derby County v Crystal Palace (A) December 8, 2011

After a run of five defeats on the bounce, excuses start to wear thin. So it was vitally important to get something at Selhurst Park, against a Crystal Palace side still elated after beating the mighty Manchester United at Old Trafford 48 hours before.

Only it was a completely different Palace side who trotted out against the Rams in front of the Sky cameras. Having gone through 120 minutes against a weakened Red Devils XI to claim a famous win, every outfield player was either rested or ruled out through injury, with the exception of defensive lynchpin Paddy McCarthy – more of whom later. Fortunately, Dean Moxey wasn't on hand to fulfil the Prophecy of the Old Boy by lashing in a left-footer from 30 yards.

After surviving the mother of all scares directly from the kick-off, when the veteran Gareth Roberts miscalculated a cross-field pass and was robbed, allowing Palace to surge into the box and almost score, Derby settled into a rhythm, playing possession football but without the penet-ration to unlock a seemingly unruffled Palace back line. Then Jamie Ward dawdled in possession in our final third and lost the ball, enabling Chris Martin to rifle in a drive, which nicked off Shaun Barker to wrong-foot Frankie Fielding.

The rest of the first half proceeded in a most depressing manner. Derby continued to stroke the ball around midfield, Palace continued to watch in an unconcerned manner and the passing got us absolutely nowhere. Tamas Priskin[22], in glorious isolation up front, was unable to affect the game. The Rams were playing neither particularly badly nor particularly well and looked ripe for the beating.

Half-time came as something of a relief – and then something happened. After what was reportedly a severe bollocking from Nigel Clough, Derby came out like men possessed and pinned back their opponents from the very start of the second half. Still, nothing would drop, so enter the young men – first Mason Bennett, then Callum Ball. The Rams were suddenly playing with four attackers and the game stretched accordingly, but it was Derby who continued to offer the greater threat.

Bennett put in his most impressive performance to date. I have previously looked upon him solely as one for the future, but it's starting to become increasingly clear that he is genuinely ready to be part of the senior squad. Yes, he has missed great chances at Boro and against Brighton and no, he shouldn't have attempted an overhead kick when well placed in the Eagles' penalty area – and that came after he laid the ball off to Priskin when he was actually clean through, if only he'd taken it on – but his linking play is really good, he is remarkably strong for such a young man and he has plenty of pace.

He is a 'number 10' player in the Wayne Rooney style – I am not saying that he is the new Rooney – mobile, picking up good positions, powerful, clever and while he still has a lot of work to do on his game, it is a relief to know that the new Elite Player Performance Plan (EPPP), which will allow Premier League players to spirit youngsters away from Football League clubs for a pittance, will come into effect too late for Bennett to be nabbed in such a fashion.

Ball also did well and must be in line for a start soon. He will feel he deserves it and who knows, perhaps he will get the nod on Saturday, either alongside Priskin or in his stead. And it was Ball who was waiting for Paul Green's wicked cross when poor old McCarthy, the staunch defender, lunged desperately to clear, only to beat his own goalkeeper

---

[22] Priskin joined Derby on a six-week loan deal from Ipswich Town in November 2011.

with aplomb.

You could say it was lucky, but I don't. The cross was so good that it had 'goal' written all over it. Ball must have scented glory and McCarthy certainly scented something less fragrant – it was brown trouser time for the centre-back, who couldn't leave it and couldn't really go for it either.

Green has been sorely missed and although Tommo somewhat controversially feels that, when Brayford returns at right-back, Hendrick, Bryson and Bailey should all be picked first in midfield, I disagree with that. Bryson and Green are very similar types of players, but Green is probably just better and put in a very composed performance at Selhurst Park.

With all the injuries to the forwards, we will probably play three of the four available central midfielders for now, but when the strikers return to fitness it gets interesting. If Theo is available, surely he plays, but does he play alongside Priskin or on his own? If you go with two strikers, which two play in central midfield?

Steve Davies reportedly even tweeted that he had a chance of playing on Saturday, which was fairly startling[23].. The club squashed that quickly and the offending tweet appears to have been deleted, but with a protective plate fitted, perhaps the striker will be back a little sooner than anticipated. Still, with an injury as grave as his was, no chances can be taken.

Nathan Tyson was yet again trumpeted as being close to a return to the team, but yet again withdrew from training with 'discomfort' in his groin.

According to physioroom.com, a groin strain is a tear to the muscle and is generally treated with the RICE protocol (rest, ice, compression and elevation). The most severe strains – grade three – typically take four to six weeks to heal. It's getting on for three months since Tyson's

---

[23] Davies had suffered a head injury during a 1-1 draw with Southampton in October 2011.

substitute appearance at the City Ground, so clearly this problem is much more problematic than is usually the case. Physioroom states that even a 'complete rupture', which could require surgery, would take about three months' rehab work to recover from. So you do wonder what on Earth is going on.

However, Tyson aside, we seem perilously close to a situation where we have a proper squad, with options and players ready to come off the bench and impact on the game.

Close… So let's hope that there are no more injury setbacks for a while.

***

Sinking in the Quicksand: Ipswich Town 1 Derby County 0 December 23, 2011

As a young lad, I remember studying the Second Division league tables one season, as Derby tried and failed to get into the play-off places. Every time we failed to win, the disappointment I felt was doubled by the realisation that three points would have taken us much closer to the top six.

Then the next time we won, I'd look again at the table and see that we hadn't really got any nearer to our goal, because rather inconsiderately, some of the teams above us had won as well. And so it would go on. We'd win one, lose one, draw one and bump along, never managing the winning run we needed to send us flying up the table.

Despite this season's current poor run of form, we are still only two wins and a draw from the play-offs, in theory – and we are still two wins and a draw better off than Nottingham Forest in the relegation zone. So even if results over the past couple of months had been merely disappointing, instead of seriously bad, we'd be there or thereabouts. Such is the way in the Championship, which is less of a league and more of a treacherous bog, in which the unwary can become trapped and flounder helplessly, until they are finally sucked under into the netherworld of League One – a tier so unglamorous that it doesn't even get its own pompous epithet.

We don't have to worry about relegation this season, even if the worst happens and we lose the two festive home games, against Leeds United and West Ham United. It's perfectly conceivable that we could get done in both matches, whereas a win in either would provide something for the fans to latch on to, as well as giving the players a much-needed lift.

Defeat in both games would be damaging. Not terminal, but certainly it would leave us down amongst the poorest teams in the division – teams, incidentally, that we have generally beaten this season.

Wins have come against strugglers Doncaster, Forest, Millwall, Bristol City, Watford and Portsmouth and it's perfectly conceivable that any two of those six could join Coventry in going down this season. You can't see a way out for the Sky Blues, who are in the middle of a perfect storm caused by the pernicious ownership of SISU. There, but the Grace of Gadsby, went Derby.

Anyway, we lost 1-0 to Ipswich, which was annoying. I saw some grumbling on Twitter – even the odd 'Clough out' strop – and quite a bit of chuntering about Paul Green being deployed at right-back, with John Brayford further on at right midfield. What is he doing playing a midfielder in defence and a defender in midfield, he doesn't know what he's doing, rah rah rah.

Yes, of course, under normal circumstances, you wouldn't expect the players to line up that way, but Ipswich have a marauding left-back in the shape of Aaron Cresswell and Clough presumably thought it important to limit his chances of getting forward by playing two men capable of getting up and down the line. Both Green and Brayford have good engines, but Green is more match fit than Brayford, so Clough presumably felt that, seeing as Green had been playing well at right-back, it made no sense to shift him out of that slot for this game. Especially given that every time I've seen Green play right midfield, he's looked like a fish out of water. So in these particular circumstances, I don't think it was such a bad decision to start like that – and that wasn't the reason we lost the game.

Derby certainly started well and gradually moved into the ascendancy during the first half. Callum Ball made a nuisance of himself and at one point outmuscled Danny Collins and Ibrahima Sonko simultaneously, which is some feat – sadly, his lay-off was then pumped miles over the bar by Ward, but the incident will have been duly noted by Clough and his staff.

We were very unlucky not to take the lead when Craig Bryson's drive was well saved by Arran Lee-Barrett, who then, seconds later, denied Jamie Ward twice. Ward claimed that the second stop was actually made by the arm of a defender on the line. Replays are inconclusive.

Speaking of inconclusive replays, did Ipswich's goal cross the line? I've heard that there is a camera angle that showed it did, but confusion certainly reigned at Portman Road and the linesman made an absolute mess of it. Why on Earth didn't he just flag, if he was convinced it was a goal? By not doing so, he leaves himself open to accusations that he was bullied into giving the goal by the protests of the Ipswich players.

Ipswich generally only threatened from crosses in the first half and sadly, Frankie Fielding was caught cold in the opening minute of the second half, making a dire error of judgement for what resulted in the game's only goal.

It's easy to forget that he's still a rookie in goalkeeping terms at the age of 23 and I for one still think that he makes enough good saves to merit his place in the team. Strangely enough, the fact that he was so underworked in the first half might have worked against him – had he actually been forced to do anything in the game up to that point, he might have been a bit sharper off his line.

Which just makes it all the more frustrating. We are not playing badly, but we are not picking up results. Things could get worse before they get better – Leeds, West Ham and Hull are all tough opponents – so if we can grind out a few points from those games, all the better. Even if we lose all three, it shouldn't be panic stations (although I can imagine the Twitter howls already); but historically, Clough's players have usually managed to raise their game for the marquee opponents, so let's hope they do so again – starting on Boxing Day.

***

Derby County 1 Dirty Leeds 0
December 30, 2011

'Your dad was a c**t and so are you' – the Leeds United supporters
'Nothing changes' – Dave Tomlinson

Individually, I reckon I could have a good – albeit lively – chat about football with a Leeds fan. Collectively, however, they are insufferable, representing as they do the Dark Side of the beautiful game.

Their values seem skewed, somehow and there's an arrogance to them. As they belt out their anthem, 'Marching On Together', you're left in no doubt that they still see themselves as a massive club, despite their years of turmoil. In fact, when we beat them at Elland Road last season, their sulky silence was only really thrown off when the Derby fans started to sing, 'You're not famous anymore.'

The Leeds team were as unlovely as I assume their fans expect them to be. Surrounding the referee, lecturing the linesmen, going down at the faintest touch, moving the ball forward five yards at a dishonestly bought free kick when the ref's back was turned, or simply spotting it in the wrong place in the hope he didn't notice – all of this infuriating stuff seems to be a part of their DNA. McCormack, Brown and Snodgrass are particularly unlovely bearers of the 'Dirty Leeds' tradition.

As the Tomlinsons pointed out, all they need is Billy Davies to take over as manager from Simon Grayson, because it would be a match made in heaven.

I would hate it if the Derby players constantly harangued the officials in such egregious fashion. They seem to believe that there is some sort of global conspiracy against them, that if the referee and linesmen could only be made to see that they were intrinsically biased against them, then justice would be done and every decision would rightfully go their way. We shuddered, thinking of the time-wasting antics that would surely have taken place if Leeds had got the first goal.

Watching Snodgrass indulge in a tantrum for nigh-on two minutes when Roberts wasn't booked for a foul the referee hadn't even seen fit to give – the linesman flagged for it – was absolutely unbelievable. In the dying seconds, the same player went ballistic appealing for a non-existent handball on the line, only ceasing his arm-waving histrionics when he suddenly realised the possibility for a short corner was on.

Of course, no team plays with absolute honesty and the odd bit of gamesmanship is part and parcel of football, but I can't remember seeing any other team so totally committed to this particular approach.

It was an open game, which either side could have easily pinched, but Derby played the better football, created more genuine openings and ultimately, deserved to win. Yet again, Jamie Ward was our chief attacking threat and his left-footed finish, first time on the rebound after his initial right-footed first-timer was blocked back to him, was sensationally well-judged. I was nonplussed for a second as I realised it had gone in – how? The angle was dead against him – assuming as I had that he would fire it across the goal for the unmarked Robinson to tap in.

The late aerial bombardment from the Whites was reminiscent of the Elland Road fixture last season, but so was the response of Shaun Barker. On that day in August 2010, the captain had to climb off the bench to play when he really wasn't fit – over a year later and he is just returning to something like fitness from the same knee problem, which was finally operated on over the summer. His shambling gait makes it seem to me that he's still limping and his defensive partner, Jason Shackell, cruises around like a Rolls-Royce in comparison, but Barker is now winning the vast majority of his headers – and made several crucial and difficult interceptions.

Between them, the two centre-backs seem able to cover most attacks; although neither is blessed with tremendous pace, they are experienced and aware enough to be positioned correctly almost every time. Much has been made of the fact that, before shutting out Leeds, Derby hadn't kept a clean sheet since the 3-0 win against Millwall in September, but we have only conceded four goals in the last five games – a major improvement on the overall concession rate of 1.39 goals per game across the whole season (32 goals in 23 Championship matches). Since the 3-1 defeat at West Ham, when the returning Barker was bossed by Carlton Cole, that average has come down considerably, from 1.56 goals per game (28 in 18).

I crunch these numbers to demonstrate the importance of Barker to the team. The return of Brayford has also made a difference and Paul Green, who seems like a fish out of water on the right side of midfield, nevertheless made his presence felt once we had a lead to defend, his tireless defensive shuttling denying space to the Leeds midfielders as they sought to find an equaliser.

Jonathan Wilson's new biography of Brian Clough, *Nobody Ever Says Thank You*, reminds us of an old Harry Storer quote. Storer, who managed Derby in the 1950s, told Clough to count the hearts on the team bus before each away game and not to bother setting off if there were fewer than five.
Nigel Clough must have received that advice from his father in turn, as there seems to be little room in his team for players who don't give their all.

***

Winning:
Derby County 2 West Ham United 1
Hull City 0 Derby County 1
January 4, 2012

I can't believe it. Having been worried before Christmas that Derby could conceivably lose all three of the tough-looking festive fixtures, I am instead writing about a run of three straight wins, which have carried the Rams back into the top ten and into the New Year on a serious wave.

Certainly after six points had been registered in back-to-back home games against Leeds and West Ham United, everybody probably would have been happy enough even if we'd lost at Hull City. As it happened, the Tigers were unable to break down a tenacious Rams rearguard and were made to pay. Adriano Basso should have saved Robinson's shot, but it's hard to feel too sympathetic given that Hull have had a recent hoodoo over Derby and given that we have had to suffer various home defeats of this ilk over the past few seasons.

Although Derby were unable to do much attacking at the KC Stadium, they showed the appetite and courage necessary to defend as a unit. Everybody put in their shift and a play-off chasing side were thereby limited to very few chances on their own patch. With James Bailey playing a shielding role in front of the back four and Bryson and Green gradually dropping deeper as the Rams dug in, Derby successfully 'parked the bus', to quote Nick Barmby.

It's not often that we've been able to do that in recent years – gritty 1-0 away wins are something we've found hard to generate. We managed four in the 2006/07 promotion season under Billy Davies, but only one last season, at Sheffield United. This term we have three already, at Blackpool, Watford and Hull.

We lack the quality to rip teams to shreds, but all too often in previous seasons we've also lacked the grit necessary to win ugly. With the exception of Ward, the current team isn't exactly full of flair, but is packed with players who work hard. A 4-5-1 system (or 4-3-3 as Johnny Metgod somewhat disingenuously termed it after Hull) will never please English fans, who remain committed to the attacking possibilities of 4-4-2, but in specific circumstances, it can be mightily effective. The ball kept going back to Hull, who probed and probed without being able to find a chink in the Rams' armour.

Of course, it's a risky business. If you set up to defend, you're basically hoping that a defender won't make a mistake and that the opposition won't manage to find a moment of magic from somewhere to prize you open. However, doughty defenders such as Shackell and Barker seem to have been born to soak up pressure in second-tier matches and the full-backs, Roberts and Brayford, are equally able to stand up and be counted. Roberts has taken some stick during his Derby career but is currently enjoying a good run and his defensive qualities are finally becoming apparent to more supporters.

After the West Ham game, the transfer window opened and speculation started to rumble. Twitter is the new bush telegraph and very soon, rumours were flying – Jamie Ward to Leicester City was the first. Ward has 18 months left on his contract, with an option for a one-year extension, which will hopefully be exercised soon.

Next, Paul Green to Wolves was mentioned, but Wolves have since signed Emmanuel Frimpong from Arsenal and Eggert Jonsson from Hearts, which suggests Mick McCarthy wasn't that keen. Green has declared that he wants to stay at Derby and I'm sure most fans would like him to stay too. However, Clough and the club are clearly playing hardball over the contract situation, as the boss went on record to say that if we were unable to match his 'financial ambitions', we would let him go and move on to develop a younger player.

The latest rumour involved a possible signing. A Nottingham Forest blogger, Reds Reporter, claimed on Twitter recently that Lewis McGugan wants to move to Derby and that his father has held talks with the Rams in the past about a possible transfer. This chap had heard from the usual nameless 'reliable source' that the move could be resurrected – the same source having previously tipped Reds Reporter off about Tyson's move to the right end of Brian Clough Way.

It would be great if there was something in it, but frankly, I doubt it. Clough has been consistent in his line for some time now that the focus this month is in reducing the wage bill by moving out players who aren't required. Whilst a talented young midfielder like McGugan would be an eye-catching signing, it probably remains the case that this season's incoming business is 99 per cent done already – as it needed to be, given how poor our form was in the second half of last season.

I look forward to my usual sitting up until the window 'slams shut' on deadline day – and I don't expect one of our best players to be spirited away at five to midnight!

***

January Transfer Window Special
February 2, 2012

Derby County went into this transfer window with their priorities firmly set and consistently stated in the media. They intended to move out several surplus players, cut the wage bill and consolidate the squad. Maybe there would be a couple of loan signings, but that would be about it.

Not a sexy message to get the fans' blood pumping, but at least it was honest.

Pretty soon, a clutch of 'non-productive' senior pros had disappeared. Stephens Pearson and Bywater were both released, to allow them to make their respective loan moves to Bristol City and Sheffield Wednesday permanent. Dean Leacock was soon saying his goodbyes to the Derby fans on Facebook and was released to join League One Leyton Orient as a free agent. Lee Croft's loan move to the SPL, which effectively ends his Rams career, was confirmed on Twitter by his glamour model partner, to very little moaning, wailing or gnashing of teeth from the Derby end.

That these players had to be released, rather than sold, says something about the financial state of most clubs in the Football League these days. There isn't so much easy credit sloshing around and Premier League clubs are generally spending less money, either to try to comply with the Financial Fair Play regulations or because there isn't any, which has a knock-on effect throughout the divisions. Not many Championship clubs have been able to spend heavily this season – not that Championship clubs were signing most of our unwanted players anyway.

After this purge, the England U19 striker Ryan Noble was loaned from Sunderland for an initial month, possibly with a view to a longer stay. Nigel Clough mentioned the possibility of another loan signing coming in before the January deadline, but also admitted that this was to cover the eventuality of Paul Green being sold. Enter Tom Carroll, a pint-sized, but gifted left-footed midfield playmaker. Carroll is another England U19 international, described by Tim Sherwood, his coach at Tottenham Hotspur, as being technically good enough to play for Barcelona.

Green's situation divided fans. Had he left, his energy and determination would have been missed. He was an important part of the recent winning run, playing well despite being out of position on the right side of midfield.

Clough made the point that the club have 'other priorities for the summer', so it may still be that Green's financial demands are not met at the end of the season, freeing up funds for other signings. Green is 28 and has given good service to Derby, but as he has now reached his peak in terms of age, this is an important contract for him. If he can get a better two- or three-year deal elsewhere, he can hardly be blamed for accepting it, as by the end of that time, he will be into his thirties as a player whose prime virtues have always been stamina and tenacity, rather than technique or vision.

In previous seasons, I'm convinced that a promotion-chasing side with loose purse-strings – Cardiff City, say, or Derby under Billy Davies –

would have taken Green, even if just to add him to the squad for their tilt at the Premier League. But only Leicester really fit into that category this season and they were more interested in adding Wes Morgan to their expensively assembled defensive unit. Clubs like Hull and Middlesbrough, who will be there or thereabouts this season, were rumoured to be interested, but ultimately either wouldn't, or couldn't, do the deal.

Elsewhere, Tomasz Cywka, still popular with many fans but not with the management, was reported to be available for transfer, probably for no more than a nominal fee. A move home to Poland seemed the most likely result, with the almost unspellable Slask Wroclaw making a bid, but a mystery Championship club – eventually unmasked as Reading – arrived on the scene with a last-minute bid. Cywka painted a dramatic picture of the deal; during a meeting at Wroclaw, his mobile went off to inform him of Reading's interest, sending him racing to the airport for the next flight back to England.

Chris Maguire, who it's fair to say hasn't made the impression we all hoped, was the subject of a loan bid from Hibernian, which was knocked back, but Clough indicated that the striker would be allowed out temporarily. Maguire could well still depart on loan after the 'emergency' window opens and it wouldn't be a total surprise if he disappeared permanently in the summer. It's certainly no good to leave him in the reserves, for whom he has scored 12 goals in 12 games this season.

Miles Addison returned from his prolonged spell at Barnsley, only for Clough to announce that he wasn't in the plans at present and would be allowed to go back out on loan again this month. That he is now considered fifth-choice centre-back, behind Jake Buxton and Tom Naylor, shows how far his stock has fallen since his inclusion in the England U21 team not so long ago. Injuries have taken their toll and he wasn't able to force his way into the Barnsley team on a consistent basis during his half-season loan spell there.

Speculation

As well as the concrete developments, there was plenty of speculation for Twitter fans to enjoy. Possibly the most outlandish rumour of all was a report that Sol Campbell would be joining as a player-coach for the rest of the season, with a view to a long-term future as a coach. This prompted one of the time-honoured 'my mate who works in a hotel just saw (insert name of chief exec) and (insert name of high-profile player) walking through the foyer' tweets, which made me chuckle. A tradition that will never die.

Sky Sports repeatedly ran stories linking James Bailey with a move away from Pride Park, stating that the player becomes a free agent in summer. I challenged journalist Pete O'Rourke on this, as when Bailey signed in summer 2010, it was announced by Derby as a three-year deal. O'Rourke maintains that the deal expires in summer, with an option to extend which Derby have not yet triggered. The window closed with Bailey still a Ram.

Bailey, Ward and Robinson are the only three squad members who seem to be in the long-term plans but who haven't yet committed to at least 2014. As long as extensions are not inked, speculation will continue. And agents will always encourage this – Jeff Hendrick being a case in point. Rumoured interest from Premier League clubs can't have harmed negotiations over his contract extension, which, as Clough pointed out, was handled by 'people who I'm sure are working in his best interests'.

The ones that got away (or were paid to leave)

It's interesting to note that of the 35 senior players Clough has parted with, only one went to the Premier League (Tyrone Mears, to Burnley) and only 12 stayed in the Championship. The majority went to the lower leagues, or to minor leagues abroad, including the Danish Superliga, Australian A-League and SPL.

Of the ones who stayed in England's second tier, none went on to become stars at their new clubs. Jordan Stewart, for example, was packed off to Greece within months by Sheffield United, while Rob Hulse, whose move left us temporarily strikerless, was in and out for QPR last season and scored just two goals during their promotion campaign.

The players Clough allowed to leave had cost a combined £17m, £16m of which was spent by Davies and Jewell. In moving them out, the club raised about £5m (almost a third of which was for Tito Villa), absorbing a loss of about £12m in transfer fees alone.

To date, Clough has been allowed to spend about £5.7m on 26 players (an average of under £220,000 per player). And it's fair to say that despite having spent less than £1m more in fees than he has re-couped, he has rationalised, rejuvenated and generally improved the squad from front to back.

Goodbye Roy Carroll, Price and Bywater, hello Fielding and Legzdins.

Cheerio Claude Davis, Martin Albrechtsen and Darren Powell, greet-ings to Shaun Barker, John Brayford and Jason Shackell.

Fair thee well, Gary Teale, Andy Todd and Mile Sterjovski, hi to Craig Bryson, James Bailey and Jeff Hendrick.

Balls to Villa, Nathan Ellington and Liam Dickinson, we'll go with Theo and Jamie Ward instead. Oh and we'll hang on to Steve Davies, thanks.

Twelve of the senior players Clough released were over 30 years old. The average age of the current squad is under 23.5.

Things are by no means perfect, but we have a good core of players, almost all of whom have plenty of years of football ahead of them, and we are well positioned to strengthen again, either in February or more likely in the summer.

***

When 4-4-2 F***ed up:
Barnsley 3 Derby County 2
February 4, 2012

Some days, your luck's out. Some days, you don't get what you deserve.

On other days – and these have been in mercifully short supply this season – you play cretinously badly and get whupped. For 45 minutes at Oakwell, Derby were incomprehensibly awful and got the hammering they deserved.

Although the bizarre circumstances of the evening contributed to our downfall, with Paul Green left out just in case somebody chose to bid for him on transfer deadline day, Nigel Clough takes a share of the blame. Unless James Bailey was injured, it was probably asking too much to change two of the midfield four while also giving a teenager his debut up front in a 4-4-2[24]. Green was a big miss, as was Bailey and the Rams were totally swamped. The swinging stable door was eventually bolted shut, but by that time, the horses were gambolling free in the hills, over yonder.

Barnsley played a midfield three of Perkins, Tonge and Korey Smith, who were able to monopolise possession, with Derby restricted to a series of embarrassingly over-pitched 'channel balls'. We were outnumbered, but also sluggish, second to everything and seemingly disorganised – a shadow of the side who have played with confidence, determination and discipline over the past couple of months.

Had we matched Barnsley's midfield three from the start, we could have denied them the space to play their football, but as it was, Carroll and Bryson were left impotent and Noble was totally peripheral as the Tykes hared into the lead. The penalty was grotesque, a mindless

---

[24] Barnsley were 3-0 up within half an hour. The losing team was Fielding; Brayford, Barker, Shackell, Roberts; Hendrick, Bryson, Carroll, Ward; Ball, Noble (Tyson). Unused subs: Legzdins, Buxton, Bailey, B. Davies. The result left Derby 12th in the table, on 41 points after 28 games.

push in the back from Brayford standing as a pretty good symbol of his side's total lack of engagement with the game in the opening 20 minutes.

Eventually, Noble was moved to the right flank, allowing Hendrick to move into central midfield and help to plug the gaps, but by then the damage was already done. The third goal was a direct result of Barnsley's zest and confidence; the through ball exquisitely judged and the finish impishly cute. Derby had barely got near them for half an hour, barely put in a tackle and as a result, the home side were playing with alarming fluency.

We simply weren't good enough in any department. Carroll must have been wondering what the hell he was doing, playing with such a rabble. It could have been four, five, even six by half-time, easily.

Derby simply have not been that bad this season, which is what made it all so shocking. It's perhaps a good thing that the next match is Nottingham Forest at home, because a performance of that nature is not an option, not with 33,000 fans screaming blue murder.

The second half was completely different and Clough held his hand up after the game, admitting that the formation he started with (and possibly team selection, too) had been wrong. Changing to a midfield three allowed Carroll to get on the ball and Derby went on to control possession for the majority of the half.

Suddenly, we were able to dictate the play and our general dominance and increased urgency was rewarded with Ward's smashed free kick and should have resulted in a penalty when Carroll was obviously clattered midway through an artful 360 spin in the box. It's one of the most blatant penalties you'll ever see – not given.

We have the players to get the most out of a single striker system. Bailey or Hendrick can hold, Bryson and/or Green can get forward and most of the central midfielders on the books can pick a pass. Ball can play as a lone striker and Tyson and Ward are capable of causing problems in wide areas.

Carroll is an interesting addition to the mix and while Tommo makes the valid point that we are essentially developing a player for Spurs, with a potentially detrimental effect upon our own players, it seems clear that he will be good to watch over the next few months.

Once they were set up in a shape that actually suited them, the players managed to find the resolve to avoid the cricket score that seemed inevitable after half an hour. While Barnsley deserved their win for their vivacious first-half performance, the locals were sufficiently rattled by the closing stages to resort to hiding the ball in the stand in an attempt to break up our momentum. As Clough has said before, 'It has to come from within' and the Rams at least proved that they won't hide, or let their heads drop, even when things have gone as badly wrong as they did in the first 30 minutes.

So we'll put the first half down as an aberration, tactically from the management and in terms of a certain slackness in the players, take encouragement from the second-half performance and move on, to Sunday. Home, the old enemy, the opportunity to smash them when they're down, a full house, the chance to make yourself a hero. It's all there for the players. They must give us a performance to be proud of and they must, must win.

And if they play like they can, they will.

***

Derby County v Nottingham Forest – Postponement and a pause for reflection February 12, 2012

In a way, the snowfall was perhaps a blessing in disguise. The untimely death of Nigel Doughty on the eve of the East Midlands derby would have totally changed the story and atmosphere of the match and I'm afraid the thought did cross my mind that it would have made it easier for morons to cause trouble – one tasteless chant and the atmosphere in the stadium could have gone extremely sour.

Forest boss Steve Cotterill told the *Nottingham Post,* 'Maybe the weather was a blessing, because I am not sure what we would have got last weekend. It could have gone one way or the other. When the emotions are high, you are never sure what you are going to get... it was better that it wasn't on.'

Before Doughty's passing, the pre-match chat was all about the disparity in the two clubs' current fortunes. *The Independent* published a full-page article about Forest's woes, explaining how the club had sunk into its current financial hole – £75m of debt to Doughty – and quoting new chairman Frank Clark's belief that Derby County's financially sustainable model was one that they would have to look to follow in the future. They are fortunate that Doughty committed £23m of funding for the next two years when he stepped down as chairman. That gives them a grace period, either to find another benefactor or get into a position where they aren't reliant upon one.

The reality of the Reds' balance sheet means that they are a long way from breaking even. Their wage bill is ruinously high and, even worse, they have veterans such as Andy Reid, George Boateng and Jonathan Greening on the books. These are exactly the types that the Rams were lumbered with when Nigel Clough took over from Paul Jewell – think Andy Todd, Robbie Savage, Roy Carroll – players on unacceptably high wages, with little or no resale value, who either need to be paid off or used as best as possible until the end of their contract.

So if the Reds are genuinely set on getting their house in order, they are going to have to go through a process which will probably be longer and even more painful than the one the Rams have suffered through in recent seasons. The sale of Wes Morgan and their best youth prospect, Patrick Bamford (to Chelsea for £1.5m), has allowed them to bring in three Premier League loanees – Danny Higginbotham, Adlene Guedioura and George Elokobi – but this is only a short-term sticking plaster, aimed at keeping the club in the Championship for another season.

Derby have been through their period of relying on loanees, who are inevitably variable in terms of their contribution. We now have a squad of our own players, pretty much all of whom are young enough to have their best footballing days ahead of them. There are no 'big names' in our squad, but the reality is that the so-called big name players from the Premier League only come down to the Championship when they are past their prime.

It took Derby years to get into our current lean, financially sustainable, mid-table shape after the trauma of Premier League relegation and there is still plenty of work for us to do if we are to start seriously challenging for promotion. If Forest do survive this season, barring the emergence of another benefactor, their supporters shouldn't be fooled into thinking that the tough times are over.

***

Past, Present Imperfect, Future Tense at Derby County?
February 18, 2012

Twitter can be a depressing place and never more so than after Derby have lost. In fact, any reasonable-minded fan would be best advised to completely avoid the platform for at least 24 hours in the aftermath of any defeat, lest their already fragile mood be completely destroyed by the inevitable litany of bitterness, anger, insults and, most annoyingly of all, hindsight, with the benefit of which, of course, many experts have all the answers.

I said at the beginning of the season that I saw Derby as a mid-table team and nothing I've seen this season has dissuaded me of that. When we've been good, we've managed to grind out some hard-won victories, dispatching only three teams by more than the odd goal (Doncaster, Millwall and Portsmouth, all at home and all of whom are struggling). When we've been bad, which has often but not always coincided with when we've been missing key players through injury, we've been pretty, pretty bad. So far, we've won 12, drawn six and lost

12. Win one, lose one. Mid-table.

So, there you go. This squad is not good enough to challenge for promotion, but rather better than the stragglers. It's not good enough for some – Pride Park league attendances are averaging just under 26,000 this season – but even the most virulent Clough critic would struggle to deny the fact that we are better this season than we have been at any time since the promotion season of 2006/07.

Since Billy Davies dragged us into the Premier League, we've never been as close to the top half of the table as we are now – 13th – come the end of a season. And even before that, George Burley's play-off season of 2004/05 was an anomaly, as the club had been performing poorly ever since relegation from the Premier League finally came in 2001/02.

<u>Derby County's Decade of Doom</u>

2001/02 – Premier League	19th (R)	
2002/03 – First Division	18th	
2003/04 – First Division	20th	
2004/05 – Championship	4th (play-offs)	
2005/06 – Championship	20th	
2006/07 – Championship	3rd (play-offs, P)	
2007/08 – Premier League	20th (R)	
2008/09 – Championship	18th	
2009/10 – Championship	14th	
2010/11 – Championship	19th	

The short-term future

The problem with the short-term future is that it isn't very glamorous or interesting to be a win-one lose-one mid-table second-tier side – and it's even hard to see that it's much better than being a relegation-haunted second-tier side. At least in a season when you're flirting with the drop, there's drama and genuine emotion. Watching a team who are about par for the course for their level isn't terribly interesting, usually.

We're short of flair but essentially solid. Defensively, we're pretty sound – we only have the 13th-best defensive record in the league at present and ever since Shaun Barker's return, we've tightened up at the back – but the midfield and forward line are not creatively gifted enough to propel us into the top six.

Due to the limitations of budget and Clough's personal preferences, the squad is fairly lean, which means that we are essentially dependent upon particular key players performing well week-in, week-out. Jason Shackell and Barker are the two leaders in the team and the most dependable men, the heart of the side. Paul Green, John Brayford and Craig Bryson are arguably the next three most reliable players – and none of them play up front.

Therein lies the rub. Until one of our star players is a striker, we will get nowhere near the Premier League.

After the disappointing performance and defeat against Reading this week, the club's PR focused on the overall improvement in results since last season, with Clough saying, 'In three years, we've never been this far from the bottom three [17 points above Coventry City in 22nd]. The play-offs are probably unrealistic for us at this stage, they always were.'

The mid-term future

A little more difficult to divine, dependent as it is to an extent upon the largesse of our investors. If the likes of W. Brett Wilson can be persuaded to chip in a few bucks, then maybe we'll get a good striker in the summer, at which point we should start to move up the table.

Again, this is something I've felt fairly confident about until recently. However, some of Clough's recent comments about relying on youth and looking for more lower-level players to develop make me wonder if my presumptions were correct, especially as these comments came after announcements about early bird deals for season ticket renewal were announced, a time when you'd think the club would be keen to state their ambitions clearly.

If next season doesn't turn out to be the one, at what point do average attendances start to dip below 25,000, as more and more fair-weather supporters drift away?

Already, we've seen sub-25,000 gates in ten of our 15 home league games this season.

In his post-Reading PR video with Rams Player, Clough said, 'The difference between the teams was Jason Roberts. Our frontman was Callum Ball… He will be what Roberts is in six months or a year.'

It's nice that Clough has so much faith in Ball, who certainly has potential, but nevertheless, that statement seems wildly optimistic to me.

The long-term future

The long-term vision for the club appears to focus on the academy, directing funds and scouting energy in that direction, with a view to producing as many of our own players as possible. That process has started already, with Mark O'Brien and Jeff Hendrick making serious progress this season. Will Hughes has been linked with Manchester United and Manchester City, while Mason Bennett has joined Hughes in the England U17 squad, but it will take years for these youngsters to become the sort of reliable, seasoned pros we would like them to be.

Long-term planning in football is very difficult. A run of bad results often sees clubs hit the panic button by sacking the manager, or splurging beyond their means on new players. Meanwhile, even teenage players have agents agitating to move them on, as we have seen with Hendrick this season.

But if the nucleus of the current side can be retained, the young players develop as we all hope they can and we add a bit of experience, there's no reason why, in a couple of seasons, we won't be a force at this level. Especially given the financial chaos which has been allowed to reign elsewhere.

After Portsmouth's second administration in two years was confirmed, court-appointed administrator Trevor Birch, who had a very brief spell at Derby County in 2007, announced that 30 per cent of Championship clubs are running wage bills higher than their entire turnover. In other words, without incurring extra debt, seven or eight second tier clubs can't even pay their staff, let alone buy more players or meet their running costs.

Clough and the board should be applauded for being far-sighted enough to prioritise the development of youth players – after all, the current success of Southampton has in part been paid for by the sale of Alex Oxlade-Chamberlain, with past windfalls also coming from selling Theo Walcott and Gareth Bale.

As Clough told the *Derby Telegraph* this week, 'We're trying to get to a break-even situation and I don't think any other clubs are trying to achieve that at the moment. It may not mean a lot to supporters, but it does mean they are not faced with a Portsmouth or a Rangers situation, or anyone else that comes out the woodwork in the future. There could be clubs who don't just go into administration but actually go out of business... We're trying to run things conscientiously and sensibly. Fans want success on the pitch – but we're trying to do both. We're not saying we can't be successful on the pitch – it might just take a bit longer.'

But all the talk of long-term planning, a promising young side, sustainable development, better times just over the horizon, etc, etc, is never going to be sexy enough to generate big crowds unless it's a game with particular resonance (Forest or Leeds, for example), or we're winning regularly. And if the fans stop turning up, the turnstiles stop clacking and the merch store takes less cash, turnover drops and the investors start to lose interest, what happens then?

The other day, I found a feature on Igor Štimac, written by Hunter Davies in 1999. This was a time when, according to Davies, an England international could expect to earn £500,000 a year, with top Premier League stars commanding a salary of £1m. Igor told Davies that in ten years' time, top flight players would be earning ten times as much. He was right.

Sadly, this financial reality means that a man of Igor's stature could not be brought to Derby in 2012 as he was by Lionel Pickering's cash in 1995 – and nor could a Stefano Eranio, Francesco Baiano, Aljosa Asanovic, Mart Poom, Jacob Laursen, or Paolo Wanchope...

As the Manchester band James once put it, 'If I hadn't seen such riches, I could live with being poor.'

***

Tactical Traumas and the Death of a Season
February 27, 2012

One of the most notable features of the current barren run is that Nigel Clough has been obliged to alter his starting formation in three of the recent defeats. In two of them, however, the damage had already been done.

Firstly at Barnsley, where our 4-4-2 failed so badly that by the time we matched Barnsley's midfield three and stopped making them look like Barcelona, they were already out of sight. Secondly, against Reading, when a 4-3-3 simply didn't offer enough punch against the visitors (who lined up 4-4-2) and thirdly against Leicester, when a lurch back to 4-4-2 gave Neil Danns an embarrassing amount of space in midfield.

Derby 0 Reading 1

Reading were simply too defensively solid and strong for Derby. The 4-3-3 we fielded looks good on paper, but on the day, Callum Ball could get no change out of an experienced Royals back four and Clough changed to 4-4-2 before half-time, with Tyson up front and Bryson on the right – without causing Reading many more problems. In this game, maybe the formation wasn't the deciding factor.

Derby 0 Leicester 1

Against Leicester, the problem was embarrassingly obvious from very early on – neither Hendrick or Bryson were capable of acting as a shield for the back four and while Nugent and Beckford were kept pretty quiet by Shackell and Barker, they got no help against the runs of Danns, who was free to romp across the pitch and pepper Frank Fielding's goal with shots at will.

Not until Carroll was shifted into central midfield to make a three did we gain any kind of foothold in the game and by that point, Leicester had already scored from a counter-attack, after Carroll lost the ball on the edge of the box in a central position and was left hopelessly out of position, exposing Green to the pace of Lloyd Dyer one-on-one. Hey presto, Green was roasted and Danns won the game, in a moment of vicious clarity.

Carroll, Bailey and a loss of balance

When Tom Carroll joined on loan from Spurs and was promoted straight into the first team at the expense of James Bailey, we started losing. This may be coincidental, but Tommo made the point very quickly that in his view, Carroll was the wrong player at the wrong time. As much as I do like the look of the player, it seems at this stage as if he was right.

When Paul Green didn't leave in January, as the club had clearly anticipated, it meant that central midfield was one of the few parts of the team where we didn't need strengthening. And what about the oft-repeated PR line about developing our own young players, not relying on loanees? Carroll's place in the team necessarily comes at the expense of one our own lads – Bailey.

If Carroll plays in the centre with Hendrick, there's not enough cover for the defence. Meanwhile, Bryson is obviously hurt, suffering with a heel injury and 'playing through the pain'. But Bailey, a natural holding midfielder with good positional sense and an excellent range of passing, wasn't even on the bench for the Leicester game.

Clough has had a dig at Bailey in a couple of recent interviews, suggesting that he started training harder after Carroll's arrival and also that he didn't play well at Southampton – but in doing without him, we are struggling very badly indeed.

Back to October and November, when our form was dreadful, we were missing Bailey. And the season's results with and without Bailey in the starting line-up make for very interesting reading:

League Record with Bailey starting
P12 W8 D1 L3 F13 A10 GD+3 Pts 25
Points per Game 2.083

League Record when Bailey did not start
P20 W4 D5 L11 F20 A33 GD-11 Pts 17
Points per Game 0.85

The difference is staggering. When Bailey has started, we've won 75 per cent of the games – promotion form – and two of the three defeats were away at the top two, West Ham and Southampton (the draw was at Burnley, when Bailey was withdrawn through illness at half-time). Without Bailey starting, our win ratio plummets to 20 per cent – relegation form.

It would be too simplistic to suggest that bringing Bailey back would suddenly solve everything. Brayford's absence at right-back has been telling and Bryson is also clearly injured, which weakens the side considerably – but it makes no sense for one of our best prospects to be completely left out of the squad in favour of someone else's prodigy.

There's no doubt that Carroll is talented, but his only previous meaningful first-team experience has come in League One with Leyton Orient and it shows. Bailey is already a good player for us, but he won't get any better if he's not picked.

This said, Clough has already mentioned the possibility of Carroll returning next season, which makes you wonder if all those Sky Sports reports about Bailey being set to leave are as wide of the mark as we assumed.

In the meantime, it's a bloody mess. The starting XI seems to be wrong for every game at the moment and things are going badly against us. The balance the side had when Bryson and Bailey played in central midfield together has been completely lost.

Green, Naylor and the right-midfield void

The best moments we had against Leicester came when Green was able to forge into the box. Which reminded you – he's actually a good midfielder. What if we had a right-back and he could go back to, if not his natural position of centre mid, at least right mid, where he was doing a good job?

We somehow appear to have arrived at a situation where there is nobody to play right midfield. Carroll, Bryson and Hendrick have all been tried there unsuccessfully and Ben Davies has seemingly been completely cast aside. So the reality is that, considering the players who are currently thought of as viable starters by Clough, Brayford's absence has at a stroke made it virtually impossible for us to play 4-4-2 successfully.

In the brilliant run over Christmas and New Year, when we beat Leeds, West Ham, Hull and Coventry, we generally played 4-4-2, with Bailey and Bryson in the centre and Hendrick left out. At that time, Brayford was fit, which allowed Green to play right midfield.

So if we're not going to loan a right-back, why not give Tom Naylor a chance, at least for one game? It can't get any worse than it's been of late and we're still 14 points – four wins and two draws – above the bottom three. Clough recently muttered something about giving Naylor a go 'if we had five or six more points'. F**k it! Give him a go now. He would have Barker and Shackell to talk him through the game, plus Green in front of him to offer support – and of course Green could move back to a midfield berth, where he'd be much more useful. Naylor might struggle and we might lose, but we're doing that anyway and we're not involved in the relegation dogfight.

The magic sponge approach

Against Leicester, Clough preferred Bryson on one leg to Bailey, who wasn't even named among the subs. After the defeat, Clough told the *Derby Telegraph*, 'If you think how many second balls [Bryson] usually picks up, but in the first half against Leicester he couldn't get any of those, which is mainly down to him not being 100 per cent at the moment.' Which begs the question, why pick him? The answer – 'It's easy to say "if he's injured, don't play him", but we still need him out there and he wants to be out there.'

That Clough went on to admit that Bryson's injury 'is the sort that gets worse during games', leaving Bryson struggling within an hour and causing hamstring and calf complications, suggests irresponsible management. It is indeed easy to say, ;if he's injured, don't play him', especially if you have other options available. We might well 'still need' Bryson out there, but if he isn't fit, we aren't seeing the real Bryson anyway – and we run the risk of losing him for the rest of the season if he damages his hamstring.

After the injury crises of previous seasons, things have improved generally this season but we are now missing Brayford probably until next season – after he broke down at Southampton, with Clough admitting that he had come back from his thigh injury too soon – and if Bryson doesn't recover from his heel injury properly but continues to play, it seems likely that he will go the same way.

The death of a season

It wasn't too long ago that Tommo and I were driving back from Turf Moor reflecting on a good point well earned, which stretched our unbeaten run in league and cup games to six matches and left us 11th in the table, just two points off sixth. Since then, it's been a very different story.

Everybody is desperate for us to just win a game, but the team selection seems to be sabotaging any chance we have, week in week out. Barnsley away could have been a comfortable victory, if we'd got the tactics right from the get-go. Reading had far too cosy a time against lone striker Callum Ball and we weren't even giving Leicester a game until we adjusted our formation to make up for the fact that, in a straight 4-4-2 shooting match, we couldn't live with them.

The season is effectively over. Another four wins and we'll be safe and that is clearly the only aim, along with 'giving the young lads experience'. Unfortunately, in a team with an unbalanced, unsettled front six, all they seem to be experiencing at the moment is the taste of defeat.

What happens next season?

***

Winning a War of Attrition: Derby County 1 Nottingham Forest 0 March 16, 2012

This was an unbearably tense affair, in which every player was called on to give everything and did so. In the end Derby had a little bit more in the tank than Forest and won by the determined application of constant pressure, rather than with a moment of great skill.

I arrived just before kick-off, after scoffing down a jerk chicken dinner from the Windrush Cafe on Woods Lane (recommended). The first thing I realised while scanning our 11 on the pitch was that Tom Carroll wasn't there, for which I offered silent thanks to Nigel Clough. For all Carroll's merits, the East Midlands Derby was obviously no place for such an inexperienced player, so Craig Bryson returned to his rightful position in the centre. Nathan Tyson lined up on the right, presumably so he could have a go at left-back Greg Cunningham, with Ben Davies on the left.

Very few chances were created in the first half, but of course, it was enthralling nonetheless. The BBC have described this period of the game as 'poor', but that was only the case if you didn't support one of the two teams. For myself – and I assume for everyone inside the ground – the action was gripping. I spent the whole time clapping like a demented seal if we did anything even remotely right.

Many moons ago (or so it seems now), I wrote a frantically cross blog about the Tyson signing, stating my belief that I didn't think he should have been considered for Derby due to the flag incident at the City Ground a couple of years ago. But months later, I finally feel ready to forget all that and accept him as a Derby player. The fact is, he's putting in the effort and ultimately, could prove to be a useful forward for us.

He came out on the wrong end of more than one crunching tackle and at one point in the first half, it looked like he was going to be withdrawn, to the huge joy of the Forest fans. To a man, they produced the rotating hands 'substitution' symbol, while chanting 'Same old Tyson, always injured' and 'He's shit and you know he is'. Tyson shook it off and kept going. Meanwhile, Guedioura and Moussi both picked up 'professional' bookings for deeply cynical tackles designed to prevent dangerous counter attacks.

The only moment of real quality came when Tyson produced a neat Cruyff turn to buy himself space for a pull-back which dropped to Ben Davies, who should have buried it. At the other end, Shackell and Green made an absolute Horlicks of dealing with an aimless long ball, making a present of it to Tudgay, who lobbed the ball into the stand.

Forest were in no mood to let us play and given their own total lack of zip in midfield, the game got bogged down. It was more like trench warfare than anything else, but I felt comfortable and relatively happy at half-time because it had become obvious that without a howling Derby error, or a moment of inspiration that was looking ever less likely, Forest were probably not going to score.

It's easy to say that with hindsight and of course, I was a nervous wreck for the entire game, but my gut feeling at the interval was that we just needed one moment of quality to beat a team who were there for the taking. This turned out not to be the case – but more of that later.

Guedioura was withdrawn for Greening, which I felt only improved our chances of nicking it. With Greening, Moussi and Andy Lard in midfield, Forest lacked mobility and were inevitably pushed back. Tudgay went into the book and then, as the Rams continued to press and with Forest trying to get an injured player back on to the pitch, Ben Davies won the ball via two fair sliding tackles, releasing Tyson on a burst through midfield which Blackstock halted, with a monstrously crude hack.

From my angle, it looked like an horrendous tackle that merited a straight red and we were then treated to the now traditional Derby v Forest melee, with everybody getting involved – although Blackstock himself walked away cradling his head in his hands, presumably in the belief that he was about to be sent off. By this time, the atmosphere in the ground was caustic and Andy D'Urso waited for a seeming age before producing a yellow card for the lucky Blackstock.

Blackstock was substituted for Ishmael Miller soon after, possibly to prevent him from being sent off, or maybe just to add somebody else who hadn't been booked, so that they could pick up a professional yellow for breaking up another attack.

Shaun Barker was then badly injured in a collision with Frank Fielding and Tudgay – credit to Derby lad Tudgay for staying with the stricken Rams skipper and encouraging the referee to stop the game. An extremely long break in play followed – enter Jake Buxton, who did very well against Watford and didn't look out of place here either.

As the game ground towards the 90-minute mark, with a seemingly endless series of Derby corners and free kicks ricocheting around the Forest box but refusing to end up in the sodding net, Tudgay got his second yellow card for smashing into Bryson. There had been worse tackles, not least Blackstock's, but he'd already been booked, it was late and he knew he'd gone as soon as it happened.

Tudgay apologised to Bryson before trotting off and the fact that Paul Green put a consoling arm around him speaks volumes. Of course, he got plenty of stick as he left the pitch, but none from me. Tudgay is a good player and really, I'm not sure why we ever let him go in the first place. It's a shame he ended up where he did. On the plus side, his sending off allowed the Derby fans to remind the Forest lot of their rotating hands 'substitution' symbol from the first half.

To be honest, I can't remember much else. All I remember is gripping the seat in front of me with both hands, my left leg jumping and bouncing around all over the place, regardless of whether I wanted it to or not.

It should be emphasised how bad Forest were. They offered next to nothing going forward and barely strung a pass together throughout the match. Although it took us 95 minutes to score, they allowed so many free kicks around the penalty area, so many opportunities for a cross, that in the end, something just had to drop for us.

Eventually, it did. As Ben Davies prepared to take the free kick, I muttered a little request for the boys to do it in spite of the Doughty chanters, not for them.

Earlier in the half, I became convinced that if I took my hat off before we took a free kick it would end up in the net, so I removed it with a flourish as the taker started his run-up. I can't remember exactly what happened, but the ball either hit the wall, or failed to beat the first man. So I didn't try the hat routine again.

And Ben swung in the free kick and the next thing I remember is seeing Camp standing there looking bereft and then realising that somehow, it had trickled in and seeing Jake Buxton, of all people, running with both arms aloft in the direction of the West Stand. I was too shocked and confused to celebrate. It was a goal, but I had no idea how it was a goal. Then I could see Steve Davies down on the ground injured and physios running towards him – nothing has been said on the Davies injury, so hopefully, he's OK – then I watched the Derby players piling on to Buxton in a massive heap and the Forest team were standing with heads bowed in a loose formation across their half of the pitch. Then I looked around me to take in the scenes of sheer jubilation in the East Stand.

If only we could somehow generate this sort of passionate atmosphere every game.

Then it was off to Jorrocks to listen to songs, sing songs and drink pints of pure celebration until late at night, easing the transition between the intensity of another fiery derby and the slower rhythms and gentler cadences of normal life.

***

The nPower Debt League
April 6, 2012

On Monday, I was lucky enough to take part in the BBC Radio Derby *Sportscene Talk-in* with Colin Bloomfield and Roger Davies. One of the most surreal elements of the experience was finding myself sitting in the studio while Bloomers read out the news bulletins, leaving me free to shoot the breeze with one of the most storied strikers in Derby County's history.

Roger is very affable and it was interesting to get his take on the current situation at Pride Park. If anything, it was nice to know that he's as much of a fan as the rest of us and is desperate to see Derby get promoted to the Premier League. One thing he did say was that it's a shame that these days, all the chat in football is 'about money, not what happens on the grass'.

I agree with him on that, but most of the callers that night wanted to talk about money in some way and here I am, writing yet another financial blog post.

Since Monday night, a couple of interesting articles have appeared online. Firstly, *The Independent* reported that the much-trumpeted Financial Fair Play regulations may not now be introduced for next season, despite Tom Glick's recent assertions to the contrary as he sought to explain the continuing policy of wage restraint at Derby County.

West Ham United, according to the *Telegraph*, were prepared to go to the lengths of seeking a judicial review to prevent the introduction of FFP this season and it's highly probable that the financially incontinent likes of Leicester City, who are desperate to debt-finance their way into the promised land, will also be opposed to its implementation.

Elsewhere, a Leeds United blog, The Scratching Shed, produced some very useful research comparing debt levels, turnover and wage bills across the division. Unfortunately, the post itself is laden with the kind of pompous hubris we've long associated with Leeds fans (blah blah 'major force' blah blah 'sleeping colossus' blah blah 'dormant power'), but if you can get past that, it's a valuable source of information and provided the numbers for the following league table of indebtedness, based on last year's figures (2010/11 season).

Nottingham Forest £75m
Ipswich Town £66.7m
QPR £56.1m (promoted)
Cardiff City £55.5m
Portsmouth £50m
Leicester City £43.8m
Hull City £40.4m
Reading £39m
Bristol City £38m
Sheffield United £32m (relegated)
Coventry City £30m
Middlesbrough £27.8m
DERBY COUNTY £25.5m
Watford £17.5m
Millwall £16.7m
Norwich City £4.1m (promoted)

No debt figures are provided for Swansea City (promoted), Leeds, Burnley, Barnsley, Crystal Palace, Doncaster Rovers, Preston North End (relegated) or Scunthorpe United (relegated).

Of course, we know that pretty much all the clubs above who are still in the Championship next year will report higher debt levels (on The Scratching Shed's reckoning, only Leeds turned a profit last time), including Derby, whose debt will climb to over £30m thanks to a further injection of interest-free loan capital from GSE. Off the top of my head, Leicester will go into the red by a further £25m – the extra money has been loaned to the club by owner Vichai Raksriaksorn at an interest rate of eight per cent – hurtling towards a total debt of £70m.

So it's clear that Derby are a long way from being the worst-run club in the division. However, there are no bonus points for being financially prudent and, more to the point, it now seems that no specific penalties are to be introduced for reckless spending yet, unless a club's house of credit cards collapses and they go into administration.

If it's true that FFP will not be introduced next season, there will be no obligation for the likes of Leicester, Ipswich and Hull to start getting their house in order – so they won't. As long as clubs refuse to sign up to the idea of regulating wage levels, the QPR/Leicester approach to chasing promotion will continue to be an option and the fate of Portsmouth could be replicated elsewhere, sooner rather than later. The fact that Derby are pretty much the only club to have prepared for the dawn of FFP by reducing their wage bill to less than 70 per cent of turnover will not give them any sort of advantage for next season if the over-spenders have their way and prevent the regulations from being introduced.

So the question is – are we happy to try to play a different, less risky game to the gamblers who are going all-in as they chase the Holy Grail of promotion?

***

Theo, Theo, Theo
April 14, 2012

With Steve Davies off the pitch, there didn't seem to be an obvious candidate to take the penalty after Anthony Gardner jabbed an arm at Ben Davies's cross, preventing Callum Ball from getting a header on goal. Set-piece specialist Ben Davies might have been expected to step up, but Theo Robinson grabbed the ball and wouldn't take no for an answer.

Watching him place the ball and take four big deliberate strides backwards, staring fixedly at the penalty spot with grim determination, you were left in no doubt that he was going to smash it.

Smash it he did. Julián Speroni went to his right, gambling that Theo would go with the more natural angle for a right-footer, but the striker buried it to the goalkeeper's left and at 3-0 up, the Rams looked set for a massive victory over Crystal Palace – maybe even one to rival last season's 5-0 romp against a ten-man Eagles outfit (nine, if you don't count the doddering Edgar Davids).

I felt my phone vibrate and when I checked it, I found two texts from Tommo. The first, sent just before the penalty was taken, said 'over the stand'.

Tommo is legendarily convinced that we will miss every single penalty we take – the most famous incident occurring in the play-off semi-final against Southampton at Pride Park, when he gave me a different reason for why every single taker would miss (they all scored) – but that's another story.

The second text said 'good pen'.

After the Palace match, Theo gave an interview to Rams Player. It was mostly made up of the usual footballer cliches and platitudes, but did include one semi-interesting quote. When asked what was going through his mind when he was preparing to take the penalty, he grinned broadly and said, 'I heard people behind me saying "he's gonna miss, he's gonna miss", but I already knew where I was gonna put it and it paid off.'

He was probably talking about the Palace players rather than the home supporters, but there's no doubt that some of the latter were doubting whether he would score too. But Robinson is a confident lad and clearly not about to let his detractors stop him from making the most of his opportunity at Derby County.

Earlier in the season, Robinson's Twitter feed was spammed with more than his fair share of abusive and derogatory comments. The situation got so bad that Theo ended up mentioning it in an interview with the *Derby Telegraph*. Even some of the more measured and respected

#dcfcfans have posted tweets reflecting the fact that they've been driven to distraction by the striker's performance and while nobody could ever fault Robinson's work rate, it's fair to say that his technical lapses can be seriously frustrating.

Against Ipswich[25], we saw all the elements of Robinson's game – good and bad. He gave the ball away more than once with bad passes, often in promising situations; his touch failed him on one occasion when it seemed that he was about to streak through on goal, but at the same time, he was unlucky not to score on three occasions – first when he stretched to divert Gareth Roberts's low cross just wide of the near post; then he was desperately unlucky not to follow in after Ben Davies's shot ricocheted back of the post just past him and most spectacularly of all, a tremendous overhead kick flashed just wide when it deserved to hit the back of the net.

Johnny Metgod, one of the more straight-talking football coaches, yeah, recently said something along the lines that Robinson 'couldn't get in the Huddersfield team and couldn't get in the Millwall team, so what do you expect' – but this was firmly in the context of discussing his encouraging goal return and continuing development as a player who cost the club about £150,000, according to a recent *Derby Telegraph* estimate.

Andy Garner believes that Robinson is in good hands with Nigel Clough (who was himself an England centre-forward in the early 1990s) and is learning all the time. He told Colin Bloomfield, 'We keep telling him he's got to keep working and running those channels... He was raw when he first came and there's things he's still got to work on, his first touch, we keep on about that, but as long as he keeps listening, he's with the right man.'

In fact, Theo's form and goalscoring have impressed so much this season that he even had the dubious honour of being the subject of an article by Sky Sports, crediting unnamed Premier League clubs, plus Leicester City, Birmingham City, Blackpool and Leeds United with an

---

[25] 7 April 2012 – Derby 0 Ipswich 0, a result which left the Rams 12th in the table.

interest in signing the player.

If Sky's story about James Bailey leaving in January is anything to go by, we can probably disregard this as agent talk at best, but nevertheless it is heartening that a player who wasn't even expected to be a first-team regular at the start of the season has now shot to the top of our goalscoring chart, has started the last ten games and is generating this sort of tabloid rumour.

He keeps producing little moments of real quality – the overhead kick against Ipswich, an incredible guided lob-volley from the edge of the box against Palace that beat Speroni all ends up and hit the angle of post and bar (my mate Stu wickedly described it as 'his first touch'), a tremendous spin-turn to leave a defender trailing in his wake at Doncaster and a very calm first-time finish in the same game, which made a difficult chance look easy.

Then there are the moments that drive you mad.

His main attributes are mercurial (acceleration, pace and a poaching ability) rather than technical (picking and executing a pass, control). In short, he's better off the ball than on it and ideally, you want to see him running behind defenders or arriving on the end of a cross in the six-yard box, rather than receiving the ball with his back to goal in the opposition half. But he can work on that side of his game and at 23, his best years are ahead of him. Let's hope he spends them with Derby County.

***

Everything but the Goal
April 20, 2012

It's fair to say that Derby County didn't deserve to lose to Cardiff City on Tuesday night, but as soon as Joe Mason's goal went in, it seemed inevitable that we would and I predicted that it would finish 2-0. Unfortunately and somewhat unjustly as it turned out, I was right (I didn't predict that their centre-back would smack one in from his own half, however.)

On reviewing the match footage, Derby were not quite as dominant in the game as Colin Bloomfield and Roger Davies felt at the time, but nevertheless it was without question a bravura performance by the Rams away to a team who they have been slaughtered by – 4-1, 6-1 and 4-1, almost a tennis score – in the past three visits.

The match stats do not lie – Derby had more shots, more corners and more possession. All well and good, but unfortunately, there was nobody to put the ball in the net when the chances presented themselves.

Nigel Clough has identified this weakness – 'a lack of quality in the final third' – repeatedly in recent weeks and I think it's fair for him to say that his defence is looking reasonably robust, while the midfield are giving us plenty of opportunities to hurt teams, either by winning the ball in dangerous areas, or by judicious short passing. It's all good until we get to the final third, which is where we fail to convert.

Clough pointed out when we were beaten 4-0 at Southampton that we actually had more 'penalty area entries' than the Saints did, which only reinforces the argument – it's not that we aren't getting into good positions, it's just that we're failing to take advantage of them, whereas promotion contenders such as Southampton, or Cardiff seem able to do so.

Last season, the lowest goals total for a top six side was 69. Looking back over the past few seasons, Birmingham went up with 54 goals in 2008/09, but only because their defence was rock solid. Billy Davies's fairly boring Rams team of 2006/07 went up with 62 in the regular season. They might have been winning 1-0 half the time, but they were scoring in the vast majority of the games. Davies's Derby only failed to score in nine league matches that season, whereas this season, we've drawn a blank 16 times. This season's total of 47 goals after 44 games is only two better than Forest, who, as if we could forget, failed to score for seven games during an amusing period this winter.

This team needs the help of a real goalscorer and ideally another creative midfielder too. Paul Green's imminent departure creates a vacancy on the right and if we can recruit somebody who can beat his man and find a white shirt with crosses and passes – along with somebody to stand in the middle and smash the ball into the net – then hopefully, we will get up and beyond the 60-goal mark next season. If we can do that, we just might have a chance of making the play-offs.

2012/13

Mining for gems in the era of Financial Fair Play
May 17, 2012

With the 2011/12 season finally over, it's time for a summer of transfer tittle-tattle, erroneous Sky Sports reports, kids confusing their game of *Football Manager* with reality and #dcfcfans claiming to have seen Glick in a hotel lobby with Kevin Davies/Michael Owen/Alessandro Del Piero.

I have no idea at this stage which players Derby County will end up signing, but am confident in making the following prediction – you probably won't have seen them play before, or maybe even heard of them (and neither will I).

I keep coming back to *Moneyball*, the marvellous book by Michael Lewis, in which the protagonist, Oakland A's manager Billy Beane, is described by scouts as a 'five-tool player' while still in school. Five-tool players are the star athletes, like Gareth Bale, say, who have physical prowess and the sporting aptitude to match and are obviously cut out for the highest level.

It goes without saying that, like Beane's Oakland, Derby can't afford to buy this kind of guy, although we could develop them through our academy (the prodigious Mason Bennett will doubtless be looming large on Premier League scouting radars already). So we have to be a bit more creative when it comes to signing new players.

Take the example of Ben Davies. Slow and lacking the skill to beat a man, Davies was not a Championship-standard wide midfielder in the most obvious respects and aged 29 when he joined, is unlikely to have any resale value. However, he possessed a certain 'tool' which Clough desperately wanted – the ability to cross the ball and take free kicks.

Davies initially seemed rather self-conscious about his set-pieces, knowing that he was under serious scrutiny every time he sent one into the box or towards goal. However, once he finally got settled, without ever dazzling anybody, Davies became one of the most prolific assist providers in the Championship last season – up there with the much more highly rated (and doubtless much better-paid) likes of Adam Lallana, Jimmy Kebe and Mark Noble.

Craig Bryson is perhaps another good example. Whilst he can pass, his key virtues are his stamina and work rate, which allow him to scurry from box to box all game long. His midfield partnership with the more studied Jeff Hendrick seems to be developing very nicely, to the point where James Bailey, a good talent in his own right, is now considered a reserve player (and probably won't be with us for very much longer). Bryson's lack of height and heft could have counted against him in some scouting reports, but Clough wanted the wispy Scot's sheer energy and would also have taken into consideration his professionalism, commitment and selflessness. At £450,000, he has proved to be an absolute steal and has earned his slot in the latest Scotland squad.

With our budget limited, for now by owner policy but eventually formally by the constrictions of Financial Fair Play, our recruitment focus has largely (though not exclusively) shifted to younger prospects with the potential to shine in our first team eventually, rather than battle-hardened, Championship-ready pros.

The first report of potential transfer activity for next season has already appeared, with a bid of Northampton Town midfielder Michael Jacobs allegedly lodged and rejected. Nigel Clough has confirmed to BBC Radio Derby that he is interested in the player – while denying that we'd bid yet – and added that teenage Liverpool left-back Jack Robinson is on a list of potential loanees for next season.

Jacobs certainly fits into the overall recruitment pattern. He is only 20 years old, but has won the Cobblers' player of the year award in his first two seasons as a first-team pro.

Clough apparently maintains a policy of collecting captains and/or players of the year from other clubs – Shaun Barker, Jason Shackell, Bryson, Ben Davies and John Brayford are examples of this and even Lee Croft had been Norwich's POTY the season before joining Derby (albeit in a relegated team). Marc Pugh, a wide midfielder linked with the Rams since January, was voted Bournemouth's player of the year this season – and so it goes on.

In the immediate future, Derby County will be a 'manufacturing' club with a production line, not a plutocrat club that swaggers on to the forecourt with chequebook in hand and a *Made in Chelsea* 'actress' in tow. Let's hope we can turn out a few Rolls-Royces – Hendrick is a very good start and in Hughes, O'Brien and Bennett, we already have a few more who don't look too shabby either.

***

Tom Glick leaves Derby County for Manchester City
June 24, 2012

Tom Glick always had an uphill struggle to win the hearts of the Derby fans. A slick commercial operator, his super-smooth American patter was anathema to some, while others were left furious or just cynical by his attempts to justify player sales and the club's failure to make signings when they were desperately needed in 2010/11.

However, while struggling to keep Derby afloat in the second tier against a backdrop of budget cuts (while other clubs were spending freely), Glick was gradually building a serious reputation for himself in English football.

As a member of the Football League board he was instrumental in pushing through the adoption of Financial Fair Play regulations, which could ultimately put an end to the sort of financial doping strategy currently pursued by Leicester City – although money men will always do their best to circumvent them by whatever means possible, as shown by Sheikh Mansour's £400m sponsorship of Glick's new employers, Manchester City.

Glick has had a difficult job to do at Pride Park, particularly since taking responsibility for football matters after Adam Pearson's departure in

2009. For a man with a sports marketing background, who was new to football and originally hired to overhaul the club's commercial operations, this was no small undertaking. With the Rams finding life in the Championship extremely hard, Glick found himself acting as the mouthpiece for an ownership group who were not prepared to throw unlimited money at the club – and were tired of spending millions of pounds just to keep it afloat.

His mistakes were sometimes embarrassing. The failure to capture Conor Sammon from Kilmarnock at the end of the January 2011 window was a spectacular gaffe, at a time when the club had just been dumped out of the FA Cup by Crawley Town and faced a relegation battle – while his plan to recruit a director of football was steadfastly opposed by Nigel Clough and eventually kicked into the long grass.

However, ultimately, Glick did help to bring about changes for the better at Pride Park. It goes without saying that many of the players Glick helped to shift off our wage bill were overpaid underachievers, while the club's new policy of youth development is to be applauded and is already bearing serious fruit. For the first time in years we are actually now in a position where several of our senior and junior players are coveted by other clubs.

*

The only problem with the theory that clubs should break even, instead of being propped up by owners prepared to plough millions into them, is that supporters who equate the old Lionel Pickering/Jack Walker model with success tend to think it means the owners are taking them for a ride.

And as long as some clubs are prepared to stick to the old ways, accepting wads of loan cash and losing money hand-over-fist in the pursuit of instant success, it will always be hard to make a case for the dull, prudent, 'slow train coming' approach favoured by Glick. However, if what Glick has described as 'an era of football financial responsibility' is indeed eventually ushered in, the Rams will be ahead of the curve.

Once it finally kicks in at the start of the 2014/15 season, Financial Fair Play will hit overspending Championship clubs with transfer embargoes, or fine them proportionately to the level of their loss should they get promoted. This said, FFP does allow for owners to invest a certain amount of money in their clubs every year and it remains to be seen how much money GSE are prepared to give Nigel Clough for players year-on-year. This summer, the answer appears to be 'none, unless you flog a few first'.

There is an extent to which the owners need to show willing, to inspire fans to get off their arses and keep the turnstiles clicking. Breaking even is fine as a business aim, but the sporting aim of a football club, ultimately, is to compete at the highest possible level and try to win things. There's also the complication of promotion and, more pertinently at present, relegation, which can destroy the most meticulously constructed business plan. Sometimes, the reality is that if you don't spend, you're going down – GSE did accept this last summer and provided much-needed money for new players, thus keeping us well clear of the bottom three in 2011/12.

All in all, Glick seems to have done a good job of preventing attendances from collapsing in spite of the team's patchy recent record. It remains to be seen whether his marketer's magic touch will be missed at Pride Park in the years to come.

'The Glick is dead' – long live the Glick?

That said, Glick has confirmed to BBC Radio Derby that he will have a hand in the recruitment of his successor, while chairman Andy Appleby has stated that the new chief executive will be 'as close to Tom as possible'.

The job description for Glick's replacement is worth a scan, as it gives some key information about the club's current policies, goals and exactly what the new chief executive will be expected to deliver.

Firstly, the owners claim to 'understand the need to maintain and further [the club's] rich history and heritage' – so it's safe to assume that the new Kappa home kit won't be red.

Next, the club's 'operating philosophy is to be fiscally responsible and prudent, with a goal of being profitable in each year of operations'. This would be a major turnaround on previous seasons. Between 2005 and 2011 Derby lost an average of about £6.33m a year, only seeing an operating profit in the Premier League season of 2007/08.

The team is expected 'to consistently compete for the play-offs, with a goal of promotion within the next four years'. By then (2015/16), the FFP rules will be in force and other clubs will be obliged to pursue a similar book-balancing model to Derby's.

The theory, I assume, is that by then, the fact that the Rams attract bigger crowds than nearly any other team at this level will give them a competitive edge. If clubs are all forced to live within their means, the clubs with the most fans will be able to generate more revenue and run slightly higher wage bills, while wages throughout the division will naturally come down to more sustainable levels.

GSE want Derby to go up to the Premier League by 'being the absolute best developers, buyers and sellers of footballers'. This explains the determination to bring through our own youth products – 'investments [in the academy] will allow us to bring up quality first-teamers that fit comfortably fit into our wage bill'. By eventually selling on the best of these youngsters, this 'development focus will ultimately allow us to make further investments in players.'

*

There are some fans who will see Glick's departure as a reason to raise a glass. I'm not one of them. He has a huge task on his hands overseeing commercial operations at the newly created behemoth that is Manchester City and wouldn't have been approached to take it on if he hadn't proved himself to be exceptionally capable at Derby County first.

If we'd sold a player to City, we'd all be sad to lose him, but also proud that one of our lads had proved himself to be good enough to secure a move to the Premier League champions. Losing an executive to them is very different, but this move should at least prove to Glick's detractors that he must have been doing something right.

That said, it's definitely the case that his new role as chief commercial and operating officer will suit him much better than the chief executive role he filled at Derby County.

***

Guest post: Report from Fan Forum at Pride Park, 2/7/12
July 3, 2012

This post comes from a good friend who was invited to the latest 'meet the season ticket holders' shebang organised by the club.

*

On Monday evening, I attended a fan forum at Pride Park with current CEO Tom Glick, finance Director Mal Brannigan, operations director John Vicars and marketing manager Faye Nixon.

I didn't really know what to expect – I was half-expecting a glitzy presentation about the new big screen and other exciting off-the-field developments. As it turned out, I was way off the mark.

Only ten fans had been invited and we sat around a table with the DCFC crew, rather than 'in the audience' as I'd anticipated. Tom Glick explained that the format was 45 minutes of our questions answered as openly and honestly as they could and then 45 minutes of them picking our brains about 'the matchday experience'. A pretty simple and effective idea that meant both the fans and the club got something out of it.

It was meant to be 90 minutes, but ended up being closer to two hours, so we covered a lot of ground – some topics more interesting than others. From heated debate about the pros and cons of a potential Jason Shackell sale to the, shall we say, slightly more mundane, 'I noticed at the last three home games of the season that there was some traffic congestion at Roundabout 4.'

The first thing that struck me about Glick is that he is an instantly likeable character. In contrast to formal media interviews, which often feel like nothing more than the audio manifestation of a press release, he was relaxed and clearly answering off the cuff with the honesty he promised.

Shackell

The first big question asked was about progress on the sale of Jason Shackell. Glick said, 'Our valuation has still not been met.' The obvious follow-up question – 'What is that valuation?' – was never going to be answered directly. The best we got was, 'More than we paid for him [just under £1m] and enough to be able to replace him with someone we feel is good enough, plus money left over to finance another signing and strengthen another area.'

Several people said they felt it sent the wrong signal to be talking about selling an established player. Glick replied that the manager feels that if he can do the right deal, then the club will benefit and move forward.

I asked how Shackell felt about being shopped around so openly and did he want to leave? Glick said no, he's happy to stay, but that he 'gets it' – 'it' being that he's a saleable asset and that's how football works. Another fan pointed out that Shackell is hardly a stranger to club-hopping.

Green

Glick thinks we will have a better team without Paul Green. 'He's one of my favourite people in the world – but from a footballing perspective, we will be a better, more balanced team with Michael Jacobs.'

Glick pointed out that Green is turning 30, an international and wanted to be first choice on a good final contract, but we couldn't guarantee he'd be first choice (in central midfield) and, as good a job as he did filling in, we needed a more natural wide midfielder. Again, there are no hard feelings, because Green 'gets it'.

Steve Davies

Stevie D's departure is still not imminent. It could still be a fair few weeks before we see any positive movement, as clubs are only just now coming back from their summer breaks.

Someone asked why we announced publicly that he wanted to leave, as this weakened our selling position. Glick said this was because we had offered him a contract extension which he had turned down, adding, 'Maybe it does weaken our position, but don't forget that he still has a year left, so if our valuation isn't matched then we keep him and he plays out his contract'.

If and when Davies goes, we're looking at a 'traditional centre-forward' and have some targets in mind. If we get one of those targets in, Callum Ball might go out on loan to get some games.

Other transfer news

Have we had any interest in Tyson? Yes. It's 50/50 whether he'll move on. Again, this will be dictated by what we're offered for him and who we can find to replace him.

We've also had offers for Brayford and Hendrick, but Clough sees them as key young players and they're not going anywhere – hence we have extended their contracts.

We're currently looking at somebody who would be a good understudy for Roberts at left-back, but could also fill a utility role (I guess a left-sided equivalent of Naylor). This was as close to a name as we got, so my interpretation was that this could be the closest deal to completion.

A fan complained that because player turnover had been so high in the past few years, he didn't feel a connection to the team. Glick said that the current team has a great nucleus of young players who are all growing together, have great relationships and will be around for some time yet. High turnover had been necessary in recent seasons, but the situation was hopefully stable now.

Scouting

I asked a question about foreign scouting – have we given up on it? The blunt answer was 'yes'! They feel that the risks are too high and said they'd had bad experiences previously. They said that you can pay people to watch players 100 times to be sure they are good enough, but if the player then comes over and feels isolated, or doesn't settle, then it ends up as a waste of time and money.

Mal Brannigan pointed out that in the past, overseas players were a good, cheap option, so you could take the risk, but now it's actually going the other way – overseas players' wage demands are through the roof, while domestic wages are finally going down (at least at Championship level).

Current squad/academy

On Frank Fielding, the club pointed out that he had played more than 100 league games at the age of 21, which is very rare for a keeper, so they feel they got a great deal – he has talent, experience despite being very young and will improve with age. Frank is another one they see being here for some time.

Bryson was mentioned as 'captain material', so my assumption is that if Shackell does go, then he is in with a shout of the armband while Barks is out.

The club are very pleased that the academy is starting to produce again. The ones we know about were mentioned, but a few younger kids who might break through soon were also discussed. DCFC were very complimentary about the work Darren Wassall is doing.

Long-term future/ambitions

Has there been interest from anyone wanting to buy the club? Yes, there are always people coming around 'kicking the tyres', as Glick put it, but it's never gone any further than that.

The Arena/Plaza development is something the club are hoping to proceed with. It may be done in stages, but it's a commercial venture that the club want to pursue in order to create a substantial revenue stream that would be invested in the team.

Promotion is still very much what we're building for and when the time comes that we're in a strong January position, the club already have a strategy in place for how we will push on.

Someone questioned whether we'd be strong enough to stay in the Premier League next time we go up. Glick replied that all three teams did it last season and his honest view is that it's easier to stay in the PL than it is to get out of the Championship. He acknowledged that getting out of this league is incredibly difficult and added that throwing money around is not a guarantee of success – Leicester, as an obvious example, spent £20m and it bought them two more points than us last season.

Goodbye Glick

Glick is at the club until mid-August and he seemed genuinely sad to be saying goodbye. There didn't seem to be even the slightest whiff of snake oil about him, despite what some fans still think about 'the Yanks'. I think he will be sorely missed by the club and I hope his successor is as open and honest. He listens and takes things on board and while not everyone will like every decision he makes, the bottom line is that Glick shows total respect for the fans and that's good enough for me.

***

'At my house, I've got no Shackells'[26] – Anger as Jason leaves Derby County
July 7, 2012

Nigel Clough has been quite open about the fact that he wanted to sell Jason Shackell for the past couple of weeks, despite outgoing CEO Tom Glick stating that Clough was under no pressure to do so.

I think it's time to examine the PR practises that have been used to massage the truth about this particular transfer, which – with no meaningful indication of who the replacement will be at the time of writing – seems potentially disastrous for the team at this stage and has even prompted 14 season ticket holders to enquire about refunds.

Firstly, Thursday's *Derby Telegraph* mentioned that Shackell was signed by Derby for £750,000. Which was interesting, because all previous reports I've seen about the Shackell deal mentioned a figure of around £1m. The *Barnsley Chronicle* reported the fee to be in the region of £1m. BBC Derby were given to understand that the fee Derby paid to Barnsley for Shackell was 'in excess of £1m'. When Shackell joined the Rams, the *Derby Telegraph* reported that he had completed a £1m move to Derby – an initial £750,000 fee topped up with add-ons to take the fee 'into seven figures'. Why, now that Shackell has been sold, is the price we paid suddenly being reported as £750,000?

Whether those £250,000 of add-ons were paid to Barnsley or not isn't the issue. The point is, when they bought Shackell, Derby trumpeted him as a £1m signing. Unfortunately, that has now backfired on them because it inflated fans' perceptions of how much the player would be sold for and has stoked anger about the deal.

Glick recently said that Shackell would only be sold if enough money was offered not only to replace him, but also to strengthen the squad in another area. Even Colin Bloomfield took this to mean that we would

---

[26] For the uninitiated, this was a pun on the first line in the song 'A House Is Not a Motel', by Love (from the all-time classic album *Forever Changes*)

be looking for at least £1.5m, maybe even as much as £2m. However, it seems that it won't be as expensive as we thought for Derby to replace Shackell. He was only a £750,000 defender, after all.

And it has now emerged that the second player funded by the deal, far from being the decent striker we badly need, is in fact likely to be a 21-year old rookie defender from Crewe[27].

When the *Derby Telegraph* asked Glick for an interview to discuss the Shackell deal, all they got was a woefully inadequate statement in which Glick was unwise enough to say the club are looking at 'young, hungry' (i.e. cheap) players:-

'Working within our budget, our focus remains on building a stronger squad for the coming season and I want all Rams fans to know that we are working hard to invest in new players across the pitch.

'By selling Jason, it allows us to reinvest at centre-back and other positions.

'Nigel has already identified the kind of young, hungry player, like Michael Jacobs, that we wish to bring to Pride Park and we hope to have further positive news soon.'

At a time like this, we don't need tired cliches, any more than we need a 'young, hungry' replacement for an 'established, experienced, high-quality' central defender.

Meanwhile, the club website quotes Clough as saying: –

'Although I am sad to see Jason leave, we have Jake Buxton, Tom Naylor and Mark O'Brien, who have all proved to be more than capable at performing in the npower Championship.'

No disrespect to those players, but none of them is anywhere near as good as Shackell and everyone knows it, including Clough.

---

[27] Kelvin Mellor. The deal never went through.

Back to the Glick line that Clough was not obliged to sell anyone. This was simultaneously true and untrue. While the manager wasn't forced to sell, in that the club didn't demand it, he was forced to sell, in that he wasn't going to be able to bring in new players unless he did so.

Cutting a few fringe players wasn't going to fund anything meaningful and we were obviously short in attack last season anyway. It's conceivable that the Shackell deal will help to fund the permanent signing of a new striker. But Clough has already raised the possibility of bringing in a surplus Premier League player on loan, so there's also every possibility that it won't. Besides, as the club's PR men have pointed out, Jamie Ward is a striker, so maybe we don't need another one anyway.

As well as Shackell, we have already lost Paul Green, with Steve Davies and James Bailey also set to leave, along with three or four other players deemed surplus to requirements. Clough has already said that a maximum of four players will come in this summer, so we can only expect three more signings in addition to Jacobs.

It's therefore fair to say that despite Glick's statement of Thursday night, our squad will actually be smaller and – depending on the calibre of the new recruits – quite possibly weaker come August than it was at the start of last season. And last season, we finished 12th.

At some point soon, these year-on-year budget cuts have got to stop. Fans have put up with austerity measures season after season and have, by and large, accepted the fact that the club has to live within its means – particularly as Financial Fair Play (FFP) regulations are about to be introduced, with transfer embargoes set to be slapped on clubs who make excessive losses.

But FFP rules do allow club owners to invest a certain amount of capital each year. Having already parted with around £30m to keep the club afloat, are GSE just tired of spending money on Derby now?
The club's next set of accounts will make interesting reading.

***

'More with Less' – Why Clough's Derby County squad gets ever smaller, younger and more versatile
August 2, 2012

From what we understand, Nigel Clough was not provided with a transfer kitty this season, instead being told that he could only spend whatever he could generate through sales. The big question is, have we now reached a point where GSE have put in as much money as they are prepared to?

'More with less' is a central tenet of capitalism. In every field of business, the powers-that-be are always looking to cut costs wherever they can and although there are a few exceptions in football – where clubs can become a rich man's indulgence (Chelsea), or the glittering front for a global marketing campaign (Manchester City) – GSE certainly don't fall into the 'sugar daddy' category.

This said, if recent comments from Tom Glick are anything to go by, there is a strategy in place to strengthen our squad in the January window – but only if Derby are in a position to genuinely threaten the top six. So further investment is apparently not out of the question, but is dependent on Clough managing to push the team into the upper reaches of the table first.

In an idle moment, I tried to pick a Derby County 'shadow XI' (a reserve team) and found it very difficult to do – this scratch team is pretty weak and patched together with youth-teamers and senior pros out of position. Four of this side played in the second half team that lost 2-0 at Mansfield, while Kwame Thomas is considered too young for the first-team squad.

GK Legzdins
RB Naylor
CB O'Brien
CB Galinski
LB O'Connor

RM B. Davies
CM Hughes
CM Doyle
LM Tyson
CF Thomas
CF Bennett

Of course, Clough can only pick 11 men on a Saturday, but nevertheless, it is worrying that there is very little squad depth, as the club's wage bill is cut yet again this season (as it has been every season since relegation in 2007/08).

With costs still being cut in pursuit of a balanced budget, it's become increasingly important that the players we do have can play in more than one position. Of this summer's signings, James O'Connor (anywhere across the back four), Paul Coutts (anywhere across midfield) and Michael Jacobs (either wing and possibly off a striker) were all brought in at least partially because of their versatility – a vital quality when you can't afford a big squad.

After a 1-0 half-time lead became a 2-1 loss at Mansfield Town, with Clough making 11 changes at the interval, the manager told Rams Player, 'The second-half team was just a little bit too weak... In principle, it's great [to field two different teams for 45 minutes each], but you do look and think...
'We've got a decent 11 out there, maybe 15 or 16, but it's difficult for young lads like Stefan Galinski to step in.'

The problem will come during a long and heavy Championship season when three or four of the 'decent' 15 or 16 are unavailable due to the inevitable injuries and suspensions. The young players will be called upon at some point and if they can't manage, we will be back to the bad old days of covering up the cracks with emergency loans. Unless, of course, we sell one of the youth products.

We can expect the Rams to continue to trade 'neutral' for the foreseeable future, with little room for Clough to manoeuvre in the transfer market until one of our best prospects – Hendrick, Hughes or Bennett – is the subject of a big enough offer.

Reasons to be cheerful… Grounds for optimism at Derby County ahead of the 2012/13 season
August 11, 2012

Brayford's back

We missed John badly last season, after he suffered with injuries for the first time during his spell at the club. He was in and out of the team with a thigh problem, coming back too early at one point and Nigel Clough wrote off Brayford's season at one time. However, he returned for the last couple of matches and looked much more like his old self.

The return of a fully fit Brayford means we will once again have a top right-back – and one who is capable of being ever-present, as he was in 2010/11. He's a brave, strong defender, quick enough, prepared to raid forward and effective when he does so, making him a potential source of assists and even the odd goal. His cracking strike against Watford, in the 4-1 win at Pride Park in 2010/11, is still one of my favourite Derby goals, simply because Brayford showed such awareness to make the opportunity for himself and so much desire to win the ball, surging through the helpless defence before smashing it emphatically into the net.

The midfield

Much has been made of the need to strengthen the attack and defence this summer, but not so much was said about the midfield, a few gripes about James Bailey's proposed departure aside. That's because when you consider the probable first-choice starting four – Coutts, Hendrick, Bryson and Jacobs – they don't look too bad.

With Bryson's box-to-box energy, Hendrick's calm passing and a bit of skill and attacking intent from either side, you can imagine us playing some pretty nice attacking football through the midfield this season – especially down the right, where Brayford will be able to link in and bomb on to his heart's content.

The youth team conveyor belt

At 20, Jeff Hendrick has already established himself in the first team and we can expect to see a few more of our own youngsters in the matchday squad this season.

Mark O'Brien played regularly at the start of last season. He defended heroically in a 1-0 win at Blackpool, but errors started to creep into his play over an extended run in the side. This was only to be expected, as centre-back is an extremely difficult position to play and not a position where you ideally want to field a teenager, no matter how promising. Nevertheless, he is clearly an asset. It's to be hoped he can put his latest injury setback behind him and continue his progress this season.

Some of Will Hughes's passes during his debut start for the first team against Peterborough United simply gladdened my heart. The boy we plucked from Repton School of all places looked serene in possession and although he didn't get the goal his performance deserved, his obvious creativity and awareness meant that he was central to much of our best attacking build-up play in the game – as well as popping up in the box on various occasions. With a little more self-confidence, he might have pulled the trigger instead of taking a touch a couple of times. He was also unlucky not to score at Portsmouth in the game before.

The 17-year old Hughes's emergence has put him ahead of his youth and reserve team buddy Mason Bennett, who, at just 16, is built like a man, making it easy to forget just how young he is. We've seen flashes of his potential, but he may turn out to be one for the season after next. On the other hand, he might just burst on to the scene during this campaign – there's no doubt that he has the talent.

As long as these youngsters aren't thrown in at the deep end too early, or relied upon too heavily before their time, it's great to know that we are becoming a club who can produce good footballers. Cashing in on talented youth products has helped Reading and Southampton make their way into the Premier League and there's no reason why it can't be that way at Pride Park too, eventually.

And finally

This isn't so much something to be optimistic about, but certainly something to look forward to – the mouthwatering prospect of Jake Buxton marking Blackburn's new *galáctico,* Nuno Gomes.

The long-haired Portuguese centre-forward has more caps and international goals than you can shake a stick at. He spent the majority of his career with Benfica, but also played two seasons in Serie A with Fiorentina, after a €17m transfer in 2000. Gomes appeared in two World Cups and three European Championships (scoring in all three). He has travelled the world, bagging goals, winning trophies galore and earning millions along the way.

But he has never, ever played against anybody quite like Bucko.

At 37, I have a feeling that Gomes may not appreciate Buxton's 'get in their faces and put them on their arses' tenacity. Without doubt, the veteran striker will go down at the slightest touch, but surely there will be an opportunity to put in a 'blood and thunder' challenge at some point. Let's see if they breed 'em as tough in Amarante as they do in Mansfield!

***

Just how good is Will Hughes?
August 12, 2012

A year ago, Will Hughes was a 16 year-old kid signing for Derby County as a first-year scholar. Before that, he was a Repton schoolboy, playing for Mickleover Jubilee.

Much has happened since then. He starred in the Rams' FA Youth Cup win at Arsenal, was called up to play for England U17s at the 2012 Algarve tournament, has been the subject of a scurrilous *Daily Mail* article linking him to Manchester City and Manchester United and, in no time at all, has established himself as a member of Derby's first-team squad.

I first saw Hughes in a youth team win at Liverpool, in which he caught the eye as an all-action, committed midfielder, willing and able to press the ball against a side who had the lion's share of the possession. Then Tommo went to see the kids play Sheffield United at Pride Park and texted me to ask who the midfielder with the bleached blond hair was, who had such good technique. By the middle of Tom Carroll's unsuccessful loan spell last season, he was asking what exactly the Spurs teenager could do that Hughes couldn't.

After his first start for the senior team, against Peterborough United at Pride Park, I wrote that some of Hughes's passing had 'gladdened my heart'. Following last week's pre-season friendly against Sunderland, the *Derby Telegraph*'s Steve Nicholson said, 'Vision and awareness of what is around you on the pitch are good qualities to have and I cannot recall Hughes giving the ball away.'

Thinking about it, I could only remember one misplaced pass against the Black Cats – an attempted through ball in a crowded penalty area – so I decided to use the 'full 90' feature on Rams Player to review the footage and see exactly how Hughes contributed, before he was substituted just after the hour.

ATTACKING STATS
Passes completed 42
Passes incomplete 2
Pass completion 95.5 per cent
Cross complete 0
Cross incomplete 1
Took man on 3
Beat his man 3
Fouled 2
Shots on target 0

Shots off target 1

DEFENSIVE STATS
Tackles won 4
Tackles lost 1
Fouls committed 1
Interceptions 4
Headers won 1
Headers lost 0

The most important stat here, clearly, is the first one. Hughes found a white shirt almost every time he received the ball. Given that conceding possession is probably the worst sin a footballer can commit on the pitch, his ability to keep us ticking over by selecting the right option and executing the pass accurately could genuinely improve the team.

Hughes shows for the ball and is not afraid to receive it in tight situations. Without being startlingly quick, he is able to trick an opponent with a darting movement and managed to beat his opponent three times. The first time, he was unceremoniously fouled, but the next time his dribble into the box left a trail of Sunderland defenders unable to lay a glove on him – and one on his backside – before he curled a shot wide.

I would be very surprised if Hughes doesn't start against Scunthorpe in the League Cup and there's every possibility that he has forced his way into the reckoning for the first Championship encounter of the season too – especially if Jeff Hendrick's wrist injury turns out to be problematic. With Hughes now very much a first-team option, Nigel Clough can think about setting up with a midfield three (chosen from Hughes, Bryson, Coutts and Hendrick).

Seeing Hughes play so well against Sunderland makes Nigel Clough's willingness to part with James Bailey a little more understandable. Bailey, however, has played well when he's been used in the first team friendlies so far and will be a very useful player to have in the squad if he stays.

It's important not to get carried away on the basis of a pre-season friendly, but the technical attributes Hughes has developed are there for all to see. He will get hustled, harried and, frankly, kicked a lot more in a competitive Championship encounter than he did against Sunderland, but hopefully, he will have the composure to handle it. The early signs are really encouraging and he clearly has the potential to make a real impression this season.

Hughes's emergence is a credit to Derby's local scouting network and also to the academy staff who have helped to bring him on. Now that he's a member of the first-team squad, let's hope his rapid development continues, because he is a very talented prospect indeed.

And so, to another season! Which did not begin auspiciously.

Derby were embarrassed in the league cup (again), going 4-1 up against Scunthorpe, only for the game to end 5-5 after extra time, with Derby going on to lose on penalties.

The opening league game, at Pride Park, was drawn 2-2 with Sheffield Wednesday, after the Rams went 2-0 up. A loss at Bolton was followed by a draw with Wolves.

Then came an unexpected, joyous 5-1 larruping of Watford.

***

Derby County International Break Update (part 1 of 2)
September 6, 2012

In the glow of the damn good thrashing of Watford, league results to date can certainly be said to pass muster. Facing two relegated Premier League sides away from home, plus a promoted team from just up the road on the opening day, has to go down as a difficult start to the season and we've acquitted ourselves well, with the exception of a highly disappointing second half against Sheffield Wednesday.

The questions raised about our defensive strength by the disaster against Scunthorpe in the League Cup have still not quite been answered. Clough and Richard Keogh will both be extremely keen to keep their first clean sheet sooner rather than later.

However, it's a different story at the other end of the pitch. Derby are carving out plenty of chances and were pretty unlucky not to beat Wolves, having created enough openings to win two games. Not to worry – the hapless Hornets copped for it instead.

Keogh and Jake Buxton are both goal threats from set-pieces and the delivery from Paul Coutts and Michael Jacobs (when selected) has been good enough to create goals. In recent seasons, a major flaw in the Rams' play has been an inability to get goals from set-plays, but these now seem to be coming in abundance.

Watford manager Gianfranco Zola was candid enough to admit that he had underestimated our ability to cause problems from free kicks and corners – other clubs will presumably now be looking closely at the videos and marking our centre-backs as tightly as they can, by fair means or foul.

On the Scunthorpe disaster, it should be noted that an awful lot of clubs have been knocked out by lower-league opponents already – not least Leicester, who got done 4-2 at home by Burton Albion. That said, Derby's capitulation was stupid and pathetic. Jacobs and Theo Robinson, who missed a penalty after asking Jake Buxton if he wanted to take it instead, have both been left out of the team since that result, with Clough suggesting that they had not shown the necessary application on the night.

After Wednesday brought a huge travelling army of over 6,000 to Pride Park, swelling the gate to 27,437, it became clear that home attendances would be starting this season considerably down on last season's, continuing the trend of recent years.

It seems that a good number of fans decided that 'enough is enough' after last year's mid-table finish, while the club's stated 'spend what Clough can raise' transfer policy was never likely to bring the hordes flocking. The sale of Jason Shackell prompted a flurry of requests for refunds on season tickets – almost as many as Cardiff received when they announced they would be changing their home kit colour from blue to red – and doubtless also prompted many Derbyshire folk to decide against splashing out on what is, at the end of the day, a fairly expensive indulgence. With the economy tanking in the age of austerity, the sad reality is that many people can't afford a season ticket and single-match tickets are pricey these days.

Although Derby's attendance for the Watford game was our lowest home league gate for a long time, it was still higher than Forest's and Leicester's on the same day. Both of those clubs attracted gates of less than 20,000 (this despite Forest recently signing a whole new team, including Simon Cox and Billy Sharp).

Hopefully, if the Rams continue to play attractive football and score goals, attendances will gradually creep up again. However, with Football League attendances seemingly down all around the country, the campaign to bring back limited terracing for 'safe standing' areas looks more and more sensible.

Safe standing is a real hit in Germany and has led to cheaper tickets being available, higher attendances and better atmosphere within the grounds. To their credit, Derby were the first English league side to publicly back the idea this summer and according to Nick Webster, the 'DCFC flagman' who is a prime mover in the campaign for safe standing, more and more clubs are getting behind the idea.

The reality is that plenty of people stand up anyway (or naturally bounce out of their seats at various times during the game) and this can conflict with those who prefer or need to remain seated at all times. So if this can be properly managed, with the fans who like to stand given their own dedicated area, surely everybody will benefit.

With the transfer window closed, it's become pretty clear that the club did make some surplus cash available for Clough to spend on top of what he was able to generate through player sales – not millions, but enough to bring in a couple of valuable extra bodies.

New players like Paul Coutts and James O'Connor are already proving their worth, while Richard Keogh is a good replacement for Shaun Barker – if the skipper can return to fitness next season, the two of them could make a redoubtable pairing.

It's worth remembering that supposed moneybags Cardiff City were seriously interested in Keogh, so signing him has to go down as something of a coup for Derby. As well as meeting with Clough, Keogh was also introduced to Barker and some of the owners, so it's pretty clear that the club went to great lengths to persuade him that Pride Park was the right place to come.

The Conor Sammon fee, reported at £1.2m, is a meaningful investment and his barnstorming goal against Watford shows that he could be a real player for Derby in seasons to come. He will be a handful at this level and it's just a shame we weren't able to bring him in when Clough originally wanted him from Kilmarnock. He'd have bagged a hatful for us by now – and we would have saved a good chunk of money, to boot.

Clough seems to be having some success in the transfer market by moving for players who, for whatever reason, are available at a cut rate. Jamie Ward (£400k) had fallen out with his manager at Sheffield United, as had Paul Coutts (£150k) at Preston. O'Connor (a seemingly genuinely undisclosed, but 'small' fee) was frozen out by Dean Saunders at Doncaster, having been a victim of last season's bizarre transfer 'experiment', which had such disastrous results[28].

Coutts has done well and I see him essentially as an upgrade on Ben Davies. Not terribly quick, but tenacious and technically good, with the ability to cross the ball well from open play or dead-ball situations, Coutts seems to be what Clough hoped Davies would turn out to be, plus he is considerably younger. Certainly, he is a better option to play right midfield than Paul Green was and doubtless came in on a lower wage.

Another point worth making is that Derby have benefited from concluding their transfer business well ahead of the closing of the window on August 31. The day before they came to Pride Park, Watford had parted with their main centre-back, Martin Taylor, as well as bringing in half-a-dozen foreign loanees, whom the manager couldn't really be expected to select at such short notice. We also arguably caught Wolves at a good time. They had just lost Matt Jarvis, while Steven Fletcher was left out ahead of his move to Sunderland. In both cases, our opponents were still trying to reorganise their squads with the season under way, while our deals were already done.

This sort of last-minute chaos is undoubtedly a cause of genuine disruption, as Derby have found themselves to their detriment in previous seasons. The abrupt sale of Shackell early in the window came as a real shock to supporters, but it did allow Derby sufficient time and financial room to manoeuvre in the window. The club promised they would replace Shackell and sign extra players to strengthen the squad and ultimately, that's exactly what they did.

Stats

Frank Fielding, John Brayford, Richard Keogh, Gareth Roberts, Paul Coutts and Craig Bryson have all started every game in league and cup to date. Clough has been able to choose from an almost injury-free

---

[28] Doncaster had allowed the agent Willie McKay to take control of their transfers. McKay brought in a glut of relatively high-profile players on short-term contracts, with an eye to helping sell them on at a profit. El-Hadji Diouf, Pascal Chimbonda, Frederic Piquionne and Habib Beye were among the influx of big names to join. Donny finished bottom of the league.

squad so far this season and long may that continue.

My pessimistic pre-season prediction of a lower mid-table finish for Derby this season was based mostly on the assumption that several first-teamers would be missing at various points throughout the season (the Scunthorpe disaster also prompted a knee-jerk downgrade of a couple of places). However, the results and performances to date show that if everyone is fit, we can be a match for pretty much anybody in the Championship.

Direct Goal Involvement

1. Jamie Ward 38.5 per cent
2= Paul Coutts 30.8 per cent
2= Michael Jacobs 30.8 per cent
4. Jake Buxton 23.1 per cent

Before the Watford game, most fans seemed to think that Theo Robinson should be preferred to Ward up front, but Ward showed us all why Clough wanted to use him in an essentially free role behind Sammon. He chipped in with a deserved goal, but more importantly, a hat-trick of assists.

Ward is clearly not an orthodox striker, but when allowed license to drift around, he becomes difficult to mark and therefore dangerous. He is a player with something about him and while he is undoubtedly effective when playing wide, it could be that freeing him from the need to track back, a responsibility which comes with playing left midfield in a 4-4-2, will help him to flourish and contribute many more goals and assists than he did last season.

Ward only scored four goals and made six assists in 2011/12. I see that as underachievement for such a talented player and he is already well on the way to improving on both totals this season.

By the time of the next Forest game, Derby's form remained unsettled, to the point of being haphazard.

They lost 1-0 at Huddersfield, beat Charlton 3-2 at Pride Park (having been 3-0 up) and then lost 2-1 at home to Burnley, meaning they had taken eight points from an opening seven games which had yielded a total of 23 goals.

What would the City Ground have in store for us this time?

***

Nottingham Forest v Derby County preview
September 29, 2012

Well, here we go again. Another East Midlands derby for the Brian Clough Trophy, with all the tension, the butterflies, the fear, the shouts, the screams, the rage, the jubilation, the f**king ref, the agonies, the uncontrollable roar when we score.

In recent years, we've had the lot. Goals galore, red cards, mass rucks, first-minute goals, penalties scored and missed, injury-time goals disallowed, ten men beating 11, pantomime villains, scarves being waved, corner flags being promenaded, fines from the Football Association, players moving from one club to the other and returning to haunt them, stirring comebacks, sound thrashings, coffee cups... all the fun of the fair, in short.

There's no logical reason that this match should matter so much to me, but by God, it does. It has nothing to do with the fact that I went to school in Nottingham, was the only Derby fan in my year and got murdered on a daily basis for it – that was a long time ago and for the most part, it wasn't really that malevolent. It has nothing to do with bragging rights at work, because I live and work in Manchester now and only know one Forest fan in this city (wouldn't you know it, we were at the same gig last night. We exchanged nods and no smiles.)

So why is it so viscerally, unfathomably important to me that we beat the bastards?

Last year, while Derby were completing the most incredible win of all at Forest, I was on a train from Holyhead, at the tip of Anglesey, heading back towards Manchester. This is what happens when you let the missus book a holiday before checking the fixture list. Schoolboy error.

Tommo faithfully texted me right through the build-up, then within seconds of the kick-off sent me the disastrous news that Frank Fielding was off and we were losing. The game was surely up and horrible fear – *we're going to get hammered* – spread through me. I closed my eyes and waited.

But the minutes passed and there were no more texts. I kept checking my phone – have I got signal? – expecting the inevitable sequel of '2-0'. It never came. Gradually, I dared to start hoping against hope.

Then came '1-1 Jamie Ward wonder goal!' – and a tumbling rush of feelings. Jesus Christ, we've equalised, f**k, we've got to hold on, how long until half-time, don't f**king lose it now. Then a garbled text about Forest complaining because Cohen was down injured, or something. Oh dear. They must have been down to ten men for a minute.

Then silence again. No more texts. And the longer it went on, weirdly, the calmer I felt. At first.

Then, with the train cruising through countryside and the Better Half slumbering on my shoulder, a text bleep. Oh no. I steeled myself and fished my phone out of my pocket. I breathe deeply and open it.

'Hendrick has missed from a yard' and my heart sank like a stone. *Shit shit shit shit shit.*

Then, minutes later, '2-1 Jeffrey Hendrick!!!'

By the time we were about to board our connecting train at Crewe, I was pretty much glued to the phone, just watching the time tick by – *it must be over, it must be over, what the f**k's happening, why isn't he texting* – then finally, another text. Please, please not a f**king equaliser... No! The Rams had done it – a quite monumental victory.

As I practically danced across the platform at Crewe station, my phone started jumping with celebratory texts from friends. Matt Ling claimed that the result automatically qualified us for the Champions League, but the one that really stood out was, again, from Tommo. It simply said:

'They were lions'

There is no reason why they cannot be lions again tomorrow in Nottingham.

That said, after flattering to deceive in games against Sheffield Wednesday, Huddersfield and Burnley, failing to take their chances at Wolves and surviving a terrifying mini-collapse against Charlton, the players have something to prove to the fans. We know they can play pretty football and look dangerous going forward, but can they go out there, show true concentration and determination, grit their teeth, keep Forest out and win?

Forest are a different animal from last season's weak and ponderous team. From the side we beat at the City Ground, out have gone Chambers, Morgan, Gunter, Derbyshire, Miller and Lynch – also the decrepit George Boateng, whose presence there was the epitome of everything that was wrong with them under Steve McClaren. In to replace these players have come what Chris from Ramspace cheekily christened a 'dirty dozen' in his blog yesterday. Glancing through the list of Forest's new signings, they are a seasoned bunch of pros who don't exactly strike fear into the heart, until you get to the centre-forwards – Simon Cox and Billy bloody Sharp.

Sharp always scores against us. I sometimes think that all you have to do to beat Derby is have a striker called Charlie or Billy – but no matter what his name, if you've got a proper striker, the reality is that we will allow him a chance at some point and he will probably take it. There is almost no chance that this game will end 0-0. You can get odds as long as 21/2 on that result, but I wouldn't touch it at 22/1.

For us, Jamie Ward is the key man (and will revel in the stick he'll get from the Red Dog hordes), but Conor Sammon has a real chance to make himself a hero. Fielding will doubtless be called upon and Richard Keogh will have his work cut out marshalling the back four, presumably alongside the doughty Jake Buxton. I firmly believe that both of our full-backs can be trusted to defend properly, even if some fans have never taken to Gareth Roberts.

We know what we will get from Craig Bryson – perpetual motion, a willingness to run his guts out for the team – while hopefully, Hendrick will be able to put his foot on the ball and exercise some control in the eye of the storm. Paul Coutts doesn't seem the type to be fazed by a big occasion and we can hope for some quality crosses and set pieces from him, which could be crucial.

And what odds on young Will Hughes taking the chance to show the watching Sky viewers exactly how good he is?

Our team have played well enough in spells this season to show that going forward, they can carve out chances against anybody else in the division. If they can match the genuine attacking threat with some real defensive resolve, it could be another magical day for those of us, as Colin Bloomfield puts it, 'of a black and white persuasion'.

***

Now that the dust has settled...
October 2, 2012

The overriding emotion was different this time. Whereas last year's 'ten men' win at the City Ground felt miraculous, this one was professional and gritty. Where the 3-2 FA Cup win in February 2009 was dramatic, this game was unglamorous – trench warfare at times, almost threatening to break into hand-to-hand combat at others. Where the 3-1 league win on a sunny day two weeks after we'd knocked them out of the cup was surprisingly comfortable – almost easy – this time, like our 1-0 league win at Pride Park last season, it was frantic and fractious.

What pleased me most of all was the way that our players managed to keep their heads while Red Dogs lost theirs all around them. Rewind back 12 months to the incident when Frank Fielding was sent off and you'll see Greening, Reid and Cohen in the referee's face, moaning for Frank to be sent off. Exactly the same sort of thing was happening on Sunday and it was obvious almost from the first whistle that Forest wanted to referee the game themselves.

For the second time in recent seasons, the FA handed this combustible fixture to an inexperienced young referee. Robert Madley did his best, but with their histrionic inability to allow him to get on with the job, the Reds made it almost impossible for him. Even Forest-supporting BBC journalist Jonathan Stevenson admitted afterwards that his team's behaviour was 'immature'. When you see Greg Halford, a man the size of the Incredible Hulk, rolling as if poleaxed after minor contact from the 5'5" tall Jamie Ward, you know that something is going badly wrong somewhere.

The caustic atmosphere of this particular derby seems to be too much for some of the Forest players. They get so wound up about the game that they turn on the ref at the first sign of a tackle, or just take the law into their own hands, as when half of their team flew at Roberts after a standing challenge on Cohen – not flagged as a foul by a linesman stood a couple of yards away – or when Blackstock went down under a challenge, then obstructed the ball and wrestled Roberts to the ground, rather than letting the game continue.

It seems hypocritical to conduct a determined campaign to pressurise a young official into giving a red card, then start crying when one of your own players walks for elbowing somebody in the face.

Credit to Madley for not setting out to 'even it up' by dismissing a Derby player or awarding a non-existent penalty, but more importantly, huge credit to the Derby players for never giving him a decision to make after Blackstock was sent off. Perhaps if the Forest players had expended more energy and thought on playing football and less on trying to influence Madley, they would have created at least one goalscoring opportunity in a first half they certainly shaded in terms of possession.

It is for the fans to get overheated and rant and rave at the ref during these games, not the players. A lot of guff is talked about fans wanting to see 'passion' and 'commitment' in local derbies, but these are characteristics best displayed by just getting the result. John Brayford, the victim of comfortably the worst tackle in the game, a disgusting lunge from Simon Cox that could have snapped his ankle, tweeted after the game, 'We came, we saw, we delivered.'

Exactly. That's called professionalism. A less demonstrative individual than Brayford would be hard to find on an English football field – so too would a right-back with more dedication to his task.

After the sending-off, what made me feel proud was the coolness with which we carved out the winning goal, then the calmness with which we continued to play, seeing out the game in relatively unruffled fashion until the dying minutes when the Hail Marys starting bombing in.

Clough's switch to 4-3-3 (or 4-5-1, call it what you will) was absolutely right, giving us the luxury of a spare man in midfield and allowing Will Hughes to start to conduct the proceedings from the centre, where he belongs. Hughes struggled badly in a physical mismatch against Halford in the first half, but came into his own once freed from the left wing. Long-term, Clough has a nice selection headache because he has three very good central midfield players who must be among the first names on his team sheet. How to accommodate them all?

By the way, whose idea was it for Forest to sign Jermaine Jenas on an 'emergency' loan? Judging from Sean O'Driscoll's post-match comments, not his. On why Jenas didn't even make the bench on Sunday, he said, 'He needs to play matches, that's the difficulty. Do you throw him in when he's not match fit? That's the dilemma in the Championship, where you don't get easy games.'

Anyway, that's their problem. Let the Forest fans cling to the fallacy of some imagined moral high ground, where their team are as innocent as babes and only lost to us because we cheated. My main wish is for the Forest team to grow up, stop playacting and surrounding the ref, let the football do the talking and give us a game, 11 v 11. Then we can burst their bubble good and proper by beating them again and doing the double double in January.

***

Paul Jewell and Nigel Clough – a tale of two managers
October 25, 2012

It may not be very kind, but I couldn't help but enjoy the fact that the axe fell on Paul Jewell at Ipswich Town after a home defeat by Derby County, almost four years after a home defeat at the hands of Ipswich brought about the end of his wretched tenure at Pride Park.

I'd rather not rake over the miserable memories of Jewell's botched attempt to manage Derby, but I do remember walking away from his last game in charge feeling utterly numb. Not just from the bitter cold of a sharp December evening, but wondering where the hell we could possibly go from that result, which left us 18th in the division after a run of one win in nine league games. His departure was a blessed relief and I'm sure that Ipswich supporters feel exactly the same today.

Jewell, who last did anything good as a manager under the indulgent chairmanship of Dave Whelan at Wigan Athletic – a job he eventually quit, citing the deterioration of his health and personal life – has dragged Ipswich into the same hole he left Derby in, bequeathing a demotivated, disorganised assortment of journeymen, has-beens and wannabes to his successor.

Pre-season talk of a long-term plan to develop that cliched new breed, the 'young, hungry' player, was junked within weeks, as Jewell signed a clutch of loan signings to supplement his squad. Four loanees started the game against Derby, along with Nigel Reo-Coker, who is on a short-term contract, while many first-team players are now into the final year of their current deals. In contrast, Nigel Clough's Derby currently field no loanees, while all of the players you'd like to think are part of the long-term plans have contracts to match.

There was a moment in the second half of Tuesday's game when Will Hughes made a run through midfield, only for Richie Wellens to pull the shirt off his back. Hughes kept going and, with the ref playing advantage, Wellens finally gave up impeding him – only for Reo-Coker to step in and body-check Hughes to the ground. There you had the difference in philosophies between the two clubs in a nutshell – Jewell's pair of cynical, washed-up old farts dealing with Clough's emerging star using the only means available to them.

Tommo thought it would be interesting to see the team from Jewell's last Derby game play the Rams team of today:-

Derby 0 Ipswich Town 1, 28 December 2008:
Bywater; Albrechtsen, Tomkins, Nyatanga, Stewart (s/o 77); Barazite, Addison, Green, Commons (Kazmierczak – 76); Hulse (Davies – 46), Ellington (Varney – 9).

Like the Ipswich team from Tuesday night, the Derby side that winter's day in 2008 was stuffed with expensive, experienced players who, for some reason, were unable to play well together as a team. There were a bunch of loanees – and consider, with a shudder, that Derby paid a seven-figure loan fee for Nathan Ellington, who pinged his hamstring in a lumbering cross-field chase in the early stages of that game.

Staggeringly, Jewell signed Ellington for Ipswich as well. Funnily enough, it didn't work out. He even bought himself another Robbie Savage-esque albatross in Jimmy Bullard, whose vast wages must, or should, have made even Marcus Evans wince.

On taking over at Derby, Clough made the excommunicated and apparently finished Savage's rehabilitation an early priority. The Rams' caretaker manager, David Lowe, also gave Sav a cameo appearance at the end of that unlikely Carling Cup win against Manchester United, suggesting that a way back had only ever been blocked by Jewell's intransigence.

By the return leg at Old Trafford, Clough and Savage were sharing jokes on the bench, before the veteran was brought on as a substitute. Clough did well to get Savage on side and get the best he could out of him rather than leaving a man on Premier League wages training with the kids.

*

Jewell couldn't resist a dig at the Derby board in the run-up to Tuesday's game, telling journalists that GSE would have 'sacked him if they have could have afforded to', so he walked away instead. If Derby couldn't afford to sack him, it was presumably because, in the year up to June 2009, the club lost just under £15m in financing what was supposed to be Jewell's promotion drive.

Commons, Green and Hulse were all very handy players, but Jewell couldn't get the best from them, mostly because they were swamped by a wave of hopeless misfits like Jordan Stewart, Martin Albrechtsen and Ellington, to name but three. Very shortly before departing, Jewell was allowed to spend yet more transfer money on Luke Varney, ensuring that by the time Clough arrived, the cupboard was truly bare.

Jewell's approach to management, on the evidence of his tenure at Derby and Ipswich, was simply to meet a dip in form by signing more players. That cannot go on indefinitely. And partly due to Jewell's wastefulness, it was never even an option for Clough.

However, while budgets have been curtailed, with the wage bill having been halved since June 2009, it nevertheless seems pretty clear that there is a solid plan in place at Derby – not one that will bring instant success, but hopefully one which will see us move forward in the long-term. Jewell, with his teams who look good on paper but mysteriously can't get results, could easily have sent two relatively big clubs over the precipice and into the third tier. Outside of the top echelon, the days of chequebook managers are pretty much over and you can't imagine that he will ever manage a football club again.

It has taken a long time, but his successor at Derby has finally developed a team who are genuinely competitive at this level, with the promise to grow together and take us slowly and surely up the table. No, they aren't going to walk the Championship, but they are a match for anybody in the division if they play like they can – and as their current flurry of late goals proves, they possess character and fitness.

Jewell's random ragbag were always likely to wilt against Derby and once their initial spell of pressure had been seen off, that's exactly what they did. The opening goal was almost an irrelevance, given that they had already surrendered so many leads this season and sure enough, they offered up an embarrassingly easy equaliser before half-time, created for us by the mistakes of two rusty loanees.

All the money in the world won't help you if you haven't got a plan – and bringing in veterans on short contracts out of desperation is tacit admission that whatever Jewell's plan was at Ipswich, it didn't work.

***

4-4-2, 4-3-3, 4-5-1, 4-1-4-1… Clough plays the Numbers Game
November 1, 2012

On Monday, I read *The Guardian*'s coverage of Chelsea v Manchester United. As a game with plenty of talking points, involving two clubs with a preposterous level of importance, the match was afforded two solid pages of analysis, dissection and pretty graphics.

This overkill approach to the reporting revealed an interesting truth. Nobody seemed to be able to agree where Wayne Rooney was playing, or what United's formation was. One reporter put Rooney on the right of a central midfield three. Another journo had him 'excelling off the striker in a 4-4-1-1', while the formation pitch map showed him in the attacking midfield line of a 4-2-3-1.

All of these were probably true, at least at some point. Rooney is such a good player that he is able to work out for himself where he needs to be on the pitch most of the time and it may also be that Fergie changed the team shape during the course of the game.

To be honest, I'm sure you could ask four different observers of the same game to name the formation of the same team and end up with four different answers. One man's 4-3-3 is another's 4-5-1, while others might claim to detect a hint of 4-2-3-1, or even call it a 4-1-4-1.

*

One thing Clough can't complain about is the amount of options currently available to him, even with a couple of players missing. In the past we have suffered from a lack of competition for places and often been forced into the loan market, but now, although the squad is not that large, there are players within it who are relatively versatile. Meanwhile, the under-21 'reserves' have six wins and two draws from eight games this season, suggesting that there are some decent young players coming through underneath the first team.

What this has led to is plenty of online fan chat about who should be playing and where. There is consensus that Hughes should play in central midfield, but not so much agreement about what shape the team should play in, or indeed the best 11.

Some would always start with two strikers. Some would start with Jacobs on the left. Others would pick a midfield three, with two attacking wide players flanking Sammon (while others seem to have decided that Sammon is absolute rammel). As for Clough, he seems to be happy to merrily switch it around during games, depending upon the situation.

All any manager wants to do is to put a team out on the pitch who are equipped to get a result. If that means packing the midfield against Brighton[29], so be it. If it means gambling in the last few minutes by switching to a back three, as we did against Blackburn[30], fine – any-

---

[29] Derby 0 Brighton 0, October 6 2012

[30] Derby 1 Blackburn 1, October 20 2012. Theo Robinson scored a last-gasp equaliser.

thing, as long as we get a result.

Then again, there's a complicating factor in that for home matches, Clough knows he is expected to be 'positive' by fielding two central strikers. With attendances declining across the division, there is a certain commercial pressure to field an attractive team and if the tactics are generally perceived to be 'negative', non-season ticket holding fans are less likely to bother turning up.

*

Playing with a single striker means that it's hard to play a long-ball game effectively, unless you have Didier Drogba up there to hit. Anything above chest height will only end up being flicked on to nobody, so the ball has to be cared for and a more patient style has to be employed. Passers such as Hughes, Hendrick and Coutts are happy to play that way.

If you just have Hughes or Hendrick plus Bryson in the middle, Bryson is less able to raid forward. Meanwhile, with Hughes nominally on the left in a midfield four, we have a fairly lopsided look. From left-back, neither Roberts or O'Connor are terribly well equipped to effectively overlap Hughes, a midfielder who wants to drift infield and play (and is encouraged by the manager to do so).

If only we had a left-back with the speed and stamina to make telling bursts forward. Roberts would presumably run out of gas if he bombed on too much, while O'Connor is playing out of position on the left, meaning that his crossing and passing, when he does get the chance from that flank, could most kindly be described as 'variable'.

After Derby beat Forest at the City Ground, Sean O'Driscoll mentioned that our key threat was down the right, where Coutts and Brayford, both in natural positions and both attack-minded players, are able to combine well and fashion crossing opportunities (and of course, that's where the goal came from on the day).

Losing Jamie Ward has been the major difficulty we've faced this season, as his hamstring injury unsettled an established team. Clough has been trying to find the best way to cope without him, while also occasionally missing Bryson and Hendrick – and only recently trusting his new winger Michael Jacobs to start.

Ward was essentially free to drift wherever he liked, popping up between the lines, linking with the midfielders and keeping things flowing. Since his injury, we have often played 4-3-3/4-5-1. With Tyson still out of favour, this has led to the unedifying sight of Robinson playing as a left-winger, which, we can all agree, is far from ideal.

Clough's take on all this is that the formation is irrelevant, it's the intent you go into the game with. Well, yes and no. If you play with one striker, your intention is presumably to win the midfield battle, be hard to break down and build from the back. If you play with two, you're more able to effectively press high up the field and take the game to the opposition, but will be more vulnerable to the counter-attacking game which away sides employ so regularly in the Championship.

Clough also likes to point out that Bryson's energy and spirit mean that he is 'almost a second striker' when we play the midfield three, given his ability to get into the box and support the attackers. The only drawback to this theory is that he can't quite finish like a striker – goal line tap-ins at Forest honourably excepted.

Derby's inconsistent season continued into November, with every impressive victory accompanied by another annoying stumble. Humiliation at Peterborough (3-0) was followed by fine home wins against Blackpool (4-1) and Barnsley (2-0), before a pair of away defeats to Millwall (2-1) and Crystal Palace (3-0).

***

Commons sense in cutting costs?
November 22, 2012

When Kris Commons left Derby County in January 2011, there was much wailing, gnashing of teeth and lamentation. In a blaze of form that season, he had scored 13 goals in 25 league games by the time he signed for Celtic in a cut-price deal, his Rams contract six months from expiry.

Derby had offered Commons a new deal and Nigel Clough said that his wage demands had been met 'to the penny', but there's no doubt he became a richer man by moving to Scotland. He even goes down in Glaswegian folklore for lining up in the team that inexplicably beat Barcelona at Parkhead – displaying a hitherto unsuspected application to his defensive duties while deployed as the more advanced of Celtic's two right-backs.

Commons's departure and Tom Glick's hamfisted attempts to sign Conor Sammon on the cheap from Kilmarnock, melded with the televised humiliation of cup defeat at Crawley Town and seriously indifferent league form, created a perfect storm for Clough and in the aftermath of Crawley, it was erroneously reported that he had left Pride Park. So it certainly didn't seem like it at the time, but actually, did losing Commons help the club to move forward?

Before that season's loan deadline, Derby signed three players who would go on to become important first-teamers – Jamie Ward, Frank Fielding and Theo Robinson. All three were confirmed as permanent signings as soon as the transfer window opened again at the end of the season, which had spluttered to a merciful, relegation-free end.

If Commons had stayed, would the money have been there for the reinforcements we needed to survive? Would Commons have stayed fit, or would he have succumbed to another injury by the time the ink had dried on his lucrative extension? Would he have scored another 15 goals and kept us up single-handedly, or has the combined contribution of Fielding, Ward and Robinson proved to be better for us in the long run?

As the great Oakland A's general manager Billy Beane[31] has said, 'Nothing strangulates a sports club more than having older players on

---

[31] *Beane's quotes are taken from* The Football Men *by Simon Kuper and a feature published on the* Daily Telegraph *website in October 2011.*

long contracts, because once they stop performing, they become immovable.' On that basis, it could even be argued that Commons should never have been offered a new contract at all.

With the wage bill dropping drastically, the profile of our squad has changed radically, from players with reputations and experience to unproven, younger, cheaper players – hopefully with the potential to develop.

Beane says younger players are 'more cost-effective... their wages are lower. With an older player you may be paying for past performance, whereas with a younger player you are paying for future performance. It is like buying stock. Young players are attractive because they are cheaper and offer more value. They may not be as good, but if they perform at a certain level it makes more sense financially.'

Number of Derby County players with Premier League experience
End of 2007/08 season – 27
End of 2008/09 – 13
End of 2009/10 – 10
End of 2010/11 – 6
End of 2011/12 – 2
Current – 1 (Sammon)*

When Blackburn Rovers are in a position to pay £8m for Jordan Rhodes – a number not much lower than Derby's entire wage bill – it is abundantly clear that we are going to have to do things differently to have any chance of competing. Back to Beane, 'If you have less than your competitors, you can't do things the way they do, or you are destined to fall behind them.'

None of our new, younger breed have Commons's level of match-winning flair, but none of them are at the peak of their powers. All of them have their best years ahead of them and as they are a mostly unhyped mob, we stand a good chance of keeping the team unit pretty much intact for the future.

When Blackburn paid that money for Rhodes, they were paying a desperation premium. They needed the guarantee of goals, now – and only Rhodes would do. As a result of the sale, Huddersfield were able to bring in Jermaine Beckford and Simon Church and sit eighth in the table, just one point behind Blackburn, at the time of writing.

Unlike Blackburn, Derby have mostly signed raw potential. And the signings have come thick and fast this season – it's just that they've mostly been youngsters. Eleven players have come in from other clubs, seven of them aged 21 or under. The average age of the new players is 21.

The recruitment has been international, with Val Gjokaj coming from Switzerland, 15-year-old Jack Tuite from Cherry Orchard in Ireland and Luke Adams, all the way from New Zealand. The latest addition is a 16-year-old striker from Scunthorpe United, Charles Vernam.

In his last interview as Blackpool manager, Ian Holloway said, 'We were talking about expanding our youth policy… [we] were using Derby as an example… What a fantastic set-up they've got. Does it give you a team that will finish top of the table? No, it doesn't, but it does give you a good chance to build summat to get you there.'

Of course, the change in policy is also to do with cutting costs, but to quote Beane again, 'Nobody is interested in the business being run well until it isn't being run well.'

The worry at Derby is that the club is still losing money – £7.7m last year, with £1m paid out in interest on debts. That means that if a big offer comes in for a player – Will Hughes, say – it becomes virtually impossible for the club to say no.

*

When people talk about players developing and improving, the most obvious examples are the youngest ones, like Hughes and Hendrick, but also think about Brayford, Bryson, Keogh, the goalkeepers, Robinson, Jacobs, Sammon, Coutts. None of them are at their peak yet. If we keep this team together, they will get stronger and stronger.

In the meantime it's nice to just be able to focus on how the team is doing and who should be playing where, without having to worry that we haven't got a left-back, or a striker, or who our next loan signing will be. In fact, we now have five players out on loan getting games, rather than continually patching up the team with whoever we can beg or borrow.

That is in itself cause for optimism.

Four more games passed before the next post, with seven points collected. Derby had to lead three times to beat Birmingham 3-2 at home, before drawing 1-1 with Cardiff, then taking what was, at the time, their regular humbling at the hands of Leicester City (4-1, on this occasion).

Then came an excellent 3-1 win against Leeds at Pride Park.

***

Sportscene Talk-in with Colin Bloomfield and Roger Davies December 13, 2012

Colin Bloomfield was kind enough to invite me into the BBC Radio Derby studios for Monday night's *Sportscene Talk-in* programme, to offer a fan's perspective on events at Derby County, alongside the towering Roger Davies.

I made my maiden appearance on the show last year, turning up nervously clutching a folder full of home-made stats, which Roger thumbed through curiously while I answered one of Colin's questions live on air. This time, I was less thoroughly prepared and possibly still slightly hungover from 'celebrating another Rams victory' against Leeds United on the Saturday night.

Overall, I thought the show was really good, with most of the callers very happy with how things are going and making valid points. However, the first caller spoke at length about a report written some weeks ago by the Forest-supporting *Daily Telegraph* journalist John Percy, which claimed that Clough had been told to raise £1.3m in January and would therefore sell Will Hughes. The caller took this as gospel and spent quite a while complaining about it. Colin consequently spent quite a while explaining that he had already raised this issue with Clough, who had denied the reports.

Anyway, Roger was in fine form and there was a cameo appearance from Darren Wassall, plugging the youth team's FA Cup game against Gateshead at Pride Park the following evening. And of course, it was Colin's last *Sportscene Talk-in* before his well-deserved big transfer to London, so he bade the listeners an emotional farewell.

The hour flew by and while I thoroughly enjoyed it, I didn't get as much time to express my opinions as last time I was on. With that in mind, I thought I'd revisit the questions I was asked by Colin on the night and see if I could expand on the answers I gave live on the mic.

The defence

Colin Bloomfield [CB]: Are you concerned [about the number of goals conceded] – is it formation, is it personnel?

DCB: We need to score two to win, that's the problem. The most obvious thing is that we lost the two top centre-backs [Shackell and Barker] and got Keogh in, so on the face of it, the defence isn't as strong. There's still an issue with left-back, in that there's no real cover, given that O'Connor is playing out of position. When he came, we were told he was comfortable anywhere across the back four, but he has said himself he's a right-back. And now that he's made a couple of mistakes, we're told he's playing out of position at left-back…

I think we could do with strengthening [in January], but I don't think we will. I think that especially now Buxton is injured, they might give O'Brien a little run.

Will Hughes

Unsurprisingly, given how well he has done this season, there was plenty of chat about Will. I thought that Jason from Borrowash was spot on in his assessment, saying that Hughes is clearly enjoying himself, other clubs are getting scared of him and other players might be attracted to play in the same team as Will – all good reasons for us to keep him for as long as possible.

Another caller, a Spurs supporter, said Hughes is good enough to be the captain of England one day and he had 'never seen anybody that good that young' – it was also nice that the caller picked up on Jeff Hendrick's potential and said the two of them together could become a fantastic partnership.

CB: Obviously we want him to stay at Derby, but do we have to be realistic if the right offer comes in? Or should we fend off the big clubs?

DCB: He's obviously good enough to play in the Premier League, that's the thing. So at some point, if we're not able to get there, we won't be able to hold him back and somebody will want to take him... There's no point him going to a big club and sitting on the bench, or playing in the under-21 team. That wouldn't be any good for his development at all.

Will's so good, it's obvious for everyone to see. The word's out now, he's getting highlighted on *The Football League Show* and all the journalists are picking him out. When he does move on, which seems inevitable that he will eventually, hopefully we get full value for him.

CB: Not a Tom Huddlestone deal.

DCB: Exactly. That would be a mark of the development of the club. The people in charge then were not the sort of people you would want associated with your football club, shall we say. But let's keep calm, keep him for January and see what happens in the summer.

The future

Colin read out a few texts from fans demanding that money is spent on new players to push us up into the top six, or even keep us in the top ten. One asked Colin whether the board match the fans' ambitions.

CB: I'm going to leave that one to Ollie. I guess you could say they're being sensible, they're being prudent, they don't want to end up like Portsmouth.

DCB: The talk for some time has been about Financial Fair Play, how we have to fit into that and how we can't lose stupid amounts of money like Cardiff and Leicester are doing and QPR did successfully – well, I say successfully – but what we don't want to do is go into a longer period where we stagnate and just stay mid-table in this division. You want to see us push towards the top of the league. This season, we're doing pretty well, but over Christmas, there's a lot of fixtures in a short space of time, you might get one or two injuries, one or two suspensions.

CB: There is a fine balance, isn't there, between sensible investment and underinvestment. It depends which side of the fence you sit on as to where Derby are when it comes to that.

DCB: It could be incremental, because we've got the nucleus of a decent squad and if we can add a little bit to it – maybe they won't do much in January, but if we can improve on last season's position of 12th, we can look at it in the summer and say, 'OK, we're in a decent position now, we've got assets within the squad, we've got good young players.'

On this last point, I'd like to add that it's fair to say that we haven't heard much talk of a promotion push coming out of the club for some time now. There's probably been an element of trying to take pressure off Nigel while the club shifted out the old, failed squad and brought in a new, younger, cheaper group.

However, fans need to feel excited about the future. If they're not revved up about a club that is gunning for promotion, they may think twice about renewing their season tickets. Why should I sign up for another season of mid-table mediocrity, some might think.

It would be nice to believe that the board want us to get back to the Premier League, but I think there's currently a disconnect in that sense between them and the supporters. Billy Beane was right when he said that nobody wants to hear about the business being run well until it turns out it wasn't being run well, but I'll also never forget the following online comment from a Derby fan – 'I don't support a balance sheet, I support a football team.'

Given a reason to truly believe they are going to see a winning team, the fans who have deserted the club in recent seasons will start to come back. A new chief executive is coming in and we will soon find out more about his vision for our future.

Just finally, I'd like to thank Colin Bloomfield for giving me the chance to appear on Radio Derby and for some great commentary moments. I'll never hear the names Mark Beevers or Danny Shittu again without thinking of Col – and will also always fondly remember the time when he excitedly quoted some stats I'd published on win percentages with and without James Bailey to the great Colin Gibson, who sniffed and said something along the lines of, 'Right...' before intoning, 'The only statistic that matters is the final scoreline.'

Best of luck in London, Colin!

***

Guest Post – Report from the Fans Forum with Sam Rush
January 9, 2013

Thirty-five or so minutes of highlights of this Fans Forum were posted on Rams Player, out of a total two-hour programme of questions. Fortunately, our guest blogger was on hand to give his impressions of the new chief executive Sam Rush's debut grilling.

I don't want to be too negative about Sam Rush, as he's clearly new to the job of president and chief executive and the crowd were quite intimidating. The problem was that he clearly had a message he wanted to get across – that he was committed and driven to achieve success, the club are moving forward in a sensible and financially responsible way, etc – and in the face of an awful lot of inane questions, he kept reverting to the same message and never really answered any of the questions particularly well.

Rush is a waffler, with an annoying habit of starting a sentence, stopping and then starting another similar but slightly different sentence. As a result, he seemed to lack confidence when compared to Tom Glick, who always spoke in a very assured, direct manner.

At the start, he seemed very keen to make the point that he wasn't a 'former agent' – explaining that representing 400 top-name players was just a small part of what his old business used to do.

There wasn't a great deal of interesting or revelatory stuff to report, but the highlights were: –

Financial Fair Play (FFP) – Rush seemed completely skeptical about it. He said that he didn't think it was punitive enough and that the richer clubs would just gamble anyway. So basically, he said that he didn't see it would really have the proposed effect – but then resorted to the standard Glick line that when it does kick in, Derby will be ideally placed, etc.

Stadium naming rights – Given how many times he steered the conversation towards this topic, it seemed pretty obvious that it's something he's got up his sleeve. The general consensus was one of apathy – who really gives a toss about the name Pride Park? – so I suspect we'll see some movement on this front.

When pressed as to how much a deal for stadium naming was worth, he stated six figures, not seven figures. Rush also said it was harder to sell the naming rights on an established stadium name – Newcastle, for example – as people refuse to call it the new name. Chelsea have apparently not been able to negotiate the stadium naming rights on Stamford Bridge, despite trying for a long time.

<u>Transfer Policy</u> – A bit of a non-topic. 'We will not sell on the cheap and if we do sell, we will screw the best deals out of the buyer.' What else was he going to say?

Rush claimed that several Premier League teams were in for Michael Jacobs and that we did well to secure his signature. He tried to argue the point about lack of depth in the squad by saying that we had the core of the team out (naming Fielding, Bryson, Ward and Barker) yet were still playing well, winning and only three points off the play-offs.

Someone quite rightly asked why we weren't investing to push on by signing a proven goalscorer and another centre-back, at which point, Rush floundered and started saying that it was down to Nigel, who seemed happy. He also suggested that Nigel might come to a future forum, which would be interesting.

Someone asked the foreign scouting question that I asked last time and Rush said, 'Yes, we do scout abroad' – so that's either a guess or a change in policy.

***

Five years on, how far have we come? (Part 1 of 2)
January 28, 2013

'Derby under Nigel Clough: 18th, 14th, 19th, 12th. Currently 13th #specialone' – Mark Douglas, chief sports writer at The Journal

It was an off-hand tweet from a north-east-based journalist who admitted, when I challenged him on it, that he didn't really know the situation at Derby, but he has a point.

On the face of it, we are going nowhere, heartened last season by (just about) not finishing in the bottom half of the Championship for the first time in four seasons since relegation from the Premier League. How much longer can we tolerate mid-table mediocrity before a tipping point is reached and fans – either by voting with their feet, or by turning up the heat inside Pride Park – start to call for change?

Most fans understood that there were reasons beyond the manager's control for his struggles in the first couple of seasons, but that we haven't looked like promotion candidates for any sustained period since 2006/07 remains a source of frustration. Even the staunchest Clough loyalist needs to see continuing league progress to justify their faith in the manager's ability.

Yes, Clough has presided over swingeing cuts to the wage bill (maybe George Osborne should give him a call) and yes, he was tasked with getting rid of unsellable shithouses like Claude Davis, but the transitional period is well and truly over now. It's time to look forwards.

But first, a quick look back. The last few seasons are among our lowest league finishes in the past 100 years. Other than the brief dip into the Third Division in the early 1980s – the club's historical nadir – this is the worst we have been since the pre-Brian Clough era.

And with certain clubs busy debt-financing their respective pushes towards the Promised Land (isn't that what PL stands for?), there seems to be little hope of the Rams suddenly shaking off their torpor and fighting their way back into the top tier any time soon.

Maybe there is some hope in the the much-vaunted introduction of Financial Fair Play. But despite all the talk of balancing the books and financial responsibility, Derby still lost £8m in 2011/12. I tweeted the football business journalist Marc Webber to ask what on earth could be done when a club who have made a policy of working towards balancing the books are left losing so much money, while still only treading water in mid-table. His reply, 'Hopefully by FL [Football League] doing better sponsor[ship] deals & feeding that money back down. But I don't think that will happen.'

As it stands, you're either in the Premier League, receiving huge cheques for TV rights, or you're nowhere – and that is unlikely to change.

Webber went on to point out that Derby are 'one of the more proactive [clubs] in trying to find new revenues with big screen & dynamic ticketing', but tinkering around with such schemes to generate a couple of extra quid clearly isn't going to bridge the gap caused by paying the players high sums – or raise enough money to pay the sort of players who would get us promoted in short order. Even a stadium naming rights deal, the possibility of which was raised at the recent Fans Forum by Sam Rush, wouldn't generate anything like enough money for us to balance the books.

Glick said he 'had a notion' that a club could be run sustainably while challenging at the top of the league, but unless FFP shakes things up drastically, it seems that the vast majority of Championship clubs will continue to spend much more than they earn for the foreseeable future.

To pick two examples, Brighton and Bristol City have both come out and said that they will struggle to meet the criteria of FFP – and there's no way on this earth that Nottingham Forest or Leicester will (hence the giant and, in Forest's case, potentially destructive pressure from their owners to get promoted this year).

Meanwhile, Cardiff recently announced £13.6m losses for 2011/12 – a season when they enjoyed the financial windfall of reaching the League Cup Final. This came on top of losses of £11.8m in the previous financial year. With their total debts likely to pass £100m by the time their next results are announced, it really is a case of promotion or bust for the Redbirds. Elsewhere, Birmingham are in financial distress and haven't even released accounts for the last two years, while Bolton, backed by a local boy done good, have declared debts well over £100m. To name but two clubs who tried to compete in the Premier League and came down in trouble. I suspect it's significant that at the time of writing, 13th-placed Derby are still above all three of the clubs who were relegated to the Championship last season, despite those clubs being in receipt of hefty parachute payments and carrying, on paper, far superior squads.

When Glick announced our £7.5m losses in 2010/11, he confirmed that we would lose a similar amount in the next reporting year. This year, however, there was no word at all on what we can expect to see in the 2012/13 figures. In the 2011/12 accounts, the club state that there will be another loss 'in line with the budgeted target', but they do not reveal what this target is. The club have decided to do no press interviews at all on the subject, saying that this is because new chief exec Sam Rush wasn't in post during the period covered by the figures.

If losses for 2012/13 are similar to those of the previous two seasons, this would take the club's total debts to over £40m, mostly owed to GSE. Rush's line on the situation was, 'The simple truth is that somebody has to cover our working capital needs, as well as make continued investments in our squad and wider infrastructure. The ownership group's strength offers the club that much-needed financial stability.'

No more talk of breaking even, or self-sustaining – GSE are going to have to keep lending the club money to keep it going and competing by financing deals for new players. Indeed, after Glick had told supporters to expect Derby to 'trade neutral' last summer, the Rams suddenly announced the signing of Conor Sammon for £1.2m just before the end of the August transfer window.

Sam Rush told the recent Fans Forum that the Sammon deal took our summer spending to around £3.5m, while my best estimate is that we generated just over £2m, mostly by selling Steve Davies, Chris Maguire and Jason Shackell. So extra money was clearly found from somewhere.

Derby's turnover was given a huge injection by Premier League TV money in 2007/8. The wage bill steadily fell in the seasons after relegation, but stayed pretty much the same between summer 2011 and summer 2012, as did turnover. Total debt dropped while the club was still in receipt of parachute payments, but has risen again ever since.

*

So in summary then, five years on from the arrival of GSE, how far have we come? Well, this season has been frustrating, in that it seems obvious that the current players can do it – it's just that they need a bit more help from somewhere, if they are to become consistent enough to genuinely challenge.

It's hard to put a finger on it. Clearly, a proper star striker and an experienced central defender would do the trick nicely, but how to get them without losing money Cardiff-style? As that isn't an option, the progress will continue to be incremental and will depend largely on the current group being kept together and maturing together (unless a windfall in the transfer market accelerates the process a bit).

Clough is far from perfect and has made some pretty ordinary decisions during his tenure at Pride Park, both in the transfer market (Croft, Tyson) and tactically (playing Leacock as a right-back at the City Ground, the Tom Carroll fiasco, etc). His main achievement to date has been to keep us afloat when lesser managers may have been unable to stave off relegation to League One – a quagmire which has temporarily claimed some big clubs of late and will doubtless claim more in the seasons to come.

Currently, he is struggling to find the right balance in the team, but this is a problem caused at least in part by the meteoric rise of Will Hughes, who couldn't have been reckoned upon as a starter six months ago, but has forced his way into the team in sensational style.

After the comprehensive FA Cup defeat at the hands of Blackburn[32], Clough came out fighting, snapping at the BBC's Ed Dawes (who had asked a gentle question about ball retention), 'Sorry, our 17 year-old's having a little bit of a bad time today against an England international they had in there [Danny Murphy] and is it a Danish international as well [he could have meant the Swede Marcus Olsson, or Norway's Morten Gamst Pedersen], yeah, sorry about that, a 17-year old alongside a 20-year old...[33] It's a shame really, cos you know, we're expected to compete when ... I think the two strikers [Jordan Rhodes and Colin Kazim-Richards] and Murphy add up to the complete wage bill of our squad. So I think that puts it into perspective.'

---

[32] Derby 0 Blackburn 3, January 26 2013

[33] Will Hughes and Jeff Hendrick

He may be overstating those players' wages slightly, but it's still a valid point and of course, he could have added that at the time of writing, Derby are above Blackburn in the league; but at the same time, Clough wasn't forced to select the 17 year-old and the 20-year old together. He could have left one of them out and picked somebody else on the left wing (Ben Davies, if he wanted more experience, or Michael Jacobs for extra pace).

But all Clough can do is put out the 11 players he has the most belief in and, ultimately, stand or fall with them. Hughes hasn't played well for a couple of games, but he's not been linked with Premier League behemoths for no reason. Maybe he needs a breather for a game, or maybe against Huddersfield Town, it will click back into place for him and he will show us why Tommo thinks he's the new Xavi again.

Once January is out of the way – generally, this window is a time for clubs under pressure to make panic purchases, not something that Derby really need to get involved with this season – next summer is really important. Finally, there are not many unwanted players left to ship out (probably Tyson is the only relatively big earner we'll be actively trying to re-home), which gives us a real opportunity to build upon the progress we've made through signing good players like Keogh, Brayford, Bryson and Ward, while developing the likes of Hendrick and Hughes through the youth system.

When Nigel arrived, surely all but the most churlish of Rams fans were hoping it would be him who managed to 'raise the roof' and bring success to Derby County. But despite being the Son of God, he isn't the Messiah and he can't do it without money to spend. At least if Clough left tomorrow, he could very reasonably point out that even if it still isn't good enough to go up, the squad is far better now than it was when he took on the job, despite the wage bill having been cut by about 60 per cent.

The legacy of Lionel Pickering – Pride Park, Moor Farm – is the foundation for a club that belongs in the Premier League. Surely one day, somebody will get it right at Derby and unlock the potential in what is still without question one of the biggest and best clubs in England. Whether it's Nigel Clough and GSE who do it remains to be seen.

***

200 'up' for Nigel Clough in the Championship
April 15, 2013

The deeply disappointing defeat at Blackburn Rovers[34] was Nigel Clough's 200th league game at Derby County. His Championship record to date looks like this: –

P 200 W 67 D 47 L 86

Average points per season 57
Average league position 15th (current position 13th)
Loss percentage 43 per cent (this season 38.1 per cent)

With four games to go, in what at one point threatened to be a good season, the Rams have dropped to 13th, five points above the relegation zone and nine points short of the play-off pace. Can you think of nine points we dropped that we could have got? I can.

The recent run of three wins[35] has, realistically, just about done enough to keep us safe for another year, but the current threat of a poor end to the campaign would not help drive season ticket sales for next season. Meanwhile, achieving the extremely modest aim of improving on last season's 12th-place finish is by no means assured.

All the talk about how Leicester, Forest and Cardiff's spending is unsustainable and reckless means nothing if a principled refusal to play the same game leads to nothing but stagnation and the feeling that there is no hope for anything better in the future. GSE may not have

---

[34] Blackburn 2 Derby 0, 13 April 2013.

[35] Derby had ended a run of eight games without a win by beating Leicester 2-1, Bristol City 3-0 and Leeds 2-1. The Leicester win was significant, as a new loan signing, Chris Martin, scored his first goal for the Rams.

realised what they were taking on when they stepped into the mad-house of English football and, especially given the global financial crisis, may now feel that they bit off more than they can chew. Let's hope not.

Assuming the players don't sleepwalk into relegation, next season, Clough needs a fast start. Maybe he needs more experience or raw character in the squad, to keep a grip on the games that we keep letting slip away – and he needs more goals from somewhere, as Conor Sammon (one goal in the last 15 matches) has become another stick to beat the manager with, for all his work rate.

It's much harder to turn around and say that Clough's had his hands tied financially when he was given £1.2m to spend on a striker – one he said at the time wouldn't score that many goals. Why not put the money on somebody he thought would score? But then again, he thought that Nathan Tyson would prosper as a number nine, which does call his judgment into question.

Steve Nicholson has challenged fans to name a striker available for the same money as Sammon who could have done better. It's not an easy question to answer, but the success of Dwight Gayle, plucked from Dagenham & Redbridge by Peterborough, shows that there are bargains to be had and scouting from the lower leagues has always been one of the things we assumed Clough was good at. Gayle's goals could well keep Posh up this season. Adam Le Fondre is another predatory striker who was available for a relative song and went elsewhere.

The higher-profile strikers Clough wanted to sign but couldn't – Hooper, Mackie, Waghorn *et al* – were beyond his budget in terms of wages as much as anything. But surely he could have got a more reliable, less injury-prone player than Tyson (£1.5m in wages over three years, if my information is correct) and a more assured finisher than Sammon for a seven-figure transfer fee?

On the positive side, Chris Martin has done some good things during his loan spell (scoring two perfectly good disallowed goals, for a start) and Craig Forsyth might prove to be a useful addition, if his loan is converted to a permanent deal. But overall, with the name of Alex Baptiste the only one currently being bandied about as a potential signing for next season, the 'Slow Train Coming', as I've called it before, currently looks in danger of being cancelled altogether.

The bottom line is that our results have to buck up because they simply are not good enough. I would argue that if we suffer a slow start to next season, the owners will be faced with a decision to make. A change at the top would be expensive and would bring its own risks, but unless GSE appointed a genuine incompetent, as they have done previously with Paul Jewell, it would be unlikely to make things much worse in the short-term.

A new manager would need to fit into the GSE blueprint. He would need to be prepared to develop young players, to be able to scout effectively from the lower leagues and the rest of the UK, rather than plucking established Championship players from rival clubs, or taking costly loanees from the Premier League. Management is a lot easier if you can just wield a chequebook and sign players that every Tom, Dick and Harry Redknapp knows are up to the task.

GSE would certainly not employ an unruly, firebrand manager – there are very few of them about anyway these days, with Paolo Di Canio the exception proving the rule – or a 'big name', who would expect to the sort of budget with which he could protect his reputation.

One option would be to appoint a bright young manager from the new school, with a fistful of coaching badges and a head full of ideas, but outstanding candidates are few and far between and I for one would find a David Brent-style character unappealing. A real communicator would be a breath of fresh air – Nigel is the polar opposite of his genius father when it comes to media relations, after all.

A new manager, should it come to that, would demand time to implement his own strategy and would require funds for new players, which on the basis of recent seasons would be available in only limited amounts (unless we enjoy a windfall from selling off one of the academy products). Any successor to Clough would have to be ready to take on a club whose fans' expectation levels have not matched by the reality on the pitch for years now.

Of course, the preferred option would be for the Clough reign to continue and as he has pointed out himself, the performances have been very good at times this season, but in what is ultimately a results business we need to see a marked upturn sooner rather than later. In an oddly funereal interview with the BBC's Owen Phillips last month, Clough said, 'I don't think we will be around, but what we are trying to do is put structure in place that will benefit whoever is here in a few years.

'The academy should almost be ring-fenced and whoever comes in next, I hope they have the sense to leave it alone and let it continue working. The problem will come if they change the philosophy totally and you have the first team playing one way and the academy playing another.'

Unfortunately, while the Slow Train Coming may be sowing the seeds of future success, nobody really gives a toss if the U21s and U18s are doing well if the first team are getting beat. It's hard to take comfort in the potential of the young players if there aren't enough seasoned pros around to overcome moribund opposition and see out games against the likes of Ipswich, Sheffield Wednesday and Birmingham, let alone Cardiff.

Nevertheless, the long-term direction of the club – nurturing youth, developing players through the ranks, trying to play decent football on the deck – is the right one to pursue. For too long we had been drifting along aimlessly, but now, there is at least a sensible plan in place. Who knows, maybe eventually, Clough could be moved into a director of football role, allowing a young pretender to take over the first team.

Long-term talk is rare in football and we should be grateful for the job Nigel has done. But the results need to improve – and he surely doesn't have the luxury of another 200 league games in which to turn it around.

2013/14

Three into two won't go
May 6, 2013

The final whistle may only have been blown on Saturday afternoon, but Derby's recruitment plans for next season are clearly already well advanced. They probably would have been even more so, had mathematical safety not taken so long to achieve (no criticism there – I have a lot of sympathy for Peterborough United, who go down with 54 points, which would have kept them up in any other season).

Clough has said that he wants to bolster the spine of the side and duly, a goalkeeper, centre-back and two strikers are among the first batch of confirmed targets. However, midfield is a different matter, as Clough has a genuine 'selection headache' to resolve there.

As Jeff Hendrick and Will Hughes get better and better, their fellow central midfielder, Craig Bryson, has reached the final 12 months of his current contract. As we all know, he has done really well for the duration of his stay, with 11 goals to add to his seemingly limitless dynamism, determination and drive. Having signed for £450,000 from Kilmarnock, he has provided full value and you would hope that, if he leaves, that the Rams would turn a profit on him.

The policy of the club, as clearly stated on countless occasions, is to go with the youth. And since we have produced at least two future international-class players from our academy, that policy is clearly already paying dividends. Those dividends may mean that we can release the more experienced Bryson in order to strengthen the squad elsewhere.

Of course, nobody wants to see good players leave, but what a difficult situation this is for Clough. Does he bench Hughes or Hendrick? Does he play Bryson out of position on the left? Or does he change the formation to 4-3-3, moving away from a team shape which has delivered excellent home form this season (it might be an idea to use that formation in away games, but that's another blog)?

There's also Bryson's perspective to consider. He will doubtless not be short of offers from other Championship clubs. Would he sign an extension at Derby if he wasn't guaranteed to be in the team, in his best position? Certainly, he will 'do a job' for you out wide, but in the same sense that Paul Green 'did a job' on the right. You lose the best qualities of the player that way.

So do we keep Bryson for the last year of his deal, thus missing out on a potential transfer fee now? Or do we just go with the two young rising stars and see where they can take us? It's one of the most interesting questions of the summer, for me.

***

Clough's Wingless Wonders?
May 21, 2013

I've been pondering more on the topic that prompted me to write my last tactics article, after reading Steve Nicholson's season wrap-up piece, in which Nigel Clough talked about the 'dilemma' of trying to fit the three central midfielders Bryson, Hendrick and Hughes into the same side:

'It was a dilemma and still is. They are three of our best players and we want them in the team. So it is about getting a system to accommodate them.

'We ended up with Craig on the left at times but not really on the left. He always played on the left of a midfield three at Kilmarnock.

'As long as he is not out on the touchline, he can do a job in that position.'

In another interview with Nicholson, Clough mentioned that Paul Coutts, who has mostly played on the right, 'wants to play more centrally as well'.

That got me thinking about the 'wingless' formation Sir Alf Ramsey used in the 1966 World Cup. With the four midfielders currently at our disposal, a version of this formation could work, on paper at least. It would not be exactly the same in execution, but it would provide a way of fitting in all of Clough's favoured midfielders while still leaving room for two forwards.

People tend to think that a sitting midfielder has to be a hardman, an 'experienced older head', or a combination of both – a Nobby Stiles, or Seth Johnson, to give a Derby-related example. Will Hughes couldn't be any more different from Stiles or Seth in playing style and plays the holding role in an an almost literal sense – holding possession, prompting and probing, making himself constantly available. Conducting proceedings from deep, he doesn't provide much of a shield for the back four, but does allow us to keep possession.

Playing without conventional wingers would allow Hendrick and Bryson (if he stays) to remain more central, to do most of the ball-winning spadework. Where we would miss out would be in genuine width – unless of course, the full-backs are young, fit and mobile enough to raid forward consistently. We know John Brayford can do that job (as, unfortunately, do one or two other clubs) and clearly, it's part of the reason why Craig Forsyth is so high on the wanted list. He has shown he can support the attacks and put in a decent cross from the left.

If we do lose Brayford, whoever replaces him will have the task of being as much like him as possible. It could well be Kieron Freeman, an ambitious young player in whom Clough clearly believes.

Another form of width would be provided by the front two. Ward is given license to roam and is as likely to pop up on the wing as in the six-yard box. Sammon has a useful habit of barging his way down the sides of the penalty areas and can provide crosses in that way.

On the downside, opponents playing with attacking widemen could cause problems against this formation and there would be a clear onus on our midfielders to help their full-backs. But Clough has always prized versatility and flexibility as assets and his players can generally be trusted to put their shift in.

In certain situations and against certain opponents, a 4-1-3-2 shape could come in handy and clearly, it could be shuffled around mid-game, if required. Ward could 'hang left' with Coutts going wide right and Sammon leading the line in a 4-3-3, for example. There would also be options on the bench in the shape of Chris Martin, Ben Davies and Michael Jacobs, or even the emerging Mason Bennett.

And who knows, we might see one or two more new faces to bolster things before the end of the transfer window as well.

***

The complete performance? Will Hughes v Leeds United, December 8 2012
June 15, 2013

By the time Leeds came to town last December, the 17 year-old Will Hughes had already established himself in our first team. After initially using Hughes as a nominal left midfielder with license to drift infield – more to shoehorn him into the team than for any tactical reason, I think – Nigel Clough eventually bowed to the inevitable and began to start Hughes in the centre.

I did an analysis of his 60-minute performance in the pre-season friendly against Sunderland – a match in which he recorded a pass completion rate of 95.5 per cent – concluding, 'He will get hustled, harried and, frankly, kicked a lot more in a competitive Championship encounter than he did against Sunderland, but hopefully, he will have the composure to handle it. The early signs are really encouraging and he clearly has the potential to make a real impression this season.' That he did and Fulham boss Martin Jol has confirmed that he's on everybody's radar, with Newcastle United the latest club to be linked with a big bid for him.

The Leeds performance seemed to confirm, to me at least, that he already had the ability to do nearly everything you would expect from a top-class central midfielder. So, for my own enjoyment in the boring post-season, I decided to review his performance in-depth.

ATTACKING STATS
Passes complete 33
Passes incomplete 5
Pass completion 87 per cent
(Assist, 14 mins)
Cross complete 1
Cross incomplete 0
Dribbles resulting in scoring opportunity 4 (100 per cent)
Beat his man 1 (100 per cent)
Fouled 0
Lost possession 2
Shots on target 2 (100 per cent)

DEFENSIVE STATS
Tackles won 4
Tackles lost 7
Fouls committed 3
(Yellow card, 69 mins)
Interceptions 1
Headers won 0
Headers lost 1
Substituted, 90 mins

Watching back, I was surprised to realise that until the 14th minute, Hughes's contribution was actually negligible. The ball pinged up and down the pitch as the two teams battled unsuccessfully to get hold of it and Hughes didn't even get a touch until seven minutes in, when his rather aimless first-time lob forward landed at a Leeds defender's feet.

But when he finally did make a contribution, it was a telling one. Derby won a free kick on halfway and Hughes instantly moved forward to make himself available for Theo Robinson, who tapped it to him, releasing him into the Leeds half with almost absurd ease. Hughes ambled forward, totally free, before artfully disguising a ball into the box for Conor Sammon, who managed to get it out of his feet and make room for a shot, which he scuffed past Paddy Kenny for the first goal of the game.

Hughes was playing as the deepest of the Rams' four midfielders and was rarely heavily involved, as Derby pushed forward and used the flanks as much as possible. However, in the 26th minute, he had a re-markable 30-second purple patch.

Sammon did really well to rush back and win the ball from dawdling Leeds in the centre circle. He laid it off to Hughes, who again found himself in acres of space and able to trundle forward. Having won the ball in the first place, Sammon had the energy and desire to charge back up the pitch, but when Hughes slid the striker clean through in the penalty area, his first touch let him down and Kenny was able to col-lect.

As Sammon showed his frustration, Kenny quickly threw the ball out, setting Leeds off on a dangerous counter-attack. The ball was played through to McCormack, who carried it into Derby's final third seemingly unopposed – but he hadn't reckoned on Hughes, who had sprinted back from the edge of the Leeds box and, having made up a huge amount of ground on the attacker, executed a perfect sliding tackle from the side, emerging cleanly with the ball, which he then calmly laid off to Brayford.

Brayford then made a hash of his clearance, which ricocheted off a Leeds man and back down the pitch, but Hughes was in position to calmly take control of the loose ball and lay it back to Adam Legzdins in goal. The teenager received an almighty ovation from the stands – and rightly so.

That little cameo of excellence would probably have been enough for Rams fans to remember his contribution fondly, but he had plenty more in the tank for the second half.

A sweetly hit strike after 58 minutes was goalbound until it was blocked, but seconds later he was threatening Paddy Kenny again, this time in scintillating fashion. Picking up the ball in the right-hand channel, he drove forward and shimmied nonchalantly past his man before blasting a shot which the goalkeeper had to tip around the post.

Hughes has no discernible pace but he takes up good positions, exhibits enviable ball control and is capable of seeing and executing little tricks, moves and passes that demonstrate a level of mental agility and technical ability far beyond that of the average Championship player. In the breathtaking moment when he swayed so stylishly and effortlessly through the Leeds defence, he was an absolute joy to watch. If it had been a goal, it would have been our goal of the season by a street.

At that point, however, the game was still in the balance. Somehow, without having so much as got into Derby's box before they scored, Leeds had equalised in first-half stoppage time. They improved considerably in the second half and at the point of Hughes's next intervention, the game really could have gone either way.

As it was, Hughes's beautifully flighted lobbed ball down the wing released Coutts and forced a corner. That resulted in a second corner, which dropped to Richard Keogh to smash a shot that Jake Buxton deflected into the net. But it had been Hughes's moment of creativity which indirectly led to that crucial goal.

Later on, Hughes tired and his influence waned. He was booked for his third foul – a late tackle committed while trying to retrieve an underhit backheel by Michael Jacobs – and in the game's final stages, he became an increasingly peripheral figure as Derby retreated into a 4-5-1 shape and tried to hang on to their lead.

Leeds peppered in a few shots, with a rasper from El-Hadji Diouf fizzing just wide and a lobbed header defeating Adam Legzdins but coming back off the post. The ball was largely travelling over Hughes's head in either direction and he was ultimately replaced, only partly to use up time, in the 91st minute.

Over the course of the game, Hughes made 38 passes and completed 33 of them, giving an excellent pass accuracy of 87 per cent. And one of the five incomplete passes was directly the fault of James O'Connor, who nervously poked the ball to Hughes in a position where it was almost impossible to do anything with it – even so, he still almost managed to find Jacobs.

However, before we get too gushy, it's worth comparing the number of passes to the top Premier League midfielders, who average about the same level of accuracy from a far higher amount of passes per match.

That we weren't able to get the ball to Hughes more often probably proves that we were not in as firm control of the game as we would have liked, at least for spells, a feeling which is backed up by the overall possession percentages for the game, which were 51-49 in Derby's favour.

It's also worth pointing out that Hughes lost more tackles than he won, understandably struggling at times with the physical side of a hard-fought game. But it would be absolutely preposterous to criticise a slight 17 year-old playing against much older and stronger players for that. And I find it fascinating that every time he was able to run with the ball, he created a scoring opportunity – one of which was converted by Sammon.

It may not quite have been the complete performance, but still, not bloody bad for a 17 year-old. That afternoon it became abundantly clear that Hughes was a major talent and a player already capable of being the man of the match in a really competitive Championship encounter. Let's hope that this season, he shows much more of the same – if he can do so, there's no reason why he can't help to propel us into the top six.

***

The Rehabilitation of Derby County
July 2, 2013

Since the end of 2012/13, the positive way in which this summer has developed has marked another stage in the gradual rehabilitation of Derby County. What was for years a club doing little more than just about get by is starting to look suspiciously like a healthy, competitive beast capable of punching its weight and winning promotion to the Premier League.

Yes, really.

As we bask in the feelgood factor of a pre-season that is actually resulting in a stronger squad, with transfers being concluded rather than just promised, think back (only briefly, I promise) to the gloomier days of September 2009.

When the proposed sale of Rob Hulse to Middlesbrough fell through, it came to light via the Wolves website that his replacement would have been an untested youngster, Sam Vokes – on loan, despite the fact that the Hulse deal was being touted as a sale in the region of £3m. This was a bit reminiscent of the Amigos nightmare and the owners GSE were not popular at the time, as a patched-up, loan-heavy team failed to meet supporters' expectations of success.

A year later, in August 2010, rattled chief exec Tom Glick, under pressure to explain what on earth was going on, was telling the media that 18-year-old striker Chris Wood was our top target, on loan from West Brom. Wood never arrived – embarrassingly, he decided to join Barnsley instead – and besides, he didn't make an impact at Championship level until a full two years later, when a goal-heavy loan spell at Millwall propelled him to prominence.

Fast forward three years to June 2013 and Nigel Clough's top attacking target is Dundee United's Johnny Russell – available for around £750,000. While all and sundry were running their mouths about the deal, with rumours of a rival bid from Celtic repeated *ad infinitum* on social media, Glick's replacement as chief executive, Sam Rush, kept schtum and quietly, efficiently got the transfer done.

In addition to Russell, Lee Grant was brought in with a minimum of fuss, not least because Derby were able to offer better wages than Burnley, a club in decline after their brief flirtation with the Premier League.

Chris Martin, whether you agree with his signing or not, was a player the manager was able to assess for himself during an extended loan spell – and was happy to bring to the Rams on a permanent basis.

Craig Forsyth, another 'try before you buy' player from last season, has since joined from Watford. These days, loanees are brought in with a view to a longer stay rather than just being used as short-term sticking plasters over gaping holes in the squad, as was the case in days gone by.

In the past there was no discernible conveyor belt of young players coming through our system, but there is now a robust academy, bringing through good local talent, as well as casting the net wider to develop prospects from further afield. This is working a treat – and when scare stories were published about a fire sale at Derby last January, with Clough allegedly ordered to sell to balance the books, rumours of big-money bids for the scarily gifted Will Hughes abounded.

But with the club on a surer footing than in the past, there was to be no Tom Huddlestone-like travesty this time. Not only are the Rams producing quality players like Hughes and Jeff Hendrick, they are apparently also in a position to hang on to them until the bid becomes too good to turn down.

*

I was worried that Craig Bryson would be leaving this summer. He was down to the last 12 months of his contract and Clough had said that players would not be allowed to go into their final year before leaving for free. I therefore assumed that Bryson would go, with Hendrick and Hughes becoming our first-choice central midfielders by default.

Instead, Bryson agreed a new three-year deal before going off on his summer holiday. Not only that, Bryson also played a major part in persuading his fellow Scot Johnny Russell to move to Pride Park. The decision to publicly credit Bryson with his role in selling life at Derby to Russell was a good one – the player deserves praise for going far beyond the minimum for the good of his club.

In another positive development, despite his years of experience in the role, Clough has been studying for his A Licence coaching badge – a stepping stone to the UEFA Pro Licence, which is a prerequisite for managers wanting to work in the Premier League. Sir Alex Ferguson was a notable exception to this rule (I would have loved to have been in the meeting when the FA told him he had to take a course on how to manage).

Elsewhere, Conor Sammon, Jeff Hendrick and Richard Keogh playing for Ireland has been another part of what I consider to be the rehabilitation of Derby County. After a dismal decade of almost constant failure, suddenly, we are a club who attracts, signs and even produces internationals.

Giovanni Trapattoni, while particularly pleased with the contribution of Sammon and Hendrick to the Irish set-up, introduced a slightly sour note when he told the press that he had been asking the guys why they don't play in the Premier League.

It wasn't pleasing to read the following quote from Trap's pre-match conference against Spain, 'If they were playing for better sides, they would have more of the ball and be more confident when they come with us. It is easier for them to leave when their contract is over because they can go for free. It's more difficult when the club must pay, but I have asked the players which agents they have because it is important for them to see if there are possibilities for them to leave.'

Derby averaged 52.7 per cent possession across last season's Championship games and had more of the ball in the vast majority of the games. However, it's certainly true that Hendrick looked out of his depth while playing in the recent friendly against England.

Nevertheless, Trapattoni's comments chafe. We know that Hendrick's representatives agitated over his current contract, much to Clough's disgust at the time – and with his current deal expiring in 2015, you get the feeling that if we aren't promoted this season, Jeff will be moved on. But let's not dwell on a hypothetical negative at what should feel like a positive time for anybody with Derby County at heart.

Ever since the Season of Doom, the club has not been remotely ready for promotion. After Clough rescued us from the ruinous mismanagement of Paul Jewell, we listened impatiently to Glick's depressing mantra of prudence, Financial Fair Play and better times just around the corner.

Rush has clearly realised that Glick's business-speak was a huge turn-off for Derby fans and steered mercifully clear of it. His comments after the signing of Russell were probably the most bullish to come out of Derby County since the Billy Davies days. Rush spoke of a club ready for a dart at promotion and the current vibe around the place genuinely seems to back that optimism up.

Last season marked the start of a genuine upturn in the club's fortunes and while Rush can't take all of the credit for that – he only started in post this January and not much happened in that transfer window – he has certainly grabbed this summer by the balls.

There is genuine excitement about the Russell deal – he could finally be the talismanic striker everybody has been craving – and to get it done so early on, allowing the player to start pre-season with his new team-mates, earns top marks for the chief exec.

At this rate, you wouldn't bank on John Brayford realising that the grass ain't necessarily greener and pitching in with us for another couple of seasons. Hopefully he will now see that his best chance of a stab at the Premier League may actually come by helping the Rams get promoted, rather than hitching a ride with a promoted side like Cardiff, or trying his luck with a parachuting relegated team like Wigan Athletic.

Even the fact that Wigan's initial bid in the region of £1m for Brayford was confidently rebuffed is a positive in itself. A player brought from the lower leagues by 'Non-league Nigel', Brayford is now generally regarded as one of the best defenders outside the Premier League and there is no desperate need to cash in on him, even though four players have already signed for a total of around £1m, with only around £200,000 recouped to date.

As Clough recently told the *Burton Mail,* 'We know we've got assets on the pitch, so we're under no pressure [to sell]. That's the lovely thing about the Brayford situation – maybe in past seasons, we would have taken the offer. We don't need to now – we don't need to take an offer for Will or anybody. We're not too far away, financially, from where we want to be this season.'

If Brayford stays and we sign another good centre-back, I might well have a little wager on us making the play-offs this year.

***

Your Application for a loan-back has been Refused...
August 22, 2013

As the transfer window slowly creaks shut, so the speculation around clubs in the Premier League and Championship intensifies. Some of it will have foundations and it does seem to be the case that Liverpool are seriously interested in our *wunderkind* Will Hughes. And why wouldn't they be?

The latest batch of reports from the national media started the bidding at £6m, escalating through £7m to £10m yesterday. Leaving aside the fact that no bids have actually been received at the time of writing, one linking factor to all of these reports is their assertion that Liverpool would apparently be comfortable with a 'loan-back' agreement, which would see Hughes remain at Pride Park for the rest of this season.

I'm sure that Liverpool would be delighted to secure one of the very best young English talents through such an arrangement, but I am convinced that unless it was accompanied by a very, very serious transfer fee indeed, it would represent very bad business for Derby.

Hughes is 18 years and four months old and is already a member of the England U21 squad. As a technically gifted English midfield play-maker with the intelligence to play at the top level, he is not so much a rarity as a real-life unicorn. His development has been incredible and it won't stop here.

It doesn't seem like hyperbole to suggest that he is a future England international in the making – indeed, Sam Wallace of *The Independent* reports, 'He is part of a small group of English players whom the Football Association hopes can be developed in the next cycle of under-21s to make the step up to senior level within the next four years'.

Everyone understands that eventually, he will move on from Derby. But letting him leave now, even for £10m, would be criminal.

For a start, he signed a deal running until summer 2016 a few months ago, so there is no contract wind-down issue to force our hand. And it seems reasonable to assume that over the course of this season, Hughes is going to improve. If he continues to represent England during the forthcoming European Championship qualification campaign, his stock can only rise. A '£10m' 18-year old is not going to lose value and may very well attract other suitors if his career continues on its current arc.

The loan-back idea is only good for the buyer. It's an insurance clause, securing the player before you actually need him to prevent any of your rivals from clocking him as he continues his development. Why would we agree to that? As Wallace says in his report, 'Liverpool are aware that the price is only likely to rise over the coming months.'

It seems ridiculous to me, but Clough nevertheless acknowledged the possibility in a recent interview, quoted in the *Derby Telegraph* thusly, 'People talk about the loan-back option should he move on. With certain players, I don't think they would cope with that, but if anything ever happens and that is the scenario… then that wouldn't be a problem for him, because he just gets on with his football.'

Perhaps, but undeniably, you would be left with a different player, regardless of how level-headed a character he may be. Rather than being a rising star, a loaned-back Hughes would be a man whose ascent was already confirmed, just not yet delivered. From the outside looking in, I cannot see how a player in those circumstances, whose big move is already secured, could possibly address his loan period with a 'smaller' club with the same level of enthusiasm and commitment.

Those who disagree could point to the Wilfried Zaha transfer last season, when the player moved to Manchester United in January and stayed with the Eagles until the end of the season, but I would argue that the circumstances were very different. At the time of Zaha's sale, Palace were fourth in the league and very much involved in the promotion race. Zaha had a very clear mission for his final few games at Palace. Even so, chairman Steve Parish reportedly kicked against the idea of a loan-back and tried unsuccessfully to delay the sale until the end of the season.

To my mind, even a bid of £10m with a loan-back should be rejected out of hand at this stage. If he is worth that much to somebody now, then there's no reason why he wouldn't be worth even more to the same club, or a rival bidder, 12 months down the line – with more experience, more England U21 caps and doubtless many more exquisite moments of guile to add to his highlights reel.

Of course, Liverpool could decide to move on to other targets, but his very Englishness, in a system which insists on a certain amount of homegrown players in a Premier League squad, means that he is an asset who will always command the attention of the big clubs. To my mind, it would be very bad business indeed to jump at the first bid that is dangled in front of us for a player of such rare ability – if indeed one is lodged before the end of the transfer window.

Derby started the new season pretty much as they had conducted the last one – win one, lose one, draw one. They shipped a late equaliser against Blackburn at home on the opening day, won 2-1 at Brighton, lost 1-0 to Leicester at Pride Park. They then beat Yeovil 3-0 at Huish Park, the game which featured a famously impressive spell of passing football that culminated in a goal for Craig Bryson.

However, any early season optimism was then thoroughly dented by a 3-0 home crushing at the hands of Burnley.

***

Guest Post: 'Your 90 Minutes' Fans Forum with Sam Rush, Thurs 12 September

I'm pleased to welcome back my guest blogger, with his take on the recent Fans Forum with Rams chief executive Sam Rush. Take it away, Mr Mystery Man.

****

This was my third 'Your 90 Minutes' forum and I was pleased to find that the format had reverted to 'ten people around the table chatting informally with the chief exec', as per the first of these that I went to in 2012, rather than '200 people in the Pedigree Suite, bellowing angrily and incomprehensibly at the chief exec' format from the one in January.

The evening's agenda was the usual 45 minutes of open questions to the club, then 45 minutes of the club's marketing people seeking the fans' opinions – this time, their chosen topic was 'matchday music'.

The shadow of the Burnley defeat hung heavy over the first half of the programme, which actually lasted well over an hour and the tone of questioning was considerably more negative than I think it would have been had the forum happened on the back of the Yeovil and Brentford goal-fests[36].

Sam clearly anticipated this and was very honest about how much the defeat had hurt everybody at the club. Nigel, more than anyone, was devastated by it.

Centre-backs/Defence

---

[36] Derby had walloped League 1 Brentford 5-0 to progress to the third round of the league cup.

There were a lot of questions about why we're not strengthening at centre-back, given that the first publicly acknowledged target of the summer window was Alex Baptiste.

Apparently, Nigel thought that Baptiste was better than what we have, but since then, we simply have not identified any targets that we think are better than the players we've got.

Adam Smith[37] had a dead leg when he came to us, hence Freeman started the season in place of Brayford. Nigel thought he deserved to keep his place after a couple of good performances. However, after the Burnley game, it's a given that Smith will start at Millwall.

The most interesting admission was that the club believe ALL the defenders have under-performed this season in comparison to last season.

Brayford

Rush said that there wasn't all that much interest until the Wigan offer, which wasn't good enough, so we turned it down. Then, just when we didn't expect him to leave, the Cardiff bid came in. The club didn't want to stand in his way, as he'd always said he wanted to go if a Premier League club came in for him.

Obviously, it's disappointing for Bray that he's not really played yet. When someone asked, 'Can we have him back on loan?' Rush very quickly replied, 'I think Nigel would LOVE him back, so don't rule it out!'

Forest Home Game / The South Stand

Plans are in place to keep the South Standers where they are for the derby and give the away fans the South East Corner. Forest will get fewer tickets than normal, but it will probably be more than the 2,002 they are giving us. This is subject to approvals, but the club are hopeful

---

[37] Full-back Smith had joined on a season loan from Tottenham Hotspur, to replace John Brayford, who was sold to Cardiff City for a reported £1.5m at the end of July 2013.

it can be sorted out that way.

Generally, the South Stand experiment has been considered a massive success so far and the longer term plan is to gradually reclaim the whole of the stand for Derby fans.

Loans / Transfer Market

Some of the Brayford money is covering the Adam Smith loan and some remains to be spent. We had to pay Crewe a fair chunk of sell-on money too *[DCB: 15 per cent of the profit went to Crewe. I estimate this as being around £120,000].*

Smith is not cheap – there was a loan fee (six figures) AND we're paying his full wages, but he had the choice of half a dozen clubs who wanted him, so we did well to get him.

Tom Naylor[38] and Jimmy O'Connor loans out – we're paying half their wages. In the case of O'Connor, it sounds like we were begging Bristol City to take him[39]! It was also mentioned that we had to 'pay off' Nathan Tyson before he would leave.

Apart from clubs with parachute payments and Forest, no other clubs in the division have done more transfer business than us this summer, so it's interesting that some people still think we haven't signed enough players.

Wage Bill

Rush stated that one of the benefits of his former role (head of a player agency) was that he knows roughly the wage budgets/structures of almost every other club and that he can state categorically that ours is 'average' and therefore, despite the Baptiste situation, we can compete on wages with most clubs. Lee Grant was stated as an example, hav-

---

[38] Naylor was loaned to League Two Newport County in August 2013

[39] O'Connor was sent to League One Bristol City on loan in September 2013, a deal which Derby stated was with a view to a permanent switch.

ing chosen Derby ahead of other interested clubs.

Rush told us that Baptiste had asked for wages well in excess of £20,000 per week, which is 'some way above our highest earner', adding, 'Could we afford £20k-a-week wages? No. Could we afford £8-10k? Yes.'

Tyson, Rush said, was 'on good money for any football club' *[DCB: I have been reliably informed that Tyson was among the top earners, on more than £10k per week].*

On the subject of spending and parachute payment clubs, one of the things that Rush was keen to get across was that people should not equate parachute payments with guaranteed promotion and that no parachute clubs went up last year. Every year, Rush said, at least one club 'like Derby' gets promoted, so there is no reason why it can't *be* Derby.

The implication was clearly that is the official strategy. Spend little and wisely and cross your fingers, rather than spend big and risk the farm.

Nigel

The most controversial question of the night was, 'How patient are the board prepared to be with Nigel given that the team is now completely his own and we've had the alleged "good transfer window" and that this is the "strongest squad he's ever had"?'

Obviously, Rush was never going to answer this fully and it was the only time of the evening where he really came across as being on the back foot.

He made it pretty clear that changing the manager was not an option they would take lightly, given how far we've come with Nigel. He recognises that Nigel polarises opinion and that is understandable with a manager who has been in post for so long. However, it's easy for fans to think that changing the manager is the answer to all problems, but for a club, it's a much bigger decision to make.

Rush did say, 'Clearly we can't have too many more defeats like Burnley' – the closest he came to an admission that Clough is not untouchable.

The pattern of inconsistent results just continued after the international break.

Derby ran riot at Millwall – Craig Bryson scoring a hat-trick in a 5-1 win – then drew 2-2 at Bolton, before another disappointing home defeat, this time 3-1 to Reading.

***

Home and Away – unexpected early season ups and downs for Derby County September 22, 2013

In July, I posted a piece intended to highlight how difficult our start to the season could prove to be, given that the fixture computer had presented us with some hard fixtures to take on in August and September. We scored only five points from the equivalent eight fixtures last season.

With this in mind, I said in my preview piece, 'Don't be too concerned if we're not among the early front-runners this year. The run of games up until the next East Midlands derby is undeniably tricky and if we can get through it with ten or 11 points, we will be set up well for a potentially good season.'

With those eight fixtures now played, we're sitting in mid-table on 11 points. However, nobody would have predicted that ten of those points would have been picked up away from home.

In statistical terms, it doesn't matter where you get your points, but for the morale of the supporters it is absolutely vital. I once suggested that if a manager of a Football League club won all his home games 2-0 and lost every away game 1-0, it would be impossible to sack him (at least until he had lost a play-off final at neutral Wembley). I never expected this theory to actually be tested, in reverse, by Derby's form.

If you win every away game, but lose every home game, can you sack the manager? Probably, yes!

Of course, in reality, the current runs of form won't carry on. We will start winning at home – next time out against Ipswich would be good, thanks – and we will lose our unbeaten away record eventually – but hopefully not at the City Ground next weekend.

Derby's next two games proved to be fateful.

They lost at Leicester yet again, this time 2-1 in the league cup. Then, on 28 September 2013, they lost 1-0 at the City Ground, a game in which Richard Keogh was sent off for two bookable offences.

The loss left Derby with a record of three wins, two draws and four defeats from their opening nine games of the season, sitting 14th in the early table.

***

Initial thoughts on the sacking of Nigel Clough
September 29, 2013

I believe that Nigel Clough should have been allowed to carry on the long-term rebuilding job he was doing at Derby County. I believe that he can be very proud of the work he has done for us and am concerned that the foundations he put in place from youth level up could now be at risk.

I think most fans understood that he was working under severe budgetary restrictions in comparison to our local rivals and to those teams coming out of the Premier League with parachutes quilted with Rupert Murdoch's millions. Not every parachute team comes down in a good way, but they all have the chance to offer wages that clubs like ours can't, which distorts the transfer market.

Clough's small squad was undoubtedly in need of bolstering. He was not able to make 11 changes for a midweek League Cup tie, like Billy Davies did this week ahead of the East Midlands derby, or Nigel Pearson, who made eight changes to the Leicester team that luckily beat us.

The board have stated that their aim is to compete at the top end of the Championship this season. They obviously feel that there is someone else out there who could drag us into the top six and have lost faith in Clough's ability to do so.

Take a look at the current top six in the league table. QPR, Burnley, Leicester, Watford, Forest, Reading. All four of the teams we've lost to in the league this season feature there. And of the six, only Burnley do not enjoy a huge financial advantage over Derby. Whether Sean Dyche's team will have the squad depth to compete at the top over the entire season very much remains to be seen.

Dyche, you may remember, did an excellent job on a tight budget at Watford, only to be elbowed aside for Gianfranco Zola once the Pozzo family rode into town with their unique plan to use Watford as an English outlet, or franchise, for their international stockpile of players. It was unfair on Dyche, but the club argued that the parameters had entirely changed. Is that the case at Derby?

For years now, Clough has struggled along from window to window, never able to make wholesale changes. He has rummaged in bargain bins and pulled out rough gems. Unsurprisingly, not every signing he has made has come off – Maguire, Tyson and O'Connor spring to mind as poor buys, but their very names demonstrate the market level he was operating in.

Clough was far from perfect. He made plenty of mistakes. He was probably loyal to a fault with some players. But he also did a lot of work to further the long-term development of a club which had lurched from crisis to crisis in the preceding few years.

Is it just a coincidence that we've seen Jeff Hendrick (full Republic of Ireland international), Hughes (England U21, at the age of 18) and Mason Bennett (England U19 at 17) develop like rockets in the last couple of seasons? I don't think so.

Yes, the team have conceded some stupid goals this season, but players such as Kieron Freeman and Craig Forsyth, who have been culpable, are inexperienced. If they were seasoned, battle-hardened pros, you could ask questions of the manager.

Again, this is the market he's been shopping in. Moulding raw talent, not managing established talent. Taking on players who have, for whatever reason, not quite made it elsewhere and trying to coax the best out of them. Trying to play the right way, which takes more character and bravery than just renouncing responsibility, lumping it in the general direction of the forwards and hoping for the best.

There were some really, really good signs in the football we've been playing this season and I had the feeling that at some point, it was going to click and we were going to go on a run. What happens now is, at this stage, anyone's guess.

It seems that we will know the identity of the new manager very soon – possibly even by tomorrow. Time will tell if the board are right or wrong. Either way, this has to go down as a very sad day in the history of our football club.

***

Initial thoughts on the appointment of Steve McClaren
October 4, 2013

If you're in mid-table,
if no one else can help

*and if you can find them,
maybe you can hire...*

Firstly, can I implore Derby County not to change manager again for another five years, because Mrs DCB has told me with some justification that for the last few days she has felt like a 'football widow'. For the sake of my future happiness, we can't be going through this upheaval every season.

Secondly, the speed with which the new managerial appointment was announced was incredible. The process, we were told, was 'well under way' at the point when Clough's sacking was revealed. It was all done so quickly that there was absolutely no time to dwell on the change.

Then the whole *fait accompli* was topped off with a *Roy of the Rovers*-style half-time intervention against Ipswich, which helped the Rams rescue a point from a game in which they were apparently dead, buried and humiliated to boot[40].

But let's backtrack to Saturday evening. At that time, Tony Pulis, having been pictured at the match with Sam Rush, was the red-hot favourite. I hope a few mug punters lost a bundle on that particular wager.

The next name to be thrown out there by one or two folk who genuinely were in the know was Steve McClaren.

Every Derby fan will have instantly thought back to the days of Agent Schteve and then further back, to the Wembley 'wally with the brolly'. Many (and I include myself in this) will have instinctively recoiled in horror.

There was no time for any speculation. By the time I was interviewed on Sky Sports News Radio on Monday morning, the dust had already settled. Pulis, thank god, was not in the frame. We were able to discuss McClaren in the near certainty that he would be in post very soon

---

[40] Derby 4 Ipswich 4, 1 October 2013. Darren Wassall was asked to coach the team, who slumped to 4-1 down by half-time, forcing the watching Steve McClaren and Paul Simpson to intervene.

– but not as a manager in the 'traditional' sense.

Sam Rush explained on Sunday night that Clough's successor would be a head coach and would work alongside a sporting director. The sporting director, who is not likely to be appointed for some time yet, will eventually take charge of the club's scouting operation and administer off-the-field matters – leaving the head coach to get on with drilling the players on the training ground. These two would work together on player recruitment, along with Rush.

Once this new structure was disclosed, the 'wally' who tanked at Forest no longer seemed like such a ridiculous idea. McClaren's coaching credentials, after all, have never been in any doubt.

During my SSN Radio interview, the presenter told me a story about a Manchester United v Derby game he covered in the late 1990s with Jan Mølby. Before kick-off, Mølby excitedly dragged the reporter down to pitchside to watch the Rams warm up, because he had heard great things about our innovative first-team coach and wanted to see his methods first-hand.

The history books show how Derby's fortunes declined after McClaren left us for Manchester United, where he helped Sir Alex Ferguson's men to win the treble. There are trophies on his managerial CV as well – the League Cup for Middlesbrough and the Eredivisie with FC Twente, who had never before won the Dutch league.

There are also notable failures. He couldn't get England to Euro 2008 and he got nowhere in the Bundesliga with VfL Wolfsburg. However, his continental and international experiences – good and bad – undeniably give him a much wider scope of contacts than Clough had.

Soon after McClaren arrived at Pride Park on Monday, Paul Simpson sauntered in and then Eric Steele's name started to float around on Twitter. Steele is an extremely highly regarded coach, nominally of goalkeepers, but doubtless his remit will be much wider than that. He spent the last five years at Manchester United and we are extremely fortunate that he was released by David Moyes this summer, was still available and, crucially, living in the Derbyshire area.

It felt, for a delirious moment, as though Sam Rush had called The A Team. If McClaren was Hannibal, Simpson was The Face, which unfortunately, for the purposes of my metaphor, makes a Murdoch of the august Steele. Mr T has not been spotted at Moor Farm, at the time of writing.

Seriously though, there was something hugely serendipitous about the fact that this group of coaches were all available when the time came – all three well-respected and liked by Rams fans for their achievements at the club in previous spells with us. Even BBC Radio Derby's shrewd old exquisitor Colin Gibson was back, ushered in on Sunday evening as a 'media consultant'.

Nigel Clough, the club was saying loud and clear, is not the only person around with personal ties to Derby County. And Gibson's instantly recognisable tones were going to help them to win the PR war.

Gibson was presumably involved in the planning of McClaren's opening statements to the media, which made plenty of references to the fantastic times from his first spell at the club. The 1990s, when we had real players. When the ground was full. When we were in the Premier League, playing stylish football, with continental, even global stars on show. We can get back there. It is possible.

This is a reset. It is much easier to be positive when you are new to a situation than it is when you are up to your neck in the swamp of details that embody it. An intense character, maybe Clough was weighed down by too many defeats, too many setbacks, the relentless pressure to shake off the past and just fly. Then again, perhaps if he'd been left to get on with it, the team would finally have clicked against Ipswich and gone on the sort of run that we know that they are capable of. We'll never know.

McClaren and co were very respectful to Nigel in their opening press statements, leaving Rush to fire a few carefully aimed darts at the departed manager. Yes, he had done well, but he hadn't done *that* well. We had been outperformed and left behind by certain clubs, Rush felt, although he didn't name names.

Usually, a new manager, head coach or whatever, arrives at a club in a time of crisis. That wasn't ever likely to happen under Nigel. We weren't going to go down under his management, but Rush has decided on our behalf that we weren't going to get promoted either – at least not quickly enough for the owners' liking.

That figures. Although it isn't always immediately obvious, they do cover considerable losses every year and the events of the past week have shown that they are not prepared to continue ploughing in their millions year-on-year to kick around in the middle of the second tier, regardless of whether promotion is a reasonable demand given our wage bill. God knows how much bleating W. Brett Wilson has had to endure on Twitter over the past couple of years, along the lines of 'spend more of your own money on our club'. Presumably, that is not what he had in mind when he decided to have some fun with our franchise.

Rush's contention is that higher budgets do not automatically equate to success. Yes, spending less stacks the odds against you, but as Crystal Palace and Blackpool under Ian Holloway have shown, it is not a permanent barrier to success.

However, the drawbridge to the Premier League is creaking ever upwards as parachute payments are gradually inflated. Take a look at the top six for the past few seasons (with the three promoted clubs in bold): –

2012/13 – CARDIFF, HULL, Watford, Brighton, PALACE, Leicester
2011/12 – READING, SOUTHAMPTON, WEST HAM, Birmingham, Blackpool, Cardiff
2010/11 – QPR, NORWICH, SWANSEA, Cardiff, Reading, Forest
2009/10 – NEWCASTLE, WBA, Forest, Cardiff, Leicester, BLACK-POOL

The same names crop up over and again. Cardiff every season for the past four, Reading two out of four, Leicester two out of four, Forest two out of four. Newcastle and West Ham bouncing straight back up. Having gone up as champions, Reading and QPR have come down again, but will not expect to hang around for more than a single season.

When asked whether it was realistic to expect to compete with teams who are much 'better off', Rush launched into a mini-diatribe about putting an end to the 'poor Derby' image – even if it is true that we have less money to spend than our direct competitors for the top six.

Rush has repeatedly said that our wage bill is average for this league. So to break into the group of clubs who are currently ahead of us without spending more, according to Rush, we need to improve our coaching, recruitment and 'football relationships'. For 'a club like Derby', as Rush puts it – one without parachute money or oodles of debt finance to blow, he means – it really is about that well-worn business cliche of doing more with less.

So, although McClaren referenced some of the stars of the 1990s in his opening press statements and the impression was strongly given that we will now finally start to look for players from abroad again, let's not think for a moment that we will suddenly be able to sign a new wave of Igor Štimacs. Established internationals now play Champions League football and command pay packets to match. Jim Smith may have come close to signing Roberto Baggio once, but those, to quote Lou Reed, were different times.

If we are to enter the global market for players, we will of course be competing with many far richer clubs. But if there is a genuine desire to expand our recruitment machine to Europe and beyond, this can only be a good thing.

Through his actions last weekend and in his press statements, Rush has made it clear that he is not here to make easy decisions and stay in a comfort zone. He is here to move the club forward. Here, in fact, to drive the club forward. There's no room for sentiment in a business which brings to mind a famous quote of Hunter S. Thompson's, 'The TV business is uglier than most things. It is normally perceived as some kind of cruel and shallow money trench... a long plastic hallway where thieves and pimps run free and good men die like dogs, for no good reason.'

It's hard to see football much differently sometimes, but we continue to try.

McClaren's debut proper came at Pride Park against Leeds United and Derby's dominance over the Whites survived the managerial change, with the Rams winning 3-1.

Next came a 3-2 victory at Watford, a 1-1 home draw with Birmingham and a 2-1 defeat at QPR, before Sheffield Wednesday were dispatched 3-0 at home.

After Derby won 1-0 at Bournemouth, McClaren had claimed four wins, one draw and one loss from his first six games, with Derby rising to 5th in the table by the end of November.

***

Regime change – is the Mac the Messiah, or is the 'improvement' an illusion? November 30, 2013

A chapter in the excellent football analytics book *The Numbers Game,* by Chris Anderson and David Sally, looks at the effects that replacing the manager does – and doesn't – have.

In Simon Kuper and Dr Stefan Szymanski's *Why England Lose* (AKA *Soccernomics*), we learned that hiring a new boss usually has a lot less impact than fans tend to believe it will, because a club's final league position is largely determined by its wage bill. Anderson & Sally cite further research which backs this up to an extent, demonstrating that in the past decade of Premier League seasons, 'wages explain 81 per cent of the variation in average final [league] position'.

That means that unless something changes very dramatically, Manchester United will never be relegated again and Stockport County will never make it into the Champions League. But there is still plenty of room for a manager to significantly influence a club's performance.

An obvious current example is United's early-season wobble under David Moyes, who has been 'driving a race car as if it's a Skoda', according to a United fan of my acquaintance. Nevertheless, they are still sixth in the table at the time of writing, only a point off fourth. The 81 per cent determined by their financial might means that they almost certainly will still qualify for the Champions League, but whether Moyes will be able to win the league at the first attempt is another matter.

You can also look at Derby's last pathetic effort in the Premier League for a different example. Although managers Billy Davies and Paul Jewell both performed dismally, signing inadequate players, flouncing and generally embarrassing themselves and everybody connected with the club, it should be remembered that our wage budget was the lowest in the division that year. Chelsea spent 6.5 times as much as us on wages that year – and, funnily enough, beat us 6-1 at Stamford Bridge. United beat Chelsea to the title that year despite a wage disadvantage of £51m, but they still spent about £20m more than Arsenal, who came third – and about £20m more than the bottom three combined. Distorted by the huge wage bills of the fat cats, the average PL club spent just under £60m on player salaries in 2007/08. Derby spent around £26m.

I've heard it said that Sir Alex Ferguson or Arsène Wenger wouldn't have been able to save us from relegation that year. I'm not so sure about that, because they would extracted much better value from that £26m than Davies and Jewell did – but nevertheless, any manager who had piloted us to safety would have deserved huge praise for their achievement. And it will be the same situation next time we get promoted.

Nevertheless, despite the huge advantage that comes with comparative financial might, it is not a given that the highest-paying club will win the league, far from it – and in the Championship, a team can finish as low as sixth and still claw their way into the Promised Land via the play-offs. And it's the manager who works with the players, picks the team and at least traditionally, signs the players (although this is changing for some clubs, who are moving to a sporting director/head coach model).

As Anderson and Sally put it, 'Player wage data are not pure measures of players' ability; they are also measures of managers' coaching and scouting skills.' If reports are to be believed, Clough would have loaned in Manchester United youngsters Larnell Cole and Michael Keane, plus Stoke City winger Brek Shea. McClaren instead brought in Andre Wisdom and Simon Dawkins, plus Kalifa Cisse and now Keane. We'll never know if Clough's recruits would have performed as well as McClaren's, although it's clear that Wisdom was a great loan signing – and interesting that both men would have signed Keane.

With a poor manager at the helm, Anderson & Sally continue, 'Results will dip, players will grow disillusioned, weak links will multiply and the fans will drift away.' I don't think there is any suggestion that the players weren't playing for Clough, but fans definitely were drifting away and ultimately, that is why Rush acted.

However, the short-term boost to attendances will only be maintained if results remain good. Firing Clough to appoint McClaren's team was certainly a shot in the arm in terms of reviving public interest in the club, but it remains to be seen over the long term whether the new men will do better than Clough and his staff could.

A study of how teams performed immediately before and after they sacked their manager in the Dutch Eredivisie between 1986 and 2004 showed that typically, the team were underperforming drastically across the four games before the manager left. On average, in the next few games, their performance reverted to what would be expected of the club. This is commonly referred to as the 'new manager bounce', or similar.

The author of the Dutch study, which is cited in *The Numbers Game*, then compared these findings to the results for teams who suffered a similar dip in form, but did not fire the manager. Their results in the next few games showed an almost identical pattern to the ones who had made a change – they improved back to the kind of level that would generally be expected of that club. Sue Bridgewater, of the Warwick Business School, did a similar analysis of sackings in the

Premier League from 1992 to 2008, with similar findings.

What this means, in a nutshell, is that 'sackings do not improve club performances. Clubs simply regress to the mean'. Temporary short-term fluctuations in form are pretty meaningless. What matters is the long-term direction of the club.

Financial clout is the most important factor, but as Rush pointed out when he made his move on Clough, you also need excellence in recruitment, coaching and tactics to make the most of your resources and these are the areas where you can make a case that he made the right decision.

However, after Clough's departure, Ted Knutson, lead trader for a sports betting company and editor of statsbomb.com, tweeted to say that the sacking was 'tremendously stupid'. Knutson has developed his own model to analyse overall team performance and while it cannot be shared with the public, he tells me that under Clough, he predicted success for Derby this season.

'Through the game Clough was fired, Derby were sixth of the 24 teams in the model, which uses statistically significant metrics to try and predict how teams will do throughout the rest of the season,' Knutson explains.

'Obviously I am just some guy with a spreadsheet, but the model is typically very good at quickly sorting out the good teams and the bad... Derby were definitely on the good side.

'Sixth might not sound like much, but given how tight Championship teams tend to cluster, Derby were well above the field and were doing a really good job at producing a style of play that would win over the long term.

'Given they are up against teams with the budgets of QPR, Watford, Wigan, Forest, Brighton, Reading and also... that Clough had actually cut the wage bill significantly over the last few seasons while continuing to compete, Derby's performance was fairly impressive.'

However, that 19 per cent that Anderson and Sally define as being within the manager's power to affect comes back to my mind when I think of the win at Watford. With the score at 2-2 and the Rams under the pump, the coaching staff conferred, debated sending on Kieron Freeman and instead decided, 'f**k it, let's go for it'. They threw on Conor Sammon and were rewarded when the big Irishman poked home the winner. I don't know if Clough, scarred as he was by the concession of so many late goals earlier in his tenure, would have gambled and sent on another striker that afternoon.

It may well turn out that Rush was right in his belief that McClaren will get more out of the squad than Clough did. However, before we get too excited about McClaren's first few games, we should remember that he has been handed solid foundations to build on by his predecessor.

In summary, I honestly think that the improvement in results we've seen in the last few weeks would have largely happened anyway if Clough had stayed. The managerial change was chiefly motivated by the club's desire to attract back the fans who had lost patience with the slow pace of progress at the Stadium Formerly Known as Pride Park[41] and decided to stay away.

The challenge for McClaren and co is to sustain the current level of performance over the rest of the season and challenge for the top six. His honeymoon period will come to an end at some point, but let's hope that tomorrow's game at Wigan keeps it going for a little longer just yet.

It did.

Derby won 3-1 at Wigan, then won consecutive home games against Middlesbrough (2-1) and Blackpool (5-1), climbing to 4th in the table.

***

---

[41] In November 2013, it was announced that Pride Park would be renamed the iPro Stadium, in a deal worth £7m to the club over the next ten years. The rebrand would be launched at the home game against Blackpool on 7 December 2013.

In praise of Chris Martin
December 8, 2013

On the walk up to the DW Stadium, I got chatting to a Wigan fan about the upcoming game and how our respective teams had been doing. You won't be surprised to learn that he was pretty unhappy about how they'd been doing and fed up with Owen Coyle[42]. Anyway, the fan asked me about our main man up-front.

I said, 'Chris Martin – and I guarantee he will piss you off. He's clever, holds up the ball and knows how to win free kicks, if you know what I mean.'

He looked at me and said, 'You mean he's a cheating bastard?'

Cheating is a strong word. But I did chuckle heartily at one point during the game when Martin was put through just inside the Wigan half and, rather than use his searing pace to storm through, had a little look to see where the retreating defender was, stepped across him and fell over. Free kick. And of course, he won a penalty on the day.

I noticed some weeks ago that according to whoscored.com stats, Martin is the most 'fouled' player in the Championship. Opposition managers and players would surely contest that statement – so let's change it and say that he has won the most free kicks, which is undeniable. Paul Ince is the latest manager to fume at Martin, who got the wrong side of the defender in the box and went to ground after the slightest of pushes from his panicked opponent. Peno[43].

This is one of the main reasons I'm growing to love Martin so much – he's the sort of player who drives opposition fans and managers insane. If he played for anybody else against us, I'm sure I'd end up calling him every name under the sun. Ince's description of the way Martin

---

[42] Wigan were 14th in the table on the day this post was published.

[43] Martin won and duly converted a penalty for the first goal in Derby's 5-1 thrashing of Ince's Blackpool, on 7 December 2013.

won the penalty yesterday was a classic – it was uncannily reminiscent of the way my dad likes to describe Franny Lee's ability to do the same back in the glory days.

If you have no pace as a striker, you have to affect the game in other ways. Martin relieves the pressure on our defence by holding the ball up, bringing the onrushing midfielders into play and by buying free kicks. Technically, he is very adept – I love some of his flicks and tricks, perhaps the best recent example being his improvised assist for Johnny Russell's goal against Leeds.

And he can finish. He seems to have put an end to our woes with penalties and can be trusted to slot the ball away when a chance comes his way from open play. The way he's going, he could just turn out to be the '20 goal a season man' we've been after for so long.

***

Eight out of ten ain't bad! McClaren's fast start reviewed
December 20, 2013

Steve McClaren's record as DCFC manager
P10 W8 D1 L1 F24 A9 GD +15 Pts 25

Unbelievable, sensational, ridiculous. I keep looking at the numbers and thinking, 'I must have written them down wrong.' Plenty of Derby fans will have spent Monday morning gazing admiringly at the league table, or chortling at a graphic which showed the Rams to be fourth-top of the European form league.

To my mind, there have been a few factors which have helped McClaren to start in such a spectacular fashion – some very much within his control, others outside of it, although that takes nothing away from what is a splendid achievement.

Turning the disorganised, demoralised rabble who shipped four in 45 nightmarish minutes to an Ipswich side accurately described by my father as 'shite' into the well-oiled, gleaming machine currently slicing through the Championship's lesser lights with such ease, McClaren has rapidly dispensed with any doubts about his coaching and managerial credentials. His job now is just to continue steering us in the right direction.

Here are a few of the reasons he has succeeded so far, as far as I can see.

Recruitment

It's tempting to say that McClaren sorted out our defensive shortcomings by signing Andre Wisdom – so I will say it. McClaren sorted out our defensive shortcomings by signing Andre Wisdom.

The Liverpool man's power, presence and technical qualities mean that he is manifestly a cut above at this level and securing him on a season-long loan was a serious coup. The Wisdom deal highlights the point Sam Rush made about 'football relationships' after he sacked Clough. Liverpool knew that when they sent Wisdom to us, the defender would benefit from top-class coaching.

Simon Dawkins was an imaginative signing and is getting stronger all the time, adding a different dimension to our play and fitting into the system nicely on the left of the front three. Unlike Wisdom, it seems likely that Dawkins's deal could be made permanent, either in January or next summer and I don't think any Rams fan would argue that he has strengthened the team. 26 years old and yet still relatively inexperienced, his is a unique story in English football. Hopefully he will have the chance to spend his best years at Derby and develop further with regular playing time.

These two deals were, it has to be said, rather better than some of the bizarre signings that McClaren made when he was at Forest. At that time, The Mac was seemingly rather out of touch with English football and ended up bringing in players who were good when he was last around – Jonathan Greening, the pensionable George Boateng and

Matt Derbyshire spring to mind. On the other hand, that athletic paragon Andy Reid proved worth his not inconsiderable weight in gold and so even at that point, McClaren's compass wasn't totally leading him astray.

After spending a few months coaching under the Del Boy of English football, Harry Redknapp, it now seems that McClaren has more of a handle on the domestic transfer market. He will also be helped in his recruitment decisions by the new head of football operations, Chris Evans. It's worth remembering that Clough kicked against the idea of a 'technical director' or 'director of football', wanting to retain control himself – mind you, McClaren will retain the final say on player signings, rather than handing responsibility over to Evans or anybody else, hence Evans's rather curious title.

Player availability

With the exception of Johnny Russell's leg-break and Zak Whitbread's calf problem, we have managed to avoid any serious injuries in the McClaren era so far (touch wood). Jeff Hendrick is back after the bad 'un he suffered at Yeovil, Jamie Ward's hamstrings have held up and nobody has been poleaxed by a demonic two-footed lunge lately. Long may this continue.

The only players still out are those returning from long lay-offs, like Zak Whitbread, Mark O'Brien and Paul Coutts. As a result, McClaren has been able to call on the same players consistently and not really had to chop and change. The core of the team have played week in, week out – and played bloody well, too.

Tactics

McClaren instantly chose to play 4-3-3 and has stuck to it. Fielding a defensive midfielder behind the attack-minded Hughes and Bryson allows them to go forward with more freedom and has always been the best way of fitting both of those players into the team.

Bryson has become an absolute beast in the 4-3-3, terrorising lumbering centre-backs and midfielders into surrendering possession and creating goals galore in the process. His Direct Goal Involvement of 41.7 per cent of Derby's 48 league and cup goals is hugely impressive.

In terms of substitutions, the most obvious example of a positive change that ultimately turned a game for us was the deployment of Conor Sammon at Watford. McClaren has also been far more prepared to use Mason Bennett than Clough was; however, his attitude towards Michael Jacobs – who was promptly loaned out to League 1 Wolves, where he has made two starts and two sub appearances – perhaps sheds some light on Clough's reluctance to use the young winger earlier in the campaign.

The fixture list

I said at the start of the season that the opening run of games looked pretty tough and that if we got through it in decent shape, we'd have a platform to build on for the rest of the season. We did that and, with respect to recent opponents like Charlton, Bournemouth and Sheffield Wednesday, they are not of the same calibre as Burnley, Forest and Leicester and came into this season with very different aims.

That doesn't lessen the achievement of winning eight of the last ten in any way and with struggling Doncaster next up at home, followed by mid-table Huddersfield and bottom-club Barnsley away, you get the feeling that the excellent run could continue for a while yet.

Luck

No team can go on a long winning run without enjoying their share of good fortune. The most recent example is Jamie Ward's free kick against Charlton, a typically milky effort which would not have troubled Ben Alnwick without the help of a nick off the wall. 'The football gods were smiling on that free kick,' said McClaren after the game.

Blackpool at home would have been a much more difficult game if the Tangerines had been able to field even one natural centre-back. As it was, stand-ins Neal Bishop and Chris Basham, both midfielders by trade, did their best, but ultimately could not cope.

Catching Wigan just after a Thursday night Europa League game gave us another real opportunity. Knowing how much the night game would have taken out of the Latics, McClaren encouraged his side to start fast. It worked a treat.

Little breaks like those have been going in our favour of late and have helped us to put together this startling run of victories.

Reason says that the run of form has to end some time – that one afternoon, our luck will just be out – but after six wins on the trot, you feel like it is just destined to go on forever, that you'll never lose again.

Of course, Derby did lose again… But not in 2013. The festive period yielded wins against Doncaster (3-1) and Barnsley (2-1), plus a Boxing Day draw at Huddersfield (1-1).

Wigan played party poopers on New Year's Day, leaving the iPro Stadium with the points after a 1-0 smash-and-grab and then there was a heavy 4-1 loss at Leicester, before the Rams got back to winning ways by beating Brighton 1-0 at home on 18 January. A 1-1 draw at Blackburn one week later kept them in 4th place, with 27 games gone.

***

Clough looks back in anger as Mac builds on firm foundations
January 26, 2014

After an unspectacular start to his fifth full season in charge at Derby County, Nigel Clough returned to the City Ground, to face Billy Davies, the hostility of a Nottinghamshire crowd who used to revere him and the Sky television cameras, trained on him with basilisk impassivity, waiting for something to happen.

There was nothing between the two teams and the tension mounted until finally, something did happen. Forest's Andy Reid fizzed in a dangerous corner, Craig Forsyth failed to mark Jack Hobbs and the centre-back powered an unstoppable header past Lee Grant. Forest led 1-0.

Fast-forward four incredible months and Brighton & Hove Albion are the visitors to the newly christened iPro Stadium. The Seagulls swing in a corner, Forsyth loses Matthew Upson and the centre-back powers in a header, which looks for all the world a goal until Grant's lightning reflexes come to the rescue. 0-0 and eventually 1-0 Derby, for Steve McClaren's 11th win in his first 16 league matches.

It was sad to learn this week, via an interview with the *Sheffield Tele-graph*'s Alan Biggs, that Clough still feels deeply hurt by his dismissal from Derby – but unsurprising. We know the man's intensity of character and his fierce belief in the value of loyalty. And of course, who else has ever managed a club with a statue of his father standing outside the ground?

That Nigel did all he could under difficult financial constraints is un-questioned. That the club is in an infinitely better place than it was when he inherited it from the incompetent Paul Jewell, nobody could deny. And signs were there even in the first few games of this season that the squad had improved again, as an impressive win at Brighton was followed up by casually superior swattings of Yeovil Town and Millwall.

Sadly, these successes in the south were only seen live by the travel-ling hardcore, while the Pride Park faithful's early-season optimism was crushed by three defeats in the first four home games. That the three losses came against some of the strongest teams in the division cut no ice with disillusioned fans, who were simply tired of what they saw as stagnation. Worse, arguably, than open anger in the stands is the apathy revealed by empty seats.

Derby had been atypically patient with Clough, allowing him the time to bring about the thorough transformation that the club so desperately needed. As a result, the squad taken on by McClaren was younger, more talented, notably more athletic and resolute than the grim as-sortment of misfits, has-beens and costly failures he took on – with a readily identifiable style of play, favouring patient, short passing through midfield, but also dangerous on the counter, with galloping full-backs prepared to supplement the attack.

It is understandable, therefore, when Clough looks at the form the Rams have enjoyed ever since he left and says, 'We must have brought some pretty bad players in… to get these results! It would be nice one time to inherit a fit, organised, talented squad of players of good character… which some people have been fortunate enough to inherit.'

There's something quite eerie about the idea of another Clough, exiled to Yorkshire, nursing his grievances over the way Derby treated him. Is this 2014, or 1974?

Of course, the vast majority of the players are still Clough signings, but it's undeniable that McClaren has, so far at least, coaxed a little extra out of them, as well as identifying three new players to greatly improved the squad. The defence, under McClaren, has tightened up. 13 goals were shipped in Clough's nine Championship matches of 2013/14, compared to 18 in McClaren's first 17 league games – eight of which came in the four games for which Richard Keogh was absent. Andre Wisdom is at least partly responsible for this improvement and is a startling upgrade on Adam Smith and Kieron Freeman, neither of whom looked capable of becoming the long-term replacement for John Brayford at right-back.

Tactically, there are clear differences too. Clough would never have gone balls-out attack against Brighton at home, with the clock ticking down and the score 0-0. McClaren sensed the visitors' happiness to nurdle their way to a dismal draw and sent on attackers to disrupt them – so committed was The Mac to the attack that he even brought on Conor Sammon when Wisdom had to come off injured, asking Jeff Hendrick fill in as a makeshift right-back, rather than doing the orthodox thing. Playing with four forwards could easily have gone wrong. But how many times did Clough's attempts to shut up shop and hang on to a result lead to the bitter disappointment of a late sickener? We started the season that way, conceding a last-minute equaliser against Blackburn – and perhaps that was the moment when many people, rightly or wrongly, lost faith.

The reputation of the new coaching team has also become a helpful factor for us when it comes to recruitment. Take our latest signing, the young Dutch goalkeeper Kelle Roos. If his agent is to be believed (so you must take it with a pinch of salt), there was plenty of interest in him from the top two divisions, but the chance to work with a coach as highly respected as Eric Steele was surely a factor in where Roos saw his future – and he would have been aware of McClaren's successes at FC Twente. Could the same have been said about Nigel Clough and Martin Taylor?

In a recent interview with the BBC, Patrick Bamford revealed how the McClaren factor paved the way for his loan move to Derby.

'Chelsea were big fans and knew how Steve worked,' Bamford said. 'Michael Emenalo [Chelsea's technical director] said he was a great coach and I would come on leaps and bounds.'

Roberto Mancini recently made statements comparable to Clough's about Manchester City's current success, telling the BBC, 'I'm happy that City is one of the best teams in England because I built this team. The players that score the goals are players that I bought – Agüero, Džeko, Yaya Toure, David Silva and Nasri.'

Mancini qualified his bid to take most of the credit for Manuel Pellegrini's work with the admission, 'After four or five years, maybe the manager needs to change team. I did my job.'

Hopefully, having gone on to enjoy success elsewhere, Clough will eventually be able to look back on his time at Derby with the same sort of detachment. He can feel satisfied with a job well done and as the club builds on the solid foundations he put into place, should try to take solace in the fact that his contribution will not be forgotten.

Besides, if I was a Sheffield United fan, I would not like to think that my club's manager spent his time wishing he had been allowed to continue in a different job, rather than being focused upon the task in hand.

Next came a couple of crazy games. Derby came back from 2-0 down to beat Yeovil 3-2 at the iPro, before collapsing from 3-1 up to draw 3-3 at Birmingham.

Things were a bit less wild in the next match, a 1-0 home win over QPR, which was settled by John Eustace's header.

30 games gone, 55 points on the board and the Rams still sat 4th.

***

Can we do it? Assessing Derby County's chances of promotion
February 16, 2014

Last week's victory over QPR has cemented Derby County into the play-off places for the foreseeable future and, following on from the similarly gritty 1-0 win against Brighton, confirmed our status as real promotion contenders who can mix it with our direct rivals.

Beating Harry Redknapp's expensively assembled side ended an unwelcome streak of six defeats against our fellow top six sides, which tended to suggest that while the Rams had too much firepower for the majority of Championship teams, the best sides were just that bit better.

However, it should be remembered that the majority of those defeats – at home against Leicester, Burnley and Reading, plus the loss at Forest – happened under the management of Nigel Clough. The defeats at QPR and Leicester have been very much the exception to what has become the rule under Steve McClaren. Twenty games after he officially took responsibility for the team, Mac's points per game average is a whopping 2.15. Over a 46-game season, running at that rate would earn a club 99 points and almost certainly the title of Football League champions. If the Rams can keep going at that rate right to the end of the season, they will finish on 89 points, which would be enough for automatic promotion more often than not.

Barring an unlikely meltdown, Leicester look to be gone and are unsurprisingly 1/3 to win the league at the time of writing, but QPR and Burnley will now be looking over their shoulders. Meanwhile, those perennial pundits' favourites, Forest, remain below us in fifth, despite not having lost in their last 13 league games. The gap back to Brighton & Hove Albion, in seventh, is currently nine points.

Looking at the odds for promotion, Leicester (1/10) and QPR (4/5) are favourites, with Burnley 8/5 and Derby 2/1. There are still a lot of difficult games to come and Sheffield Wednesday, our next opponents, have been on a real mission to strengthen their squad in the past few days, leading some pundits to suggest that they could hinder our promotion push.

However, our record against the lesser lights this season has been absolutely phenomenal and while the East Midlands derby and the game at Turf Moor both have the air of 'six-pointers', it is by continuing to take full advantage of games against poorer teams that Derby will stay in the promotion hunt. The eye-catching thing is that all season, we have only lost once to a team not currently in the play-off spots – the slightly unlucky 1-0 home defeat to Wigan Athletic – and the majority of our remaining games come against teams who are haunted by the threat of relegation, or just floating along in mid-table.

A lot will change in the coming weeks. There are always surprise results and players get injured – losing Charlie Austin has been a massive blow to QPR and even signing a glut of new strikers doesn't guarantee that his goals will be replaced, as we saw when they failed to break us down at the iPro last week.

The momentum continued, with two more 1-0 wins over Sheffield Wednesday and Bournemouth, before the first genuine stall of the new McClaren era.

First, Derby lost 2-0 at Burnley, a game in which Chris Martin was given a second booking for 'simulation', having been fouled in the box. In his absence, Derby then lost 1-0 at home to Millwall.

They failed to score in their next two games, a pair of goalless draws with Bolton at home and Reading away, meaning that they went into the East Midlands Derby on 22 March 2014 without a win or goal in their previous four.

Was this a good time or a bad time to face the auld enemy?

***

Nottingham Forest preview, with Seat Pitch blog
March 19, 2014

If you're anything like me, you'll already be getting a few butterflies about Saturday. I was thinking about writing a preview, when I received a tweet from Forest blog Seat Pitch, asking if I would be interested in answering a few questions. I said sure, why not – and while you're at it, I have a few of my own.

DCB: Despite a run of only one league win in eight, Forest have only dropped from fifth place to sixth. What are the reasons for the dip in form – and is a potential Derby v Forest play-off clash still on?

Seat Pitch (SP): The simple answer is injuries. We've suffered with injuries throughout the season — Chris Cohen, Dexter Blackstock and Kelvin Wilson — and having glimpsed how good our midfield trio of Andy Reid, Henri Lansbury and David Vaughan actually are when fit, they've all been sidelined. Add to that the loss of Jack Hobbs and our defence isn't as strong as it was might be.

Subsequently we've been without Guy Moussi, Eric Lichaj, Rafik Djebbour and Radi Majewski — of those four, only Lichaj appears to be a long-term absentee now, but our midfield has been decimated.

Of course, Billy Davies's sides traditionally go on a bad run of form around this time of year and it's come off the back of 14 games unbeaten. Hopefully, it'll turn around soon — we're still in the play-off positions as it stands.

DCB: Can Jonathan Greening still play? I assume he's been used in front of the back four, in a similar role to that which John Eustace usually fills for us?

SP: Greening has come back in from the cold, after spending most of the season as an under-21 coach, to cover the midfield deficiencies. His performance at the base of the diamond against Doncaster was widely praised by Forest fans who've rarely seen the best of him since he signed in 2011. However, he's only started three games this season so it's hard to judge the 35-year-old.

DCB: Do you think that Billy Davies will stay if Forest aren't promoted this season?

SP: There are two schools of thought. The first says that Leicester stuck with Nigel Pearson and look at them now – next season should be progression and stability and without the injuries we've suffered this season. The second says that Davies has been backed to the hilt, injuries are an excuse for poor performances and his behaviour is not becoming of someone representing a club with the history and heritage of ours. I'm not sure he'll be around if we don't go up this season, but that's just speculation.

DCB: If you were to go up, are you at all worried by the example of what happened that last time Davies got a club promoted to the Premier League (I hardly need remind you who, when and what happened)?

SP: I think Davies himself would acknowledge that Derby got promoted too soon and that they weren't ready for the step up. The investment we've seen in the past few years means that we have the making of a squad that might hold its own in the Premier League. Of course, whether Davies will fare any better or not remains to be seen.

DCB: Forest recently reported losses of £17m for the 2012/13 season. Do you expect similar losses to be sustained this season and are you worried about a potential transfer embargo being implemented next

January if so?

SP: I don't think anybody was particularly surprised that we lost so much money last season and I don't imagine it will be any better next season. Long-term, those kind of losses are not sustainable, but promotion is the aim and that's the gamble we're taking at the moment. While the prospect of a transfer embargo next January is worrying, it looks like Financial Fair Play might be reassessed, given that many clubs in the Championship will be facing a similar penalty.

DCB: In recent seasons, the East Midlands derby has thrown up some incredible stories, with some unfortunate behaviour being exhibited at times. Do you think that Davies's touchline ban (assuming the appeal fails) and the absence of Nigel Clough could lead to a slightly less frenzied and fraught atmosphere on the pitch on this occasion?

SP: With Davies's FA hearing now postponed until next week, he'll have the option of being on the touchline — he chose to remain in the stands against Doncaster last weekend. However, Davies and Nigel Clough seemed to remain cordial in the FA Cup tie last month [Clough's Sheffield United beat Davies's Forest 3-1] and Steve Mc-Claren doesn't have a history of animosity with Davies, so I doubt it'll be as controversial as recent years.

DCB: We'll see! Just finally, does any Forest fan anywhere have '27 Derbyshire' on the back of their shirt?

SP: Until recently, there was very little chance of that happening. But then he scored what is possibly the goal of the season against Leeds. Nobody's going to forget that for a while.

***

Forest preview, part II – interview for Seat Pitch blog
March 21, 2014

SP: What were your expectations for 2013/14?

DCB: Having signed some decent players over the summer, I felt we had an outside chance of the play-offs, although with plenty of clubs spending more than us on player wages, it would be a challenge. Nigel Clough's dismissal early in the season paved the way for the appointment of Steve McClaren and his record of 51 points in 26 games has propelled us to third, exceeding even the most optimistic supporters' hopes.

SP: What is the fans' general opinion of McClaren?

DCB: I think the jury was definitely out when he was appointed – not least because of his recent failure at Forest. However, until a surprise home defeat by Millwall, the team barely put a foot wrong under Mc-Claren's stewardship – the current run of four games without a win is as bad as it's got, so there really hasn't been anything for supporters to complain about. The loan signings of Andre Wisdom and Patrick Bamford have really strengthened the squad and the appointments of two former Derby players – the respected ex-Manchester United coach Eric Steele and the popular Paul Simpson, who operates as a kind of under-manager to McClaren – were calibrated to foster a kind of 'family' feel. Important, when you've just dismissed the Son of God.

SP: Have there been many changes since last season?

DCB: Yes. The manager and half of the team have been replaced, expectation levels have gone through the roof, even the stadium name has changed.

Of the team which drew 1-1 with Forest at the ground formerly known as Pride Park last January, the goalkeeper has been dropped and both full-backs have left the club. Richard Keogh remains at centre-back, partnered by the dependable Jake Buxton. The midfield three from that day are all still present and Bryson and Hendrick will probably function as our engine room on Saturday, although Will Hughes may miss out with a groin strain suffered against Reading. Goal-free workhorse Conor Sammon led the line last season, but has been relegated to the bench ever since the arrival of the technically superior Chris Martin.

SP: What can we expect tactically?

DCB: A fairly fluid 4-3-3, with Martin as a target man, Simon Dawkins and Jamie Ward as wide forwards and Bryson and Hendrick support-ing from midfield, although the precise balance of the midfield depends upon Hughes's fitness. Full-backs Wisdom and Craig Forsyth will add width to the attack wherever possible. If – heaven forbid – Forest take the lead, McClaren will not be afraid to go with what is essentially a 4-2-4, by throwing on Sammon, Bamford or Johnny Russell.

SP: Who are the key players to watch out for?

DCB: John Eustace, who usually fulfils an important role as a midfield anchor man, is suspended for this match and with Hughes doubtful, we may well see a debut for loanee George Thorne. Thorne has signed a long-term contract at West Bromwich Albion, but we have no idea how good he is and the East Midlands Derby is quite an occasion on which to make your first appearance for the Rams.

Patrick Bamford started his Derby career in fine style and his magnifi-cent, match-winning strike at Sheffield Wednesday was his fifth goal in his first seven appearances. He hasn't scored since mid-February, but given that his family tree is Garibaldi red and firmly planted in Sher-wood Forest, the script demands that he should score on Saturday. That said, he may well be used as an impact sub rather than from the start.

SP: What's going to happen on Saturday?

DCB: I don't know, it's anyone's guess! When you think of all the crazy s**t that has happened in these games in the last few seasons, it would be pretty brave to make a prediction.

Logically, given Forest's record as the division's draw specialists and our recent stuttering form, a draw is the most likely result. Looking at the current table, with automatic promotion highly unlikely and with Forest six points behind us in sixth, honours even would actually suit us fine. Hopefully, we will see a cracking game of football with no red cards, no histrionics and no flaming howlers from the referee.

***

After the Flood:
Derby County 5 Nottingham Forest 0
March 25, 2014

It's hard to know what to say about a result as historic, as comprehensive, as seismic as Saturday's. Several other bloggers commemorated it very well with their instant reaction, the local and national media did their thing in recording the facts and I'm sure a DVD akin to 2004's *Forest Felled* – Tommy Smith and all that – will be on the shelves of the club shop before too long.

As fans, we will always remember Saturday as the day when everything, just for once, really did go right. Everything flew in, there were no hitches, barely any resistance, to be honest. It was easy, a non-contest, even hilarious at times, like when another Forest shot went out for a throw-in – yes, that happened more than once – or when a lovely Derby move ended in Johnny Russell kicking fresh air and falling on his backside – at 4-0 or 5-0 already, I forget quite how many, everyone could see the funny side, Russell included.

Much of the media attention focused on the Forest end of the result. That Billy Davies was sacked within 48 hours was inevitable – even a far less emotional owner than Fawaz al-Hasawi would have found his hand forced by such a disaster – and while a certain amount of *schadenfreude* from Derby fans is entirely justified, I don't think we should focus on him, or them.

This result was a thoroughly deserved triumph for Derby County, a riotous affirmation that the club is in good health on and off the pitch and a blissful example of the stylish excellence of our passing football.

Our recent mini goal-drought belied the range of serious threats present in our front five. Whichever combination of wide forwards and attack-minded midfielders is selected behind the technically excellent target man Chris Martin, they can all score. There are options to suit different occasions, to unlock different defences.

Simon Dawkins unsettles opponents with his dextrous dribbling. Johnny Russell is quick, tenacious and – as we discovered on Saturday – has the deadliest of drives in his locker. Jamie Ward is, when fit and firing, an unpredictable menace to any Championship defence. Patrick Bamford, meanwhile, is in a different class to your average Championship forward. A flair player, he is a languid, stylish footballer with superb technique.

All four are potential match-winners – as is Martin.

Then there's the line behind the forwards. Will Hughes, a potential future England midfield playmaker. Jeff Hendrick, improving all the time and possessing the ability to change a game with a driving run or an astute pass. And Craig Bryson, one of the most devastatingly effective attacking midfielders in the division, with his unbelievable stamina, anticipation and steely determination. All three can create and finish opportunities to score.

When all eight are fit, it's a hell of a job for Steve McClaren to pick five to start – then you have the other three on the bench to come on and affect the game, if needed. Against Forest, Dawkins was missing and Ward injured during the first half, but Bamford, with his sublime assist for Hendrick, and Russell, with his unstoppable strike from the edge of the box, ensured that they were not missed.

It's no wonder that teams come to the iPro Stadium determined to park the bus. That can work sometimes, as we've seen – but Forest, drawn out by the concession of an early goal, were forced to take us on and were totally outclassed in the process.

Hughes was able to watch from the bench before a late cameo designed only to let the hat-trick hero Bryson wander off and take a standing ovation from the fans. Hendrick, whose stop-start season has been disrupted by injury, was at the heart of much of our best football, linking in well with the forwards and the defensive midfielder George Thorne, who was calm and comfortable on the ball, in what should on paper have been a really difficult game in which to make his debut.

The defence, ever since the signing of Andre Wisdom, has tightened up amazingly – 20 goals were shipped in the first 12 league games, but only 23 have been conceded in the 25 since Wisdom made his debut. It was ignored due to the fact that we hadn't scored for four games, but before Forest we had only conceded three goals in our previous seven matches, keeping five clean sheets.

Richard Keogh and Jake Buxton now form a reliable partnership at this level, with Buxton's concentration and appetite for defending making him a good foil for Keogh, who shows an admirable desire to lead the team from the back, vocally, but also in terms of bringing the ball out of defence when he can and looking to pass it. Buxton, too, possesses a deceptive range of passing for one who has worked his way up from Conference level to flourish in the fifth-best supported division in Europe.

Lee Grant is looking ever more composed and unruffled between the sticks, thanks to an increasing familiarity with the settled back four in front of him and surely also thanks to the input of Eric Steele. Left-back Craig Forsyth is perhaps the least polished member of the side, but is improving and doing extremely well when you consider that he is learning a new position – at Watford, he was primarily used as a wing-back or midfielder.

All these players, working under a team of experienced and effective coaches, have combined to become a real force in the Championship. They have not quite been good enough to keep up with Leicester – who chalked up £65m of losses in the last two seasons while buying their way to the top of the table – and Burnley, who have found one of those classic two-striker combinations that works with devastating effect. But they have been a real match for everyone else.

Apart from the 1-0 defeat at Forest, the only other game we've lost to anybody currently outside of the top six was the surprise home loss to Millwall, a result so freakish that it could almost have been created by a puckish God of Statistics as an 'outlier', to better highlight the trend. The lottery of the play-offs beckons and it will not be easy to get promoted that way, but whoever we have to play in the semi-finals will not be relishing the prospect.

'We are where we are' was one of Davies's favourite phrases and Derby are where they are – third – entirely on merit.

It is what it is.

And it probably isn't remembered greatly that Derby lost their next game, 2-1 at Ipswich. Who cares?

March ended with a bang, though, as Derby routed Charlton 3-0 at "Fortress iPro". And April proceeded in fine style. Although the Rams lost 1-0 at Boro to open the month, they went on to record a fantastic five victories on the spin. Blackpool away (3-1), Huddersfield home (3-1), Doncaster away (2-0), Barnsley home (2-1), Watford home (4-2).

Sadly, automatic promotion was never on the cards despite the Rams' excellence, as Leicester and Burnley powered away from the pack, but a 1-1 draw with Leeds on the final day left Derby in 3rd, with a club record tally of 85 points for the season.

The play-offs beckoned.

***

Eustace v 'Newstace' – George Thorne's impact analysed
May 4, 2014

Much has been written about the impact of Steve McClaren's four key signings this season. Patrick Bamford's has been the most spectacular – it's a shame that his sublime strike against Sheffield Wednesday didn't at least make the top three contenders for goal of the season – while Andre Wisdom's defensive and offensive contributions have been rightly applauded and Simon Dawkins has proved to be an important attacking option.

George Thorne had to wait for his turn and you couldn't help but wonder, for a while, whether he would go the way of Michael Keane and be unable to force his way into the side. There is only room for one holding midfielder in the current system and John Eustace, whose experience and leadership has been a big part of our success this season, hung on to his place in the team for some time after Thorne joined from West Bromwich Albion.

However, once Eustace was suspended for picking up one too many yellow cards, Thorne never looked back. He made his debut in the East Midlands derby and I remarked at the time that it was a heck of a game to be thrown into – not that it seemed to faze him.

Pretty much from the get-go, his most important attributes were very clear – he wanted the ball from the defenders and would use it well, helping us to knit passing moves together through the midfield. Tall and strong, he would be the one who took defensive responsibility, allowing the other midfielders to raid forward with more freedom, although he would creep up to the edge of the opponents' box in relatively risk-free situations as well.

I thought I'd compare some of Thorne's stats for the season with Eustace's and although it should be remembered that Thorne has only made nine starts, while Eustace has made 28, I still feel that some striking differences are worth pointing out.

Thorne has hit roughly double the amount of passes per game that Eustace did from the same position. When it comes to accuracy, Thorne has been far better than Eustace and has in fact become the best passer in the team, even beating Will Hughes (albeit over a far smaller amount of games).

Is this because Thorne has a risk-averse, short and simple passing style?No. Thorne plays more accurate long balls per game than Eustace, any of the defenders, or Lee Grant. His high accuracy percentage has been maintained despite his showing the ambition to pick out team-mates from range. It's worth adding that whoscored.com credit Thorne with more 'key passes[44]' (13) in his nine starts than Eustace managed in 35 league appearances (10).

So it's clear that Thorne is contributing more with the ball than Eustace did, but how about the defensive side of the job?

Thorne's tackles per game are notably higher than Eustace's – 3.4 compared to 1.9. It's the same when it comes to interceptions – 1.8 per game for Thorne, 1.3 for Eustace. Younger and more athletic, Thorne is able to directly affect the game much more than the veteran.

That's not to denigrate Eustace, who has done an excellent job. The stats can't show the positive effect of his experience and leadership on the pitch; however, I can remember a few occasions this season when Eustace was simply bypassed by quicker players, not least Tomasz Cywka, who ran past him before scoring for Barnsley at Oakwell.

Whatever division we find ourselves in next season, holding midfield will be a key position to strengthen. Eustace has been a tremendous professional, but at 34, is now perhaps ready to use his experience and knowhow to pursue a coaching career. Thorne's much more active contribution highlights this. He has been outstanding, but it remains to be seen whether WBA would loan him to us again.

----

[44] A pass which leads directly to a shot.

Trying to find another 'Newstace' will be a key priority for Chris Evans and his scouting set-up this summer.

***

Derby v Brighton – Play-off semi-final preview
May 7, 2014

Before the season kicked off, I thought we had a chance of making the play-offs, but never would have dreamed we'd canter home a strong third, with a match to spare. I suspected that the final day at Elland Road would end up being a crucial encounter, not a dead rubber.

The semi-final pits the Championship's most potent attack – and doesn't that have a nice ring to it? – against one of its tightest defences. It makes for a potentially fascinating clash of styles, in which the Seagulls' defensive discipline will be forensically examined, while on the other hand Derby's much-vaunted creativity will be given a very stern test. It's a case of youth versus experience, fire versus ice.

Here's a direct statistical comparison of the two sides in various key areas.

<u>On the ball</u>

Average possession	Derby 55.2% Brighton 55.3%
Pass success	Derby 79.6% Brighton 79.2%

Other than Brighton, only QPR have enjoyed more possession per game than Derby this season – and Brighton just by the finest shade. However, in the post-Guardiola at Barcelona age, there has been a bit of a backlash in the media against possession as a stat – what does having the ball and prodding it around the back four mean if you can't put it in the net?

In front of goal

Goals	Derby 84 Brighton 55
Shots on goal per game	Derby 15.1 Brighton 13.7
Shots on target per game	Derby 5 Brighton 3.9

Derby have generally made their possession count a lot more than the Seagulls. We create more chances, hit the target more and score a lot more.

While the Rams have goal threats from all angles, Brighton have been almost entirely dependent upon Argentinian striker Leo Ulloa for their goals. Only six clubs have scored fewer than Brighton this season, including all three relegated sides, which makes their sixth-place finish remarkable.

At the back

| Goals conceded | Derby 52 Brighton 40 |
| Shots conceded per game | Derby 13.1 Brighton 12.6 |

Derby tightened up considerably towards the end of the season, conceding only nine goals in the last dozen league matches, but Brighton have been almost sadistically mean throughout, boasting the second-best defence in the division behind Burnley and conceding less than a goal per game. They kept 20 league clean sheets this season, shutting out both QPR and Burnley home and away in the process. This compares favourably to 13 clean sheets for the Rams.

Brighton will believe that Derby will offer up a chance at some stage. If they can take it and nick the aggregate lead, they will become devilishly difficult to break down.

Direct Goal Involvement leaders

DERBY[45]

---

[45] (All competitions)

Chris Martin	37.8% (23 goals, 11 assists)
Craig Bryson	36.7% (16 goals, 17 assists)
Jamie Ward	17.8% (7 goals, 9 assists)
Will Hughes	13.3% (4 goals, 8 assists)

BRIGHTON[46]

Leonardo Ulloa	30.9% (14 goals, 3 assists)
Stephen Ward	14.5% (4 goals, 4 assists)
Jesse Lingard	10.9% (3 goals, 3 assists)
Kazenga LuaLua	10.9% (1 goal, 5 assists)

Although Lingard has pepped things up with a bit of youthful verve since joining on loan from Manchester United, really, Ulloa is the Seagulls' only consistent goal threat at present. Under the normal run of things, if you stop Ulloa, you stop Brighton – although Craig Mackail-Smith will feel the script is written for him to make a goalscoring impact, having been out injured for so long.

Conclusion

I want to believe that the younger, more exciting, more positive team will ultimately have too much for a miserly, craggy side whose success in making it this far has been built on being tough to break down. The ageing legs in the Brighton side are starting to creak, with three important players either out or playing with injuries, whereas Derby had the luxury of resting fully-fit key men last weekend.

In the first leg, it is simply important that we don't get well beaten and although I'll be as nervous as hell tomorrow night, looking at it rationally, I don't believe Brighton have enough firepower to really harm us.

Go into the second leg level, or even trailing by one, and I am happy to predict that with the backing of a fervent home crowd, we will ultimately break them down and go through to the final.

***

---

[46] (Championship goals only)

Play-off final preview: Derby County v Queens Park Rangers
May 22, 2014

After Brighton were soundly thrashed on a delirious day in Derby, thoughts around the county (and beyond) turned to who we 'fancied' in the final. The consensus seemed to be that Wigan offered more to worry about than 'Arry Redknapp's QPR.

A reasonable shout, given Wigan's strong squad and resurgent second half of the season, but I found it interesting that the 'megabucks' Hoops were seen as the preferable option to face at Wembley. Yes, they underachieved in finishing fourth, but probably the only reason we aren't playing Burnley at Wembley instead of QPR is the shoulder injury that Charlie F***ing Austin suffered in January.

On the ball
Average possession   Derby 55.2% QPR 56.5%
Pass success   Derby 79.6% QPR 79.8%
Long balls per game   Derby 68 QPR 79

The only two teams to have enjoyed a higher average possession per game than us over the regular season were Brighton and QPR. What we must avoid at Wembley is a repeat of the semi-final first leg at the Amex, when Brighton managed to dominate possession and pen Derby in for spells. Although we hung on and won that game, it was as much down to the home side's ineffectiveness in the final third as it was to do with our defensive resolve. QPR are better than Brighton and will not forgive us if we let them have too much of the play.

In front of goal
League goals   Derby 90 QPR 62[47]
Shots on goal per game   Derby 15.1 QPR 14.2

---

[47] Goals scored and conceded include the play-off semi-finals

In the absence of Austin during February and March, QPR lost five matches, failing to score in four of those defeats. However, the signing of Ravel Morrison proved to be a shot in the arm for the team and he rapidly became the Hoops' second-top scorer behind Austin.

Austin and Morrison can now be fielded together, with plenty of experienced back-up options to turn to if a Plan B is required.

*

I don't think there's any doubt that a fit Craig Bryson would go straight back into our team. There will be debate about whether Hughes or Hendrick should take the other midfield berth, but despite Hughes' exquisite finish against Brighton, how on Earth do you drop Hendrick at this stage? With Bryson and Hendrick in tandem, we have a serious midfield engine room, while Hughes is the sort of player that a cynical old bastard like Joey Barton would simply love to mark, but may be less keen to see coming on fresh after 70 minutes have elapsed.

However, the opposite way of looking at it is that Hughes would be more likely to wind Barton up and get him into trouble – and it was a moment of magic from Hughes that effectively killed the semi-final, after all. How on Earth do you leave out a player as good as Hughes?

As for QPR, well, they're just a bunch of overpaid old farts, aren't they? Well, yes and no. Yes, they're certainly overpaid relative to their performance level and yes, the likes of Barton and Richard Dunne are past their best, but they're still more than capable at Championship level. Elsewhere, you're looking at good pros in their prime. Rob Green, Nedum Onuoha and Danny Simpson will not see the Championship as their natural level and if QPR lose on Saturday, Austin could well hitch a ride to the top flight with somebody else.

I'd say the best description of the current QPR side would be 'Dad's Army Premier League Lite'. Some are past their peak, others, although still in their 20s, are yesterday's big thing – barely any are young enough to have their best years ahead of them. Under Redknapp, they would make for a very satisfying end-of-level-baddie to slay at Wembley indeed.

Redknapp could be missing a few international stars, although you have a feeling that the long break since the semis will enable some of them to return to fitness. Niko Kranjčar played extra time against Wigan with a hamstring problem, but is expected to recover for the final.

Direct Goal Involvement leaders (Championship goals only)

Derby
1. Chris Martin	38.5% (25 goals, 12 assists)
2. Craig Bryson	34.4% (16 goals, 17 assists)
3. Jamie Ward	17.7% (7 goals, 10 assists)
4. Will Hughes	13.5% (5 goals, 8 assists)
5. Patrick Bamford	12.5% (8 goals, 4 assists)
(all competitions)	

QPR
1. Charlie Austin	37.1% (21 goals, 2 assists)
2. Junior Hoilett	16.1% (4 goals, 6 assists)
3. Ravel Morrison	14.5% (6 goals, 2 assists)
4. Bobby Zamora	12.9% (3 goals, 5 assists)
5. Matty Phillips/Joey Barton	8.1% (3 goals, 2 assists)

As Brighton rely on Leo Ulloa, so QPR, for all they spend on wages, depend heavily on Austin for goals. 'No Austin, no obvious goal threat,' as QPR writer Paul Warburton has put it.

However, Hoilett's darting runs in off the wing are another issue to contend with, while Morrison's six goals and two assists have come in 17 appearances (15 starts), so on average, he has either scored or set one up in every other game. Let's hope that the final is his 'other' game.

As for us, when you compare Martin and Bryson's productivity to the more famous, wealthier names in Redknapp's squad, you can't help but marvel at the fantastic work they have done this season. For all of his technical qualities, would you take the elegant Kranjčar (two league goals this season) over the tenacious Bryson – a man who extends the concept of box-to-box into goalline-to-goalline and has been rewarded handsomely with goals and assists galore in the process? When you think about it, what is a player as gifted as Kranjčar even doing, playing in the English second tier at 29?

Martin and Bryson aside, there have been contributions from plenty of other Derby players. Even if QPR can prevent Martin from scoring (Richard Dunne has indicated that this is their chief concern) and Bryson hasn't fully recovered from his back injury, there are threats from both wings, the midfield area – even from the full-backs. Any of them could score.

On the other hand, QPR also have plenty of players who might pop up with a goal and their bloated squad is one of the reasons why only Austin registers a high DGI rating. In total, 23 players have chipped in with at least one goal or league assist for QPR this season.

From the bench

'Arry can call on a host of established names, including Kevin Doyle, Bobby Zamora, Aaron Hughes and Yossi Benayoun. I have a sneaky feeling that Benayoun could start, simply for his big game experience, although the manager may decide he has enough of that elsewhere in the side already.

Yet another member of the 30+ brigade, Karl Henry, can be introduced if Barton and O'Neil aren't being sufficiently 'nasty', while Tom Carroll – once of this parish, but not as good as Will Hughes – is an option if extra guile is the order of the day.

It's hard to determine exactly who will start for QPR, or even be on the bench, because they've got so many sodding players.

Conclusion

The riot of youthful exuberance that is Derby's current side did for Brighton with such irrepressible zeal that it's hard not to feel some optimism going into the match that they called a £60m game when we won it in 2007 – and was this month hyped as a £220m game by the *Derby Telegraph*, once they'd factored in the expected benefits to the city's economy.

I daren't call it as a prediction, but just as Brighton simply weren't strong enough to stand in our way, I hope that an ageing QPR side won't have the legs to stop us over the 90, or even 120 minutes. Let's not consider the possibility of penalties. We'll probably need to score at least twice – which shouldn't be a problem, given our record.

It would be stretching it to say that a QPR side copiously stocked with players on huge salaries looks patched up, but they don't quite have the settled, round peg/round hole feel of the Derby team. Building on the spine of Green, the back four, Barton and Austin, 'Arry has rotated his huge squad, so we'll have to wait to find out who he chooses to fill in the gaps.

Nearly every neutral out there wants us to beat QPR, whose owner Tony Fernandes has provided an object lesson in how not to run a football club in the last couple of years. Given that Financial Fair Play regulations are apparently going to be active from next season in the Championship, staying down would be something of a disaster for Fernandes, parachute payments notwithstanding.

They say that football is a numbers game. Fernandes and Redknapp's interpretation of that theory has been to pay as many players as possible as much money as possible and it would be heartening for everyone in football if the crushing advantage they have on paper adds up to nothing on the day and the best team – as opposed to the highest-paid, randomly assembled assortment of big names – wins.

That said, they are nevertheless as strong a team as you could expect to face in the Championship. If we can beat them, we will have thoroughly deserved our promotion to the Premier League.

***

Moving on from the Nightmare at Wembley:
Derby County 0 Queens Park Rangers 1
May 25, 2014

I said immediately afterwards that it was one of the worst moments of my life. Especially because I was sitting two seats away from the QPR fans – who, after 75 minutes, all looked like they were about to be guillotined. With my head in my hands and my eyes closed, all I could hear was the jet engine roar of 39,000 people who couldn't believe their luck.

I freely admit that if this defeat ranks among my all-time lows, on balance, I've had a very good life. It was only a game of football and nothing could be more frivolous. But it was the shock of the thing, the total injustice of it. The bizarre collective brain fade that seemed to visit itself upon the back four at the crucial moment when promotion was within our grasp happened in a game in which Lee Grant had nothing to do. No. Thing. Not a save, not even plucking a cross from the sky, as far as I can remember. Charlie Austin scuffed a shot wide when well placed, but QPR, with their incontinent spending on players, had barely laid a glove on us and looked palpably inferior even before Gary O'Neil was rightly sent off for a deeply cynical professional foul.

It was defence against attack, to the point where we forgot that we might actually have to defend at some point and f**ked it up, colossally, at the crucial moment. QPR could have played until Doomsday and never scored unless we gave them a major hand and, very sadly, we completely fell to bits for no obvious reason. It was like watching a horror movie in slow motion and the joke club, with the embarrassing Champions League wage bill and no discernible plan, had spawned it in the last minute. It was all our own fault.

I said after about 40 minutes, 'We can beat these.' After O'Neil's dismissal, I said, 'It's all about us now.' I was convinced, until the defenders lost their minds simultaneously, that we would win and was just annoyed that it would take extra time to do it. Never mind the £140m involved, it was simply a game of football that we would have won 99 times out of 100. They had no right to win, morally. They were negative, insipid, limited, boring, cynical and slow. They stuck up their defensive guard and played for penalties. They will stink up the Premier League next season.

That we failed to take advantage of such a huge opportunity is a real, real shame. Yes, you could argue that we will be well placed to go again next season, but this was the season where the stars, it seemed, had aligned. Hughes, Bryson and Hendrick could all conceivably be picked off by richer clubs now. Thorne, Wisdom and Bamford will have to be replaced. The club have made much of the new recruitment head and his network – well, now is Chris Evans's time to shine, so that the club are ready to take on a new season in which they will be expected to challenge for automatic promotion.

OK, it's arguably been the best season overall since the Jim Smith era. OK, the club has progressed massively in the last five years, but it may be that the 2013/14 side, which showed such promise, turns out to be an ephemera. That's the trouble with loan signings. If they get you where you need to go, fine. If not, they're gone. Can we get another right-back as good as Wisdom? What about the defensive midfield role – in the absence of Thorne and (presumably) Eustace, can we find somebody else for that specialist position, or do we have to change formation entirely?

As it stands, next season's first team is Grant, Freeman, Keogh, Buxton, Forsyth, Hughes, Hendrick, Bryson, Russell, Ward, Martin. But as we know, Jeff can't do the holding role and it's not where Will belongs either. It may be that we actually shouldn't be opposed to the idea of selling one of the midfield trio so that the funds can be used to balance the team up differently. I'd keep Hughes, if we could.

In fact, although it may seem churlish after a season in which he got most things right, I'm going to criticise McClaren just slightly for his substitutions today. Why, when we needed a killer pass to prise open a stingy old back four, did we take off our playmaker? Furthermore, why wasn't Bamford introduced for Ward earlier[48]? I'm fairly sure McClaren had decided to save him for extra time.

Forest fans will lap it up, of course, but firstly, ask them where the f**k did they finish. Secondly, how's that Financial Fair Play compliance thing going and will you be laughing when you're under transfer embargo next January? And thirdly, 5-0.

So now, it's all about next season. The team will be at least subtly different, possibly radically different, depending on the bids we receive for the midfield talent. So much could happen. We were lucky with injuries this year, which may not happen again. Three more teams come out of the Premier League with huge parachute payments to burn on plucking the best Football League prospects, or even fresh blood from abroad.

Our revenues will have increased through extra season ticket sales, plus there's the play-off gates – the gentlemen's agreement about the Wembley loser taking the winner's share of ticket receipts adds something like £1.5m to our coffers. That's a pittance compared to what Fulham, Cardiff and Norwich trouser from the PL for failing to stay up, but will still give us an advantage on some of the Championship sides who finished below us this year.

We should – should – now be strong enough to be there or thereabouts again next season. But will we get as good a chance as this again? We would be very fortunate to bring through two players as good as Hughes and Hendrick from the youth set-up in the next few years and if they are sold, they can't be replaced like for like. However, it's good that, as a healthy club, we shouldn't be faced with the loss of our next Tom Huddlestone for a pittance.

Derby County is one of the biggest and best clubs in England. We are, however, excluded from the Premier League party because we have been underachieving for years. Those dark days should have been put behind us today.

---

[48] Hughes was replaced by Craig Bryson on 68 minutes. Bamford wasn't sent on until after Bobby Zamora had scored, in injury time.

My dad and I struggled to speak for most of the way back, but when we finally managed to essay some sort of comment on the game – I think we'd reached Codnor – it was that they all played OK. Just OK. Nobody was able to grab it by the balls and make themselves a hero.

I have no doubt that the club is in an infinitely better place than it was five years ago, but due to the ridiculously uneven distribution of finances in English football, we now need promotion if we are to progress. Ultimately, we have to get to the place Southampton are in, benefitting from a top-class academy and keeping hold of our best products until a Champions League club comes knocking with £20m+. Size-wise, there is no reason why we cannot become a top-ten Premier League club in time.

It's all there for us, to burn through this bloody division of has-beens, mediocrity and ineptitude. This should have been the season, but it wasn't. Now we move on and the expectation is that we can make it happen next season.

2014/15

The O-Ring Theory: Derby County's squad assessed
June 7, 2014

I did a spot on the BBC Radio Derby *Sportscene Talk-in* earlier this week and was asked by Owen Bradley where I thought the club should strengthen this summer. Without any hesitation, I said that the first priority should be right-back.

'More important than Thorne?' Owen replied. The discussion on the show had, to that point, been dominated by the future of the West Brom holding midfielder.

I'm not saying that we shouldn't sign Thorne at the first possible opportunity – if it's a deal we can do, we should do it – but Andre Wisdom's return to Liverpool leaves us with a gap to fill.

In a post I did a while ago – a *Football Manager 14* review – I looked at some of the theoretical principles explained in Chris Anderson and David Sally's *The Numbers Game*. The O-Ring principle – named for the Challenger space shuttle tragedy, in which a multi-billion dollar enterprise was undermined and destroyed by the malfunction of one of its cheapest parts – dictates that the weakest player in your side is the one who has the biggest chance of derailing your chances of success. This principle was established by an analysis of top leagues across the world.

Here is my attempt at a position-by-position 'O-Ring' analysis of the current team:-

1. (weakest) Right-back – Kieron Freeman, returning from his loan spell at Sheffield United, is currently our only senior right-back. Andre Wisdom proved a massive upgrade on both Freeman and the Spurs loanee Adam Smith, adding presence and pace to the defence. Without a suitable replacement, we're at risk of losing much of the solidity we developed under McClaren last season.

2. Defensive midfield – John Eustace has been retained for another season, but George Thorne proved to be a significant improvement on the veteran. If we can land Thorne on a permanent deal, it would be a huge boost to our promotion prospects. If not, we still need to bring in another holding midfielder to compete with Eustace, unless there is an intention to change the core starting formation.

3. Centre-back – With Mark O'Brien and Shaun Barker both still recovering from very long-term injury problems, there are only two recognised, fit senior centre-backs on the books at the time of writing. Given that our success last season was built on scoring so heavily, it follows that a tighter defence would give us an even better chance of going up. Again, the vital importance of clean sheets is statistically demonstrated in *The Numbers Game*. On average, conceding no goals guarantees you more points (2.5 PPG) than scoring twice (about 2.0 PPG).

The recruitment of a competent centre-back to go straight into the team, while ruthlessly harsh on the committed pairing of Keogh and Buxton, would be one of my transfer priorities – especially when you consider that Wisdom effectively acted as a third centre-back at set-pieces and in defending crosses. A backslide to the days when any ball hopefully lobbed into our box made you reflexively cringe would be most unwelcome.

4. Wide forward – Having four players able to play wide forward helped us last season, as a tiring Ward or Russell, say, could be exchanged for a fresh Bamford or Dawkins late on in a game. Bamford has now returned to Chelsea, leaving us with a gap we could perhaps fill with another exciting youngster from the Premier League on a long loan.

5. Left-back – Craig Forsyth did very well last season but is the only recognised senior player in his position in the squad. I'm sure the club will have targets in mind, even if only as emergency loan cover should Forsyth get injured.

6. Centre-forward – A difficult one, because Chris Martin was exceptional last season, so unless we were to change formation and play two up front ,there is no need to strengthen this position, in theory. However, if Conor Sammon wanted to leave for first-team football, we

would have to think about recruiting another striker.

Ideally, you would have a developing academy product acting as an understudy to Martin. Step forward, Mason Bennett?

7. Central midfield – We certainly don't need to look at strengthening central midfield when we have Bryson, Hendrick and Hughes. It is a source of great frustration to me that we can't seem to fit those three players together into a system that works, but all three are at their best when somebody with defensive instincts is there to do a disciplined shift behind them.

8. Goalkeeper (strongest) – Lee Grant's return and Eric Steele's coaching have solved this problem for the medium to long term. A group of young keepers led by the Dutchman Kelle Roos are developing behind Grant, so we seem to be settled in this position for now.

***

Guest post: Derby County's 'Your 90 Minutes' night at the iPro Stadium July 24, 2014

Our guest columnist enters the iPro Stadium to meet Rush and the gang.

On Wednesday night, I was invited to attend another of the club's regular 'Your 90 Minutes' sessions. Representing the club were Sam Rush, commercial director Lisa Biesty, finance director Stephen Pearce, marketing manager Faye Nixon and concessions manager Nick Richards.

The evening was split into four parts: a session from Lisa on commercial ideas, an update on finances from Stephen, an overview of new ideas for matchday food and drink from Nick and finally an open Q&A with Sam.

One interesting aside from Sam during the commercial discussion was that the season ticket base dropped by a quarter during Nigel's era. Given that prices were frozen for much of that time, it's clear that the financial director (who came from Chelsea FC) was horrified by the situation. A club with a fanbase as big as Derby County's absolutely has to be making more from its season ticket revenue.

Stephen Pearce seemed a personable chap and is clearly very astute. He covered the investments they are making in Moor Farm and the academy – all exempt from Financial Fair Play accounting – which should hopefully lead to the academy getting Category 1 status (the audit is still under way according to Sam).

FFP was covered, but there didn't seem to be much to report. They expect QPR and possibly the Premier League to mount a legal challenge against the fine they will be hit with, but any teams remaining in the Championship (e.g. Forest) who have failed to comply will be placed under a transfer embargo. There are ongoing discussions to change some of the criteria, but it needs 17 clubs to agree and currently, consensus has not been reached. If and when changes are made, it will likely be small adjustments to the figures, rather than wholesale changes.

The Q&A with Sam was probably the easiest ride since the Teacups at Blackpool Pleasure Beach. The timing of the meeting was such that we had absolutely NOTHING to moan about. We'd come within a few minutes of the Premier League last season, all the major players and the manager had signed contract extensions, Thorne had signed[49], plus plenty of new exciting talent recruited for the development squad. All smiles.

I planned to bring up some contentious stuff, such as, why did we sack our chief scout after six months? Do we really think our defensive frailties will be fixed by a League One signing in place of a Premier

---

[49] George Thorne joined Derby from West Brom on a permanent deal on 19 July 2014, for a fee of around £2.75m.

League loanee[50]? Does the fact that all the youngsters we've signed – Shaquille McDonald, Alefe Santos, Kelle Roos, Ivan Calero, Alban Bunjaku – come from Full Contact Soccer Agency mean that we're not actually casting our net that wide? But with the prevailing mood, it all felt churlish, so needless to say the questions went unasked.

Sam was delighted to have signed Thorne and felt that the deal was good business for both clubs. He made some comments about the media not really helping and pointed out that while journos were reporting we'd made two bids, the West Brom chairman wouldn't even take his calls!

Rush said that we had an option of waiting it out until August, which may have driven the price down a bit, but Thorne had already made the decision that he wanted to be at Derby. Sam thought that if we'd tried to play it cool, that he may have had his head turned by other clubs, who would have started to sniff around if his agent put the word out that Derby were playing the long game.

Chris Evans was praised for his hard work in securing some of the other players. Calero had flown home to talk to a Spanish club, so Evans flew after him and talked him into coming back to Derby. He was also credited with doing similar with other players, including Santos. A comment from the floor was that he'd perhaps been reading Brian Clough's autobiography!

Pearce confirmed that funds are earmarked for Premier League loanees again, but until the clubs come back from their pre-season tours and name their squads, we won't know what's available. At that point, he expects Premier League managers to be phoning Steve Mc-Claren begging him to take players – not the other way around. A good place to be.

In general, Sam's message was that he feels the club is back under control and going firmly in the right direction. All we have to do now is win some football matches.

---

[50] Cyrus Christie was signed from Coventry City to replace the departing Andre Wisdom. The fee was reported at around £200,000.

22 July:
Zenit St Petersburg 2 Derby County 0

Where were you when you heard the news? We'd been willing the deal over the line ever since Wembley and finally, on 18 July, it was done. The man who would knit it all together, the final piece in the promotion jigsaw – the midfielder who would provide the steel and solidity at the base of the system to allow everybody else to concentrate on what they did best – attack.

It was the transfer deal that proved the owners' intent, which made us logical favourites to go up. McClaren wanted the exciting team from 2013/14 to stay together – contract extensions for Bryson, Hughes, Hendrick, Keogh, Buxton *et al* were important and not always easily agreed, but clinching a deal worth in excess of £2m for George Thorne gave us the chance to carry on exactly where we had left off – and maybe to go one better this time.

Four days after the deal was announced, Thorne trotted out as part of a full-strength team at the Sports Zentrum Karlsdorf in Austria for a friendly against Russian giants Zenit. Thirty-four minutes later, he had received treatment twice – first for a dead leg, then for a jarred knee – and was withdrawn.

The club initially said Thorne had merely been substituted as a precaution. 'George took two knocks,' Paul Simpson told the *Derby Telegraph*. 'He is limping and feeling a bit sorry for himself, hopefully he will be OK.'

Within a couple more days, we heard the awful truth. Thorne had ruptured the anterior cruciate ligament in his left knee and would be out of action for up to nine months. The season's bright promise was seriously compromised before it had even started.

McClaren: 'George will be back, he is still young. He has to stay posit-ive and we have to deal with it and move on. Injuries are one of the pitfalls of football and the team need to respond. People have to step forward, fill in, do a job and we carry on.

'We've still got a very strong midfield department. George gave us good balance, but other players have to step forward and provide that balance.'[51]

McClaren started the season with a midfield trio of Hughes, Hendrick and Bryson. Everybody hoped and expected that Derby would hit the ground running after Wembley, but with their plans disrupted by Thorne's injury, they stuttered in the early stages of 2014/15.

Rotherham were seen off on the opening day, just about, then a goal-less draw at Sheffield Wednesday was followed by defeat at Charlton.

John Eustace was recalled to shore things up and Felix Magath's cal-low Fulham were swatted 5-1 – but a home draw against Ipswich ad-ded to the sense that the season hadn't really got started.

Forest, on the other hand, had roared out of the traps under the Mes-siah, Stuart Pearce. Everybody and his (red) dog saw this match as Forest's chance to avenge the 5-0 and the bookies – who are never wrong, remember – had them down as promotion favourites.

To the City Ground…

***

---

[51] Quoted in the Derby Telegraph

Nottingham Forest 1 Derby County 1
September 15, 2014

Before the 5-0, there was a 0-1. Before that, a 1-1 and a 1-0. Before that, another 1-0 and a 2-1 – before that, another 0-1.

The East Midlands derby can explode into life at any time, but March's instalment was in part so enjoyable because in recent years these games have been tough, evenly-matched, tense occasions to be endured – it is very rare to be able to relax and actually enjoy it. In place of tension, that day, was high farce.

The tension returned in spades for this gritty draw, a match in which both sides cancelled each other out sufficiently to ensure that neither deserved to win.

Since the dismissal of Billy Davies, Forest have completely refreshed their starting 11 and with a club legend now at the helm, they started this season in boisterous fashion. Their fans went into this match feeling very confident and when I pointed out that there were reasons for Derby to be confident as well, I was trolled on Twitter by various Red Dogs who laughed at my 'desperate analysis'.

Those who bridled at my suggestion – backed up by statistics – that Stuart Pearce has introduced a more direct style of play may wish to read the thoughts of Forest supporter Steve Corry, who was surprised and disappointed by what he describes as his team's 'obvious long ball tactic'. The strengths I referred to in my preview – the pace, power and width – and the direct attacking style, looking to cross it in for the dangerous Britt Assombalonga or Michail Antonio, were there for all to see.

Back-post crosses have been a regular source of joy for Forest this term, hence the deployment of the tall Ryan Shotton[52] in place of Cyrus Christie. Richard Keogh saved a certain goal by getting his noggin in the way of one such ball in, later Antonio got to Jack Hunt's deep

---

[52] Shotton signed on loan from Stoke City on 25 August 2014, with a view to a permanent switch.

cross, but couldn't direct his header goalwards. Steve McClaren even referred to a 'back three' of Shotton and the centre-backs after the game – the right-back only ventured forward when presented with a compelling case to do so.

At the other end, Psycho's Reds were well marshalled and compact, denying the Rams space in which to play. There was the odd flicker of the neat interplay we expect to see, but with Forest pressing aggress-ively – as you'd expect from a team managed by Pearce – very rarely any threat of a goal.

Pearce and McClaren had spoken of their mutual respect in the build-up to this game and this attitude, mostly, filtered through on to the pitch, as both sides were clearly wary of each other and desperate not to concede.

As the second half drifted, you started to get the feeling that it was within Derby's gift to nick it. Then there was a pathetic pitch invasion from a bunch of overgrown children and then a Forest goal on the counter-attack. That, you feared, with the pretty football not working, was that – but atypically, we actually went and forced an equaliser home from a set-piece instead.

And that is the thing to take away from this game, which was not ex-actly a classic. We went to a club who have started the season with a bang, into an intensely hostile atmosphere and dealt with almost everything they threw at us. OK, there were some hairy moments – mostly whenever Antonio got the ball and ran one-on-one at a clearly ring-rusty Shotton in the first half – but ultimately, even after a combin-ation of attacking substitutions and Jake Buxton's second yellow card left us with no midfield, they couldn't get through us, or round us, or over us again.

Neither team did enough to win. That is fine from a Derby perspective, as recovering to draw this match was a good outcome and meant that we had passed what was without doubt one of the hardest tests we will face all season. Yes, there was a complete malfunction at the back for the goal, but overall, the defence stuck to their task doggedly, hence my instinct to vote for Keogh as man of the match. Granted, they conceded too many free kicks around the box and could have paid for that on another day and certainly, Shotton should have been booked, but I struggle to recall Forest creating more than one clear chance, or Lee Grant having to make a really difficult save.

There are many more hard games to come, of course – the return leg of this fixture among them – but if Forest really are as good as it gets in this league, then we have nothing to fear.

And in the weeks that followed, that was how things played out.

Derby's 1-0 win at Blackpool on 21 October sent them to the top of the table, with 26 points from 13 games.

***

25 October:
Derby County 1 Wigan Athletic 2

The Rams came into this game on a splendid 12-match unbeaten run in all competitions and leading the league, but they had experienced some problems at home. There had been away wins at Blackburn, Bolton, Reading and Blackpool – but Cardiff somehow escaped from the iPro with a 2-2 draw, before the frustration of a goalless stalemate against struggling Millwall.

Wigan were having a bad season, but gave Derby problems from the off by refusing to allow them to pass out from defence. They even won a (debatable) penalty, saved by Jack Butland[53], before John Eustace volleyed in Johnny Russell's free kick from close range – The Eust celebrating his poacher's strike with serious gusto in front of the South Stand.

---

[53] The England U21 goalkeeper joined on loan from Stoke City in October 2014, to cover for the injured Lee Grant.

But after Wigan equalised, McClaren opted to twist, withdrawing Eustace for Leon Best[54]. Rather than having the desired effect, the switch to two up front left the Rams more open and they were punished with seven minutes to go. Butland could only parry an effort from Adam Forshaw back into danger and James McClean's mishit volley looped and bounced agonisingly into an empty goal ahead of the chasing Craig Bryson.

As McClaren said, 'Our forte, what makes us different, is that we play football – we build up from the back… They pressed, we couldn't deal with it.'[55]

At this time, the feeling in some quarters was that Eustace couldn't provide enough attacking impetus in home games. Losing to Wigan, drawing with Millwall and Ipswich, struggling to break down Bournemouth until they had a man dismissed, the Rams were hitting brick walls at the iPro. Perhaps they needed a younger, faster, more skilful player in the holding role, at least at home?

That player was already in the building, having signed for the Rams on loan from no less a club than Real Madrid.

***

8 November:
Derby County 5 Wolves 0

After Wigan, Derby suffered another setback, losing in injury time at Brentford to what I still maintain was a pretty fluky winner from Stuart Dallas. However, they got back on track by beating Huddersfield at home, more comfortably than the 3-2 scoreline suggested.

---

[54] Best signed for Derby on a season-long loan from Blackburn Rovers in August 2014.

[55] Post-match quote published by the BBC

Wolves, a strong passing side, were supposed to offer much more of a test than the Terriers – but Derby simply battered them.

Omar Mascarell, by now preferred to John Eustace in midfield, flighted in a free kick for Ryan Shotton's opening goal, then Jeff Hendrick drove home from outside the box as Wolves slept. Johnny Russell, allowed the freedom of the penalty area, controlled the ball on his chest and rifled gleefully home after Kenny Jackett's men couldn't clear a corner. 3-0 before half-time.

It was threatening to become a rout and it did. Will Hughes laid in Hendrick for a lovely fourth and then Russell steered home a cross from Craig Forsyth to compound Wolves' agony. It was wonderful. Mascarell got rave reviews as Derby swaggered back to the top of the table.

This performance did a lot to convince the supporters and the wider public that the Rams were serious contenders for promotion to the Premier League.

McClaren, 'The key thing was the discipline they showed... It was a game we controlled by being a good team without the ball... To do that to a very good team shows what this group is capable of.'

***

13 December:
Middlesbrough 2 Derby County 0

Derby were still going strong at top of the table at the start of December, with 38 points from 20 games. They had lost four times up to that point – most gallingly in an appalling performance at Elland Road on 29 November. The temptation to write that defeat off as a mysterious blip was strong, particularly after the Rams swept Brighton aside 3-0 the following Saturday – a handsome display in the first 20 minutes producing a memorable goal flood.

The visit to Boro, however, abruptly punctured any complacency. Derby were absolutely slaughtered. The only surprise was that Boro didn't score more, particularly after McClaren's half-time double rage substitution, which saw Leon Best introduced in place of Omar Mascarell, who had been pressed mercilessly throughout the first half.

With Boro already leading 1-0 through Patrick Bamford, Ryan Shotton was dismissed in the act of conceding a penalty. Grant Leadbitter converted emphatically and that was that. Only due to Lee Grant's superb shot-stopping did the Rams avoid a hiding, in a game which confirmed Boro's promotion credentials and left Derby thoroughly embarrassed.

McClaren, 'What's got us where we are and will keep us where we are is our quality of football and building from the back, going through the lines and creating opportunities. We failed to do that today.

'They did what many teams have done to us… Just dropped, remained compact, invited us to play and hit us on the break.'[56]

On the double substitution, 'Martin was doing a good job, but there was no one running beyond, we weren't playing forward enough. So we put Besty on just to try to get some penetration in behind them, same with Jordon Ibe[57], instead of playing in front, trying to play behind them. And we never got to find out really whether it would work because of the sending off.'

***

---

[56] McClaren's post-match quotes are sourced from the BBC website

[57] 18-year old wide forward Ibe joined Derby on a season-long loan from Liverpool in August 2014.

Does Derby County's dip mean it's time for John Eustace to return?
December 23, 2014

John Eustace is something of a cult hero these days – helped by his enduringly popular parody Twitter account. And there's a growing feeling that he should be recalled to the starting XI at the expense of Omar Mascarell[58].

What Eustace lacks in attacking quality, the theory goes, is more than made up for by his defensive and organisational nous. He is the coach on the pitch, the leader of men who will drag younger and less experienced players through tough patches, tough games, tough weeks, the inevitable, gruelling troughs of the season. Long forgotten is the result of his last start, the deeply disappointing 2-1 home defeat to Wigan – although the decisive goal was actually conceded after Eustace had been substituted.

At Leeds, I was standing on the front row – close enough to be featured on Rams Player, politely asking Adryan how he was feeling throughout the lengthy duration of *that* dive – and at half-time in that match, I saw Eustace put an arm around a clearly unhappy Jeff Hendrick as they walked into the tunnel. How we could have done with that steadying influence on the pitch, I thought[59].

In the first half against Boro, Derby prodded the ball feebly around their own third of the field, unable to hurt the home side in any way. Mascarell wasn't able to get the Rams playing, the midfielders in front of him couldn't get on the ball and both full-backs looked dithery, ponderous and unsure of themselves in possession. And Patrick Bamford's goal stemmed from a misplaced pass out of defence from Richard Keogh.

---

[58] Mascarell signed for Derby on a season-long loan from Real Madrid in August 2014.

[59] Derby lost 2-0 at Elland Road on 29 November 2014. Adryan's outrageous dive and risible histrionics after a challenge from Johnny Russell were rightly pilloried on social media.

Opponents have learned the importance of stopping us from passing the ball out from the back. The losses to Leeds and Boro, the draw with Norwich and even a 20-minute spell against a hopeless Brighton showed very clearly that tactically speaking, we have been rumbled. There is now a standard anti-Derby game plan – press high, press hard, press fast, force the defenders to go sideways, backwards, stifle the passing game at source, force mistakes from the least competent passers, starve the creative players – and we are struggling to do much about it when it is executed well.

My complaints at half-time in both the Leeds and Boro games were that we needed to play faster if we wanted to work our way through the lines. The back four wanted too many touches and the midfielders weren't doing enough to make themselves available. It's not easy to do, but if we're going to play 'the Derby County way', as we've rather loftily christened it, then we can't complain if teams set up to stop us from doing it. We just have to do it so well that they can't stop us.

I am 100 per cent behind the desire to play short, passing football, but I did not like what I saw against Boro or Leeds or Norwich, much of which was heads-down, slow, passive, losing football. It's counter-intuitive to suggest that selecting a slower, more defensively minded player could actually help us to play better passing football – but maybe it's a question of balance, of having a solid foundation upon which that slick forward play can be built up.

Mascarell is a lovely player, given time and space. Unfortunately he is not going to be given that time and space, so he must do more to earn it, move the ball faster and make himself an easier option for the defenders to find. He has found the adjustment from the Spanish lower leagues[60] to the Championship difficult. That's not surprising – he'll never have experienced anything like the match at Elland Road before and he couldn't cope on the day. Boro was an equally tough assignment and again, he struggled.

It may be that Mac simply wants to look to the future. However, if The Old Warrior is no longer the answer, I'd suggest that Mascarell needs

---

[60] Mascarell had mostly played for Real Madrid Castilla, the reserve team

additional competition from outside the current squad. The defensive midfield berth is critically important for our system – we need somebody who can protect the back four, allowing the other midfielders to go forward with more confidence.

George Thorne was, is, perfect for us and I firmly believe that we'd be clear at the top of the table now had he been available for selection all season. Tommo nailed it when he said, 'Thorne took us to another level, because he can hit any kind of pass, carry the ball and is hard.' However, in Thorne's absence and with Mascarell struggling to stamp his authority on games, do we have to go back to The Eust for now – or do we keep faith with the younger, faster, more technically adept player and hope that he can adjust and grow into his role?

Eustace will take a strategic yellow card for the team. When he puts in an emergency tackle, the opponent is stopped. He can pass the ball given a chance, but more importantly, will sit in almost as a third centre-back, allowing the full-backs to push on. Eustace is highly unlikely to pirouette away from a marker with sumptuous ease, or even cheekily lob the ball over Cesc Fàbregas's head, as Mascarell has done – but he is also experienced enough to know when a pass simply isn't on.

That said, Eustace's total lack of pace remains an issue and is not something that can always be redeemed by his positional sense.

I've written before about this selection issue – Cavalier v Roundhead, Romanticism v Realpolitik, Mascarell v Eustace – and have always previously backed Mascarell. I want to believe in pure passing, but my oh my, do we look milky when we lose the ball and there's no enforcer there to rescue the situation. Young Mascarell can look every inch a multimillion-pound man on the ball, but without it, he is all too often caught out of position and not always strong enough to win his tackles. He drifts, often trying to make himself available for a pass ahead of the ball, instead of sitting. He is yet to develop the paranoia, maybe even the cynicism which is essential in a reliable holding midfielder.

So, here we are – it's Christmas. Form has stalled. Injury problems are starting to mount up. The team seems tired, edgy, jaded, in danger of losing direction – in need of somebody to stand up and drive them through the gruelling Championship winter.

Cometh the hour, cometh the man.

Cometh The Eust.

Eustace was indeed restored to the side for a Boxing Day trip to St Andrew's, where Derby thrashed Birmingham 4-0.

Any notion of a 'dip' in form seemed pretty silly by the time of the next post, as Derby went on to avenge their earlier loss at Leeds by beating them 2-0 at home, before winning 1-0 at Ipswich in the first league game of 2015.

Now Derby sat second, with 48 points from 25 games.

***

The Rock of Eibar – Spanish football writer Chris Moar on Derby County's new signing Raul Albentosa
January 16, 2015

Chris Moar covers Spanish football for various outlets, including @BeInSports and @MailSport. He was good enough to answer a few questions on big Albentosa for us – welcome, Raul!

DCB: The Albentosa story was a surprise to us all here in England when it broke, although the player had been linked to a few Premier League teams in the tabloids – so clearly somebody was trying to drum up a market for him to move here. You've tweeted to say that the deal is a 'coup' for Derby – could you expand on why you feel that way?

CM: Derby are gaining a defender who understands the tough task of chasing promotion. In fact, he was promoted with Eibar last season. So, not only are Derby acquiring a good defender, but also a very strong mentality that could rub off on other players.

DCB: Derby's style is to try to play out from the back, with the centre-backs expected to be happy to receive the ball and look to use it, rather than clear it. Will this suit Albentosa, or might he have to adapt?

CM: In this regard, he will fit Derby's defence like a glove. Playing from the back suits Albentosa excellently – it's one of his main traits. He often steps a few yards outside of the defensive line to prevent attacks with interceptions and tackles. Once winning the ball, his distribution is quite strong. It allowed Eibar to recycle possession and they used him as a proxy defensive midfielder at times. He may not possess the best passing accuracy *[DCB: 67 per cent, inline with Eibar's team average for the season]*, but this is sometimes down to having to hoof the ball when Eibar are on the ropes.

DCB: In England, it would be impossible for a Premier League team to lose its key central defender to a Championship side. How come Albentosa was available for €600,000 (about £470,000)?

CM: In terms of the fee, I think one has to consider the club you are dealing with. Eibar are the smallest club in the top two divisions and, although they are financially healthy, they are by no means rich. €600,000 will do them the world of good, especially with their upcoming stadium renovations.

DCB: It seems that Albentosa was overcome with emotion at his final press conference at Eibar. Can you explain why he would be so sad to leave? What is special about Los Armeros?

CM: Eibar gave Albentosa a chance to play at the highest level. Prior to that, he was becoming somewhat of a journeyman in the lower divisions. The squad unity at the Basque club is something worth commending – every player knows they are important, whether as a starter or on the bench and the fans give them a lot of love. It's a family club and that could be the reason why he was overcome with emotion.

DCB: Can you give me a bit of background on just how small Eibar is as a club – from what I've read, it seems to be almost the equivalent of

Alfreton Town flourishing in the Premier League.

CM: Eibar are, as I said, the smallest club in the top two divisions. Ipurua (their stadium) holds just 5,200 – they're trying to expand on this, but that would involve knocking down people's houses, as the stadium is surrounded by various domiciles.

Up until two seasons ago, Eibar were a third division side with no real quality or ambition. Enter Gaizka Garitano – their 39-year-old manager – and fast forward a couple of years. He gets Eibar into the first division for the first time in their history by finishing first in what was one of the tightest second division seasons ever.

After promotion, they had to raise €2m to ensure that they could meet a (harsh) financial quota imposed by the Spanish football governing body. A small fee for many clubs, but Eibar had to crowdsource – I think that is a testament to their size *[DCB: former Eibar loanees David Silva and Xabi Alonso both contributed]*. But what they lack in stature, they make up for in heart.

DCB: There's been a bit of confusion about the technicalities of the deal – I understand that the buy-out money had to be lodged with the league by the player, rather than being paid directly to the selling club. However, Derby reportedly paused at that point and tried to deal with Eibar directly. What difference did it make?

CM: Dealing with Spanish clubs is the devil, in all honesty. You have to bypass buyout clauses, deal with the LFP and RFEF (the governing bodies) and then the player has to pay out his clause to coincide with the tax quotas. I think Derby wanted a simpler, more direct transfer because it is quicker and less alien to the club. Derby are used to making straight deals between clubs within England – it may just be that they do not want to dive into untested waters. Ultimately, you get the player either way, it just means that the Spanish way will take a few more days and it's a bit of a pain for the player.

***

Derby County v Nottingham Forest preview
January 16, 2015

Before the last East Midlands derby in September, five league games had gone and Forest were top of the formative table. They were bookies' favourites for promotion and all was right with the world at the wrong end of Brian Clough Way. Psycho, one of the City Ground's greatest servants as a player, had walked down the Trent on water to take over as manager, Fawaz[61] was a genius, the glory days were rolling back into Nottingham, like so much mist off the river. There was an expectation that the record-equalling 5-0 Derby win in March would be avenged.

So, Statto here had a look at the numbers and after having done so, I suggested that maybe, just maybe, Forest were not quite as good as their early results had made them look. I pointed out that their five-match unbeaten run had included the nearest thing that you will ever get to a genuine gimme – Blackpool at home on the opening day – and a nervous draw at Bolton, which had provided Dougie Freedman's strugglers with their only point of the season at that stage.

I felt that my analysis was pretty reasonable, but after posting the article on Twitter, I soon found out that many Forest supporters thought otherwise. I hadn't solicited 'bantz' by tagging them in my post, but those who brought up reasonable points, I debated with, as I will with fans of any club. 'This won't be easy' was my conclusion and it wasn't – but we weren't beaten and it turned out that my 'desperate analysis', to quote one Forest fan, wasn't so far off, after all.

As it turned out, the fast start for Forest proved to be a false dawn. Pearce, who had been hailed as the Messiah, is now under very serious pressure – and it seems increasingly possible that defeat on Saturday will trigger Fawaz's itchy sacking finger yet again, leaving the

---

[61] Fawaz al-Hasawi, Forest's chairman from 2012 – 2017.

Red Dogs looking for their sixth manager in the past 30 months.

I thought it was interesting that after his side lost 3-1 at home to Birmingham, Pearce used his post-match interview with BBC Radio Nottingham to demand a 'manly' response from his players, 'There's that element of leadership and confidence in the group that's been eroded a touch. I spoke with them... and said, "Look, it's time to roll our sleeves up, gentlemen and man up a little bit, you know, in regards to what we're trying to achieve... I think we've got quality in the squad, if you've got that, you just need to find that real leadership and... we need to grow a pair... go out there and put on a manly performance and not let people come here and take charity from us."'

After that call to arms was issued, Forest surrendered meekly in the FA Cup at League One Rochdale and lost 2-0 at home to Sheffield Wednesday.

Since Derby and Forest last met, Forest's league record is as follows:-

P19 W3 D8 L8 Pts 17 GD-10

That is relegation form, when Forest were supposed to be challenging for promotion, at least according to the expectations of the owner and the supporters. They are now under a transfer embargo, having failed to comply with the Football League's Financial Fair Play rules and even under the new, watered-down FFP system, they are hampered. There will be no more exuberant £5.5m splurges – instead, they have been limited to a couple of loan signings this January and are pretty much going to have to work with what they've got for the rest of the season. And then two of their best youth products will complete their moves to Newcastle United[62].

*

The pressure-cooker atmosphere of this derby causes many strange things to happen – none stranger than the 5-0 in March. Teams simply

---

[62] Karl Darlow and Jamaal Lascelles had been sold to Newcastle in August 2014 and loaned back to Forest for the season.

aren't supposed to fold like that in these games and if one side takes a slim lead, they tend to declare, on the grounds that discretion is the better part of valour. Nearly always, the losing team show some fight, even if they're in awful form at the time. Think back to 2011, when a poor Nigel Clough Derby team lost 1-0 at home to a Forest side who went in as favourites. The Rams weren't beaten for want of endeavour and the goal didn't come until fairly late on. It's usually a real scrap and we shouldn't expect it to be any different this time.

That said, Pearce's era, when 'manliness' was expressed through a puffed-out chest and a crunching tackle, is gone. These days, anything approaching a 'reducer' is penalised by a red card, especially in the East Midlands derby if it's being handled by a jittery ref. It is through composure and quality on the ball that the best chance of success lies. Remember young Will Hughes's eerie calm on the ball at the City Ground in 2012, when Dexter Blackstock was sent off and Craig Bryson eventually scored the winner.

Derby can be countered – we are good on the ball, but we're not exactly Barcelona – and no doubt Pearce will try to prep his side to press hard and high up the field, to stop the defenders from having an easy pass on to a forward-thinking player. That is the way to stifle and overcome Derby, but it is a risky game – fail to press as a disciplined unit and we'll cut through you. Run out of steam and you won't be able to keep it up and will have to retreat into your shell, waiting to be prised open. Are Forest fit enough, committed enough, strong enough to come to the iPro and put on the kind of performance it takes to get a result?

I thought the difference between the two clubs' current situations was perfectly summed up by Daniel Storey, in his piece for this site earlier this week. He believes that on paper, Forest's squad is stronger than Derby's and when I asked him whether he would take any of our players, given a free pick, he only nominated Hughes.

On the surface, that sounds crazy, but the point he is making is that these are two strong Championship squads and that talent-wise, there probably isn't a huge difference between most of the players. The difference, as he went on to point out, is that Derby's system is finely tuned to maximise each individual's strengths and, most importantly, that the players have made an 'emotional commitment' to the club – they buy in to the coach's plan, they see the results, they are unified.

Storey watches Forest at the moment and isn't quite sure what the hell is going on – we watch our team and can see exactly what they're trying to do and how each cog fits into the machine. The absence of John Eustace impacted on the fluency of some recent performances and is an issue going into this game, but still – I remember not so long ago watching Derby County sides that had no discernible identity. Those days are gone.

The East Midlands derby is a game apart and we all understand the significance, but actually, even if it's drawn or (heaven forbid) lost, the overall pattern is clear. On the one side, there is equilibrium, togetherness, motivation, positivity. On the other, there is instability, confusion, frustration and fear.

The momentum is all one way and it would take a colossal effort from Pearce's players to reverse it. Derby should – should – be able to see them off and I am confident that they can, but when it comes to these games, nothing is guaranteed.

***

17 January:
Derby County 1 Nottingham Forest 2

By January, the idea that Stuart Pearce was the man to lead Forest to glory had been exposed as a fond delusion. As their season unravelled, Fawaz al-Hasawi's axe was sharpened and readied – surely now, it fell to second-placed Derby to deliver the final blow. At least when Billy Davies's team lost to us so heavily, it meant that they were finally rid of Billy Davies. Where was the silver lining this time?

At half-time Derby's progress to victory couldn't have seemed more serene, an own goal separating the sides and Forest looking listless, sunken into themselves, ready for another beating. It never happened.

Will Hughes was withdrawn injured and with him disappeared the Rams' control of proceedings. Omar Mascarell, desperate to do well, charged around conceding free kick after free kick – seven, in total – and from one of them, Forest lobbed the ball into the box and it trickled sickeningly in. A soft equaliser, but you couldn't deny that it had been coming.

On came new signing Darren Bent[63] in place of Jamie Ward, but it was never entirely clear where he was supposed to be playing – up front and somewhere vaguely to the right of Martin seemed to be his grasp of the situation, leaving a clear gap on the flank.

At 1-1, the game had petered out with both managers apparently more than happy to share the spoils. Despite Derby's puzzlingly inept second half, a point was in the bag when, in injury time, they shipped a goal for which almost the whole team shared blame.

Lee Grant claimed the ball, Bent signalled for a quick kick – rather than hanging on to it, Grant delivered. Bent didn't win it. A routine defensive header took Craig Bryson and Jeff Hendrick out of the game as both had charged up the pitch after the ball. Mascarell, already booked after a series of largely pointless fouls, missed a challenge he simply had to win and suddenly, out of nothing, Forest were clean through. Ben Osborn was still at an angle from which it seemed hard to score, but smashed his shot with power and Grant dived right around it.

It was a simply mind-boggling malfunction from all concerned. Inexplicable, unprofessional, unacceptable. Thanks to the Rams' ineptitude, Al-Hasawi had to postpone Pearce's sacking, while Derby were left to brood on a dreadful result and a deeply worrying second-half performance.

McClaren, 'We said at half-time, the only way they'll score is through an opportune moment, not severe pressure, they won't play through us

---

63 Bent signed for Derby on loan from Aston Villa on 2 January 2015.

– a set-play, a ball into the box.

'We gave too many set plays away, we stopped playing football, we kicked too long, we didn't win second balls in midfield.

'What we did at the end was absolutely crazy... We're running around everywhere, I don't know what we're trying to do... We were really immature at the end of the game.'[64]

Although what I described at the time as the 'colossal f**k-up' of losing to Forest was a nasty blemish on what was otherwise shaping up to be a successful season, it did not derail the Rams. Their next three games were all won. Blackburn (H, 2-0), Cardiff (A, 2-0), Bolton (H, 4-1). The goal blitz against the Trotters left the Rams in second, with 57 points from 29 games.

But it was their next match, at Bournemouth on 10 February 2015, which proved to be a pivotal moment in Derby County's decade.

***

10 February:
Bournemouth 2 Derby County 2

We had always muttered under our breaths about what would happen if Chris Martin got injured, but Martin never got injured. Until, in the 15th minute at Dean Court, *ping* – the big man's hamstring gave out.

Darren Bent was Martin's replacement and played his part in a first half which was probably the most exciting, impressive spell of two-sided football that Derby were involved in all season.

The teams went toe-to-toe at high tempo and scored a really good goal

---

[64] Post-match quote sourced from the BBC website

apiece – Bent assisting Tom Ince's[65] cracking strike by chasing down and robbing Bournemouth's centre-back – before a bad error by Jake Buxton undercut the Rams' performance just before the break. The Cherries went in 2-1 up, their supporters chuckling and doubtless rather relieved at their good fortune.

In the second half, Derby got a second equaliser, Bent slamming home from a tight angle after a neat passing move involving Craig Forsyth and Simon Dawkins. The Rams could even have gone on to win this humdinger, but in the process, they suffered a blow that, although they didn't feel it instantly, would entirely alter the course of their season.

McClaren, 'Bent has come on and showed his quality. Losing Martin was huge and we had to change things around, but Darren gave us something different.

'He has had to be patient and wait for his chance but he will get the opportunity to play some games now.'[66]

***

The importance of Plan B(ent) for Derby County's promotion prospects
February 11, 2015

For much of the earlier part of this season there was a sense among fans that Derby required a 'Plan B', for when 'Plan A' – the 4-3-3 system – wasn't working.

The Rams are third-top scorers in the division overall, second-best from open play and improving from set-pieces due to the superior delivery of Omar Mascarell. Nevertheless, there have a few frustrating

---

[65] Wide forward Ince had signed for Derby on a season-long loan from Hull City on 2 February 2015 (transfer deadline day). Manchester United attacking midfielder Jesse Lingard joined on loan on the same day.

[66] Post-match quote sourced from the BBC website

home games in which visiting managers have set out – with varying levels of success – to stifle Derby.

Chris Martin, for all of his many qualities, is not exactly blessed with pace. With Craig Bryson's lung-bursting runs apparently now a thing of the past, we have struggled to get runners past the often deep-lying number nine at times, which has allowed opponents to shuffle up, condense the space, press hard on to our defenders and prevent us from enjoying the room in which to play.

Will Hughes is so good that he will generally find pockets anyway, but still – there will be times when it simply isn't happening and we struggle to break teams down through intricate short passing and meticulous link-up play. And I've noticed recently that Derby's average amount of shots per game has been dropping, quite rapidly in fact.

We're third in the league and scoring an average of almost two goals per game, so the statistic has to be put into context – but it's still a bit of a worry that Derby are now only 17th in the division in terms of total shots per game and ninth-best for shots on target per game. So there's evidence to back up the hunch that fans had been discussing for some time, before the arrival of a truly predatory striker, Darren Bent, to replace the ineffective Leon Best.

Bent has bagged three Championship goals from a total of 133 minutes in the white shirt, plus the assist for Tom Ince's excellent strike at Bournemouth. His longest spell on the pitch came at the Goldsands, due to the hamstring injury which will presumably deprive us of 'The Wardrobe' for at least a couple of weeks. So now Bent has his chance to get a run of games.

The ideal scenario would be that, with Bent opening space with his often immaculately timed runs and Ince prowling freely from a wider starting position, we will to stretch teams more and create more shooting opportunities; but even if we're unable to, the hope is that with these two new players possessing real attacking quality, we will continue to take enough of the chances that we do create to keep winning games.

***

24 February:
Derby County 2 Charlton Athletic 0

The high-water mark.

Another home game, another regulation swatting of a bunch of also-rans. Two stylish early goals, rapier-like, cutting through the Addicks like they weren't there. The game was over as a contest in no time – from 20 minutes on, it seemed to just be a case of how many.

No further goals came, but who cared? The Rams were top of the league by two points, unbeaten in seven and averaging 1.97 points per game – comfortably better than the average required for automatic promotion over the previous ten seasons (1.87).

Best of all, George Thorne was back. This was his second start since that dreadful injury and he managed 70 minutes before he was replaced by Omar Mascarell – possibly with a knock, but his withdrawal, we were assured, was nothing to worry about. It had been Thorne's fizzed, lazer-guided pass into the feet of Jeff Hendrick that allowed the Irishman to slip a through ball for Jesse Lingard to notch the second goal.

McClaren, 'We've still got a lot to do, but our midfield is very strong, our bench is good, we can make changes and our loan signings have come in and done well. So I hope we haven't seen the best of this team, I think that's still to come.'[67]

***

---

[67] Post-match quote sourced from the BBC website

7 March:
Derby County 2 Birmingham City 2

After the Charlton win, the Rams headed on a road trip south for two away games. It was not supposed to end in double defeat.

Fulham had struggled badly and were not supposed to be able to brush us aside as easily as they did – consider that we had beaten then 10-3 on aggregate in the season's two previous meetings[68].

Worse than the three dropped points at Fulham was the injury – *ping* – to Darren Bent, which deprived McClaren of his only serious back-up for the hamstrung Chris Martin. Those anticipating news of loan cover were left disappointed, as Mac chose to continue with Johnny Russell up front – the club giving fans the impression that either Martin or Bent would return before too long.

Meanwhile, Thorne was out again, his two-match cameo ended by a thigh injury. The initial prognosis was that he would be missing for no more than a couple of weeks. Nothing to worry about.

With Russell leading the line, Derby dominated at Brighton, yet contrived to lose 2-0. So it was with some relief that they returned north to host Birmingham City – markedly improved under the leadership of Gary Rowett, but still, no great shakes.

McClaren decided that now was the time for a change at the back. Spanish defender Raul Albentosa, signed by the Rams in January, had endured a difficult start to his Derby career due to injury and personal issues. Now he was finally handed his first league start, in place of Jake Buxton.

For 90 minutes, the Rams dominated. Ward converted the rebound after Darren Randolph pushed away Russell's drive. Hughes was denied what would have been a goal of the season contender, finding

---

[68] Derby had walloped Fulham 5-2 in the fourth round of the league cup at Craven Cottage, in October 2014.

the angle of post and bar with a delicious left-footed shot from 20 yards. Ince collected Hughes's pass, dribbled inside and found the bottom corner to make it two – then Russell couldn't quite get enough power on a shot with the goal gaping, allowing a defender to clear off the line.

That spurned opportunity for a third goal should not have mattered, but it proved incredibly costly.

With a minute and a half of four minutes' stoppage time played, Ince received the ball on the right, inside his own half and facing his own goal. He was rapidly closed down by two players – credit to them for still trying when the game was to all intents and purpose over. Looking around desperately for a pass, Ince trundled backwards and was dispossessed – his clumsy attempt to atone for his mistake prompting the Birmingham man to fall over in the box for the silliest of penalty concessions. Ince was booked, protests were waved away and, 68 seconds after the award of the spot-kick, Paul Caddis converted.

The referee added every second of that delay to the existing stoppage time and Birmingham spent it winning a free kick, which was then scrambled behind for a corner. Which a scrambled Derby couldn't clear. With time up, the ref had decided to allow this passage of play to reach its conclusion – which was Clayton Donaldson's bundled equaliser, after 95 minutes and 12 seconds – 72 seconds over the allotted four minutes.

Derby raged at the referee, but their implosion was their own fault. It had been triggered by an unforced defensive error and compounded by one of their oldest problems – an inability to defend set-pieces. A shame they couldn't have used the energy they wasted on snarling at the official to keep the ball out of their net and win the match instead.

McClaren, 'Anger is the feeling at the moment, pure anger... Not dealing with the set-play at the end, one ball, survive... That can define a game, it can define a season.'[69]

----

[69] Post-match quote sourced from BBC website

The win that had seemed inevitable would have put Derby two points clear at the top. Instead, they were now one of four teams on 66 points, with ten games to play.

The last-second sickener against Birmingham meant that Derby hadn't won in three games. They at least avoided defeat by drawing 1-1 at Norwich, but only after Jamie Hanson's corner flew straight into the net. And things got worse.

Promotion rivals Middlesbrough completed a league double over the Rams by winning 1-0 at the iPro and then Derby were defeated 2-0 at Wolves, a televised game in which Lee Grant made an inexplicably awful mistake to concede the second goal.

Suddenly, Derby had picked up just two points in six games and their automatic promotion challenge had stalled.

Next came the visit of Watford, who went into the game as league leaders, five points ahead of the fifth-placed Rams.

***

Watford preview
April 2, 2015

When I wrote my season preview piece back in August, I tipped Derby to finish in the top six. So, I think, did nearly all other Rams fans, so I'm not claiming to be some sort of visionary. However, I did add: –

'We'll play good football, we'll win a few in style, we'll let a few goals in – will we have the luck we need this time?'

Now to run through some stuff you already know.

George Thorne was the key to it all and losing him for virtually the whole season rocked us on our heels before we'd even got started. I still believe that, had he been fit, we'd have walked it. Drafting in Omar

Mascarell at late notice was a risk and he didn't turn out to be as effective a holder as Thorne, with John Eustace, despite his lack of pace, a more suitable replacement – before he got crocked too.

Losing Chris Martin when we did was a blow, but we probably would have just about coped, had Plan B(ent) not then also gone out of the window – the sight of poor Johnny Russell charging gamely around on his own up front was pitiful in the main, while the attempt to blood young Jamie Hanson was, in hindsight, not a good move.

To lose all three senior holding midfielders and both senior strikers was colossally unfortunate and while having only two mainline strikers was always a risk, how do you persuade somebody to come in when they have Martin and Bent in front of them and they're likely to be third choice?

That's just the injuries. When you consider some of the freakish nonsense that has dogged us during the recent games, you start to feel like you're going insane. What the hell was the referee doing in the Birmingham City game, allowing that amount of added time? Why on earth wasn't Danny Batth sent off at Molineux, when everybody understands – or thought they did – what happens when the last man denies a clear goalscoring opportunity? How the hell did we lose 2-0 at Brighton when we were the better side for the whole game?

I don't think any of us wanted to go into the play-offs again and deep down, we were all praying we'd go up automatically. Now, the top two suddenly seems nearly out of reach for the first time and we're forced, extremely reluctantly, to consider another mini-tournament, with a final most probably against one of Bournemouth, Watford, Norwich or Middlesbrough – all of whom are really good sides, in their differing ways.

Faced with the form we're in, it's hard to remember that everybody else is going to lose games and drop points as well. Boro and Bournemouth have both been through recent wobbles, but have now apparently come out of them on the other side. Norwich underachieved in the first half of the season and only started to find consistency more recently, under Alex Neil – their form bodes well for them and fixtures, on the face of it, also favour their chances.

Watford have been in good nick of late, but over the season they have been poor against the top sides, so the trip to Derby is as much of a test for them as it is for us. Then they face Boro.

Everybody assumed that Brentford would capitalise on our loss at Wolves by beating Millwall at home, but they only just scrambled a draw in the end and remain below us. Ipswich were apparently out of it after a winless run, but beating Watford away has pushed them back into sixth.

We know what we need to do on Good Friday.

Watford struck first, through Matej Vydra, but Derby went on to take the lead with goals from Darren Bent (pen) and Tom Ince before being pegged back to 2-2, despite the Hornets having had a man sent off in the first half.
The missed opportunity meant that Derby had endured a seven-game winless run, dropping from top spot to sixth in the process.

That drought ended at struggling Wigan, where the half-time appearance of Chris Martin turned the game. The Wardrobe netted and the Rams won 2-0, moving to 71 points from 41 games and sitting fifth in the table.

Their next visitors were Brentford, who sat seventh and one point behind the Rams. Big game.

***

11 April: Derby County 1 Brentford 1

This was truly painful to watch and confirmed Derby's complete lack of readiness for promotion. By this stage, everything, frankly, had gone to shit.

Injuries, defensive blunders, inexplicable refereeing decisions – not much had dropped Derby's way since the end of February and all of this came while the national media and regional press in the north-east continued to report that Steve McClaren was expected to take over at Newcastle United in the summer.

Yet McClaren, apparently a Premier League manager in waiting, was all at sea – with seemingly no idea of how to turn the tide and prevent the Rams' season from falling apart.

By this stage, 33-year-old left-back Stephen Warnock – signed in January as cover, on an 18-month contract – had been drafted into the team. Jake Buxton and Ryan Shotton were both out, with Zak Whitbread only just returning from long-term injury problems, so Craig Forsyth, who had been dropped for a couple of games after committing his share of the defensive errors which had become endemic, was now asked to fill in at left centre-back. Albentosa was at right centre-back, with Keogh shunted to right full-back to make way.

The Christie, Keogh, Buxton, Forsyth unit which started the season had now been completely changed, with a centre-back at right-back and a left-back at centre-back.

Thorne was injured again, joined now on the sidelines by Mascarell and Eustace, both of whom were out for the season. In their absence, there was no senior player capable of operating as a holding midfielder.

And Hughes was suspended.

Martin had returned for 45 glorious minutes at Wigan – his appearance, first 'Wardrobe' moment and a super goal completely transforming the atmosphere in the away end after the Rams' abysmal first-half showing. Having come through that, Martin was declared fit enough to start alongside Bent against Brentford, in a 4-4-2 formation.

It failed utterly. Brentford, a sharp, spirited side with some clever players in the advanced roles of their 4-2-3-1 system, rapidly got on top and scored a classic counter-attacking goal to take the lead. Jeff

Hendrick tried to advance down the left and was dispossessed. Nobody had thought to cover for him, so with a couple of simple passes forward Derby were wide open at the back. Although Alex Pritchard had plenty left to do he did it with style, curling a fine finish from just outside the area past the helpless Grant.

After that, Derby's passing was atrocious, the footballing principles apparently binned, midfielders gone missing, panicked defenders ridding themselves of responsibility, removing the threat of another errant short pass costing another goal by smacking the ball in the general direction of Bent. It was as though McClaren's mind had been annexed by the ghost of another member of the Former England Managers Club.

Martin was palpably knackered long before the end and should not have been asked to play 90 minutes. Only once was Bent put through on goal, while the Bees created several great chances to put the game to bed, only for their young striker Andre Gray to pass them up. He could easily have had a hat-trick, while only a Forsyth goal-line clearance prevented Jonathan Douglas from killing the game in the 68th minute.

And yet. With the game seemingly stone dead and buried, Derby dredged up one last attack in stoppage time. Hendrick received the ball about 30 yards out, looked up and, with Brentford standing off him, hesitated, then reluctantly tried a shot. He shanked it and it flew low to the back post, where, against all the odds and any sense of justice, it landed at the feet of Bent, who managed to half-trap it and then react quicker than anyone else to poke it past the despairing David Button.

It was a grotesque act of larceny.

McClaren, 'We're not in good condition, we're not in good nick at the present moment. We've got four fit defenders, we've got five midfielders out… And Chrissy Martin coming back but not fully match fit.

'It's now that you've got to show some mettle. They played with a freedom. We played with fear.'[70]

The draw kept Derby in fifth place, ahead of Ipswich, Brentford and Wolves by a solitary point. And finally, a horrible run of six games, which had included meetings with five of the top eight, was over.

Now there were four games left. All we had to do was play relegated Blackpool, plus Huddersfield, Millwall and Reading, all three of whom were struggling at the wrong end of the table.

Plainer sailing, surely…

***

Team for Tuesday? McClaren's selection headache continues as Derby County flounder
April 14, 2015

With their favoured system disrupted by injuries, Derby find themselves not waving, but drowning at the season's business end. Steve McClaren must now somehow find a way to rescue a campaign that is rapidly unravelling before his eyes.

In the chaos and tension of a promotion run-in which has involved a slew of fixtures against the best sides, it has proved impossible to reorganise effectively after the loss of key players. They've all looked better than us, with the exception of Wolves – and against Brentford, some of the players selected didn't even look fit. Somehow the 'strongest squad in the league' has started to look like it's down to the bare bones.

Now, though, we face four games against teams in the bottom half of the table, whose league campaigns are over (with the possible excep-

---

tion of Millwall). As we saw against a dreadful Wigan, even a Derby side firing at something like 60 per cent are better than the division's stragglers – so we should still be able to pick up the necessary points to finish fifth or sixth. Whether we can then upset the form book and beat at least one, more likely two of the current top four to go up is quite another matter.

McClaren has admitted that he faces a trip 'back to the drawing board' to work out what to do, so I did a quick straw poll via Twitter to see who the fans would pick to face Blackpool. Of the 20 fans who responded, no two picked the same starting XI – with 18 players mentioned at least once.

The votes were as follows. Grant, plus:-

1) Hendrick 19
2) Keogh 19
3) Bryson 18
4) Whitbread 17
5) Martin 16
6) Ince 15
7=) Warnock, Hanson 14
9=) Albentosa, Bent, Russell 11
12=) Shotton 7
12=) Forsyth 7
14) Ward 6
15) Lingard 5
16=) Dawkins 4
16=) Christie 4
18) Barker 1

There aren't many players who are an automatic pick at the moment and for those who are, it's more because there's nobody else to play in that position. I sat down to pick a side myself – usually, it's pretty easy to at least establish a basic spine. Not today.

You've got to pick Hendrick, essentially because he at least seems to be fit. Alongside him, it has to be Bryson – but he's not 100 per cent. Do you continue with those two as a midfield pair, or use the kid Hanson behind them as a shield, despite his lack of experience?

In defence, do you put Keogh at centre-back, or is he going to have to continue at right-back? Is Whitbread genuinely fit to start? Can Warnock's ageing legs cope with a midweek game? Would it be better to put Forsyth back in his usual position? Do you continue with Albentosa, or draft in Shotton – at centre-back, or right-back?

Up front, are we starting four attackers, or three? If three, do we go with the 4-3-3 shape, or a midfield diamond with two central strikers and more attack-minded full-backs? Is Martin really fit enough to be risked from the start, or would we be better to leave him on the bench? Russell was ill on Saturday, has he recovered?

Nearly everybody polled picked Zak Whitbread, who hasn't been tainted by the recent struggles – and is naturally left-sided. Shotton is another option to come back in, but not too many supporters named him in their preferred team – probably a reflection of his patchy performances when he has been selected.

The past month and a half has been chastening for all of us but despite all the body blows, the season is far from over. There is an opportunity now to get on a run of form, starting tonight. Whoever McClaren picks, surely they will be too strong for Blackpool – and the return of Will Hughes will strengthen the head coach's hand ahead of Huddersfield.

***

18 April:
Huddersfield Town 4 Derby County 4

Blackpool were already down by the time Derby thrashed them 4-0 at the iPro. Automatic promotion was long gone, as Bournemouth, Norwich and Middlesbrough streaked away from the pack, so the win provided three more points on the road to a top six finish and the play-offs again. With three games left to play, Derby had a four-point cushion over Brentford in seventh and Wolves in eighth.

I made it to Huddersfield early enough to meet my friend Trev for a couple of pints in a real ale bar. And when Tom Ince unleashed an absolute rasper to put Derby ahead in the 16th minute, it very much felt like the party was continuing.

However, a Rams team who had become alarmingly flaky in recent times outdid even themselves in a seven-minute capitulation that was truly shameful. Cyrus Christie, brought on as a sub for the injured Zak Whitbread, was robbed and Huddersfield serenely passed the ball to Oscar Gobern, who scored unchallenged (albeit with the aid of a blatant handball, missed by the officials). Within five minutes, that time-honoured weakness, defending corners, reared its head in the ugliest fashion imaginable as Derby conceded twice. The first was a farcically free header for Mark Hudson, the second was flapped directly into the net by a buffoonish Lee Grant, although it went down as a goal to the taker, Reece James.
Derby were 3-1 down at the break and I stood in shock, contemplating whether to simply forget about it, walk back into town and take up our stools at the bar we'd just left.

We didn't and we were rewarded, kind of. Derby scored three goals while attacking the away end, which in normal circumstances, would have meant absolute calypso time. First, Simon Dawkins cleverly finished Stephen Warnock's cross to pull one back, then Jesse Lingard passed home from the edge of the box on the hour and all of a sudden, a rocking away end was contemplating a winner. Fools that we were. Derby's passing from the back had been shaky throughout and the limited Ryan Shotton, a strange signing if ever there had been one for a team like Derby, gave the ball straight to Nakhi Wells, who eventually scored despite a frantic scramble to keep the Terriers out. Schoolboy defending, for the fourth time in a single game.

Derby were level again within minutes, but I refused to celebrate the goal. I was seething. And it looked as though Derby had blown it when Ishmael Miller netted in stoppage time, only for the linesman to flag offside.

Somehow, we had contrived to draw. And the self-inflicted psychodrama seemed not to matter too much, because neither Brentford nor Wolves managed to capitalise, with both clubs drawing their fixtures. Only two games left to play and Derby remained fifth, six points behind fourth-placed Norwich, one ahead of Ipswich in sixth and four ahead of Brentford and Wolves in seventh and eighth. The gap was effectively five points, due to Derby's vastly superior goal difference.

Despite ourselves, we were almost there.

McClaren: "We need one more win and that's our only focus – but the way we are defending at the moment, anyone could beat us. We are not in a good condition but we are scrapping."[71]

***

2 May: Derby County 0 Reading 3

When I spoke to Brentford supporters for a podcast before the final match of the season, I got the clear sense that they felt, morally, they deserved to make the play-offs instead of us, after we had been so disgustingly bad in the game against them and indeed for the past two months in general. It was hard to disagree.

By this time, I didn't believe for a minute that we would win the play-offs, but to make them was the minimum I had ever expected from the season. Sure, it was disappointing the way things had panned out, but you never knew – people pointed out that we'd been in fantastic nick going into last year's play-offs, unlike QPR. Once you got there, anything could happen.

After all the injuries, mistakes and unlucky breaks, we were still sixth. Now, all we needed to do was draw with sodding Reading – who had been crap all season, except for in the FA Cup and in securing their four away wins for the campaign – at Boro, Norwich, Ipswich and Wolves. Results like that showed they had the players in the squad to mix it with the best, on their day, but surely the last game of the season

---

[71] Post-match quote sourced from the BBC website

was not going to be their day. It wasn't about Reading.

And it never was about Reading – it was all about us.

How with only seconds gone, Will Hughes, the supporters', players' and club's player of the season, turned and played a blind pass straight to whippet striker Kwesi Appiah, who had started the season on loan at Cambridge United, who streaked past the hopelessly exposed, ponderous Albentosa, coolly put the desperately covering Keogh on his backside and arrowed the ball unerringly past Grant.

How Warnock, fielded as a defensive midfielder out of pure desperation, was substituted after half an hour.

How Bent, who had scored three penalties for Derby and missed none, was given the opportunity to equalise after Russell was brought down, but hit an unconvincing spot-kick within reach of Adam Federici, who did the rest.

How the fans booed.

How a still unfit Martin was brought on – with Russell the only realistic sacrifice, whether he deserved it or not, whether it was for the best or not.

How feckless punts aimed in the general direction of Bent flew dismally out for goal kicks, any pretence at 'playing our football' long gone, Mac's principles – the much-trumpeted 'Derby County way' – utterly betrayed.

How pathetic defending at a set-piece ended in a simple goal for the opposition – again – and how Grant made a tit of himself jumping up and down protesting after conceding a penalty which Reading were never, ever going to miss – the final embarrassing insult to add to the grievous injury we already knew had been sustained.

The finality of it was brutally shocking, the realisation not long into the second half that this was it – a season which had promised so much would deliver nothing, Derby surrendering their play-off berth to a euphoric Brentford as they totally ran out of steam.

McClaren, who still faced weekly questions about his future, had hoped that they might 'crawl over the line', but this was the proverbial bridge too far. They had buckled under what Martin memorably termed the 'monster of expectation', which had grown due to their own excellence in the previous season – an excellence which had been hinted at in spells during this campaign, but never fully replicated.

The players looked crushed on the final whistle. It wasn't as if they didn't care, but their lack of basic competence on the day was deeply worrying.

McClaren[72], 'We petered out... Today was a culmination of the last two months where we go from first down to wherever we finished... We ended outside the play-offs because we deserved that.

'We ran out of energy in the end... Not enough experience on the field... We've been top four or five times and didn't go on. This time, we've dropped, really dropped... Today, it's just one game too many.

'This is a journey, this is not the destination, now we have to review the last two months.'

---

[72] Post-match quote sourced from BBC website

Acknowledgements

Firstly, I have to thank Liam 'Tommo' Tomlinson, who gets a lot of name-checks in this volume (despite me doing my best to edit them out) and is still the first person I message when the brown stuff really hits the fan at Derby County. Hopefully, we will be back in the Alex for a proper post-match chat after some dismal 0-0 draw soon enough.

Thanks also to Chris 'Ramspace' Smith, who gets a few mentions here. With his brilliantly accessible style of writing, wicked sense of humour and passionate love of music, which colours all of his writing, he was the Rams blogger who most influenced the Derby County Blog in its early days. We eventually went on to recording the Derby County BlogCast together, which is always a hugely enjoyable thing to do.

Thank you to Rob Fleay, who was my 'mole' at the Fans' Forums in this period, providing excellent in-depth reports from the events. Not content with being the Svengali who encouraged my teenaged attempts to become a lo-fi post-rock icon, Rob continued to help 'produce' me after I turned my 'Lazer Guided' focus to writing about the Rams.

I'd like to pay tribute to Colin Bloomfield, who was hugely encouraging of my work during this period and always extremely personable and kind – a true gentleman. Colin was a fine commentator on the Rams for BBC Radio Derby and his passing in 2015 was a truly sad loss.

Thanks to my dad, who got me into this mess by taking me to the Baseball Ground in the 1980s. To use his favourite descriptor of the Rams, we were shite then, we've been shite more or less ever since, but neither of us would swap it for anything. And to my mum, who can't stand football, but who always encouraged me to express my creative side in the hope that one day, I would become a rock star and buy her a Porsche 911. It's still not too late!

Finally and most importantly, to my wife Sarah. In October 2013, after Nigel Clough had been sacked, I implored Derby not to fire another manager in the next five years, after Sarah told me with some justification that for the last few days, she had felt like a 'football widow'. 'For the sake of my future happiness, we can't be going through this up-heaval every season', I wrote.

I think it's safe to say that Mel wasn't listening. But somehow, I managed to avoid getting the boot. And on our wedding day, I didn't even know that we'd beaten Birmingham City, until Tommo told me after the speeches.

About the Author

Ollie Wright was born in 1979, in Derby.

While training as a journalist, he founded www.derbycountyblog.com in 2010 and, with the exception of a blog for Sky Sports about the progress of Ghana through the 2010 World Cup, has focused his football writing exclusively on his beloved Rams ever since.

He is a regular guest on BBC Radio Derby and hosts the Derby County BlogCast, a podcast series recorded with Chris Smith and special guests.

The majority of his work is now published first at www.patreon.com/derbycountyblog.

Printed in Great Britain
by Amazon